ROUTLEDGE LIBRARY E
AGRIBUSINESS AND LAND USE

Volume 3

FARM RENTS

FARM RENTS

A Comparison of Current and Past Farm Rents in England and Wales

D. R. DENMAN
AND
V. F. STEWART

Routledge
Taylor & Francis Group

LONDON AND NEW YORK

First published in 1959 by George Allen & Unwin Ltd

This edition first published in 2024
by Routledge
4 Park Square, Milton Park, Abingdon, Oxon OX14 4RN

and by Routledge
605 Third Avenue, New York, NY 10158

Routledge is an imprint of the Taylor & Francis Group, an informa business

British Library Cataloguing in Publication Data
A catalogue record for this book is available from the British Library

ISBN: 978-1-032-48321-4 (Set)
ISBN: 978-1-032-47946-0 (Volume 3) (hbk)
ISBN: 978-1-032-47952-1 (Volume 3) (pbk)
ISBN: 978-1-003-38670-4 (Volume 3) (ebk)

DOI: 10.4324/9781003386704

Publisher's Note
The publisher has gone to great lengths to ensure the quality of this reprint but points out that some imperfections in the original copies may be apparent.

Disclaimer
The publisher has made every effort to trace copyright holders and would welcome correspondence from those they have been unable to trace.

Farm Rents

*A Comparison of Current and Past
Farm Rents in England and Wales*

BY

D. R. DENMAN
M.A., M.SC., PH.D.

AND

V. F. STEWART
M.A.

Ruskin House
GEORGE ALLEN & UNWIN LTD
MUSEUM STREET LONDON

*Printed in Great Britain
in 11 pt. Imprint type
by East Midland Printing Company Limited
Bury St. Edmunds, Peterborough, Kettering
and elsewhere*

INTRODUCTION

The substance of this book is a report upon a survey of farm rents in England and Wales made by the Department of Estate Management of Cambridge University. Field work on the survey began in the winter of 1956 and was finished by the summer of 1958. In origin the survey is neither Governmental nor academical. Professional opinion inspired it. Landowners, farmers, central and local Government authorities were attracted by the idea and its intentions were promoted by a representative committee under the chairmanship of the Ministry of Agriculture, Fisheries and Food.

From the outset the survey has been strictly conducted as an independent investigation, free of obligation to any particular one of the agricultural interests represented on the promoting committee. At the request of the committee the Department of Estate Management undertook the survey. Suggestions and help were sought and received from the bodies and institutes represented on the committee, notably from the Ministry of Agriculture, Fisheries and Food, but, for the conduct of the survey and this presentation of its findings, we of the Department of Estate Management are entirely responsible. In the interests of impartiality this report is no more than a factual statement of findings. Some may think we have been over scrupulous and consider the calculated absence of any attempt to pursue the economic, social and political implications of the findings an unfortunate and unwarranted weakness. While we are ready to sympathise with this point of view, we would rather suffer its stricture than appear partial in the presentation of this report. The knowledge that Mr. J. T. Ward of Wye College, University of London, was simultaneously preparing a theoretical and analytical study of farm rents also influenced our minds. His recent book,[1] although illustrated by statistics available immediately prior to this survey, deals with basic principles readily applicable to the data given in this report and a treatment of rental theory here with Mr. Ward's recent text available to the reader would have been an unnecessary repetition.

The text of the report is written and the Tables arranged to cater for those who want no more than the principal results, for the detail-

[1] *"Farm Rents and Tenure"* by J. T. Ward. Estates Gazette, 1959.

hunters, and for the statistically minded, who, understandably are suspicious of all tabulated figures whose statistical significance cannot be judged. The principal results are readily ascertainable from the Tables alone, and in their simplest form from the Summary of Principal Results (p. 21). Those who seek detailed and more informative facts must read both text and Tables. Readers concerned with the statistical significance of the figures will find of prime importance the description of the size, structure and selection of the samples, and the results, and conclusions of the analysis of variance given in the text and the Appendix. Less penetrating judgements can be made from the numerical content of the cells of the Tables. The numerical content can be ascertained directly from certain Tables (such as Table App. 2) prepared as numerical keys to less elaborate Tables, or indirectly from figures in the Tables giving the percentages of the total number of holdings in the samples or of some other total in the cells; in each Table cells whose figures are contributed by evidence from less than 10 holdings are marked with an asterisk.

Apart from the National Farm Survey 1941-43 this survey is the most extensive enquiry into farm rents yet undertaken in Britain. The area represented is $6\frac{1}{2}$m. acres distributed among estates greatly varying in size and character. Without the willing assistance of a very large number of landowners and their professional advisers, and the co-operation of the Ministry of Agriculture, Fisheries and Food and local Government authorities the task could never have been accomplished. We are deeply conscious of the debt of gratitude we owe to them. We are particularly grateful for the advice, suggestions and helpful criticisms offered by members of the Country Landowners' Association, the Royal Institution of Chartered Surveyors, the Chartered Land Agents' Society, the Chartered Auctioneers' and Estate Agents' Institute, the National Farmers' Union and the Ministry of Agriculture, Fisheries and Food, who represented their respective institutions and departments on the promoting committee. We are indebted also to our colleagues in the Department of Estate Management who assisted in the field work, the compilation of the Tables, the tedious task of proof-reading and in the preparation of the text for the publishers.

D. R. DENMAN

V. F. STEWART

Cambridge University
1959.

CONTENTS

TABLES

Note:
All tables in the text of this book are listed here in the order of their appearance. In each Table the information tabulated has been supplied from the sample of 12,661 holdings, unless otherwise stated. Figures in cells where ten or less holdings have contributed to the evidence are marked in each Table by an asterisk (*) as an indication that they are less significant than the figures in the other cells Cells to which the tabulation contributes no evidence are marked with a dash (—).

DIAGRAMS

SELECTED GLOSSARY OF TERMS
USED IN THE TEXT

ADJUSTED ACREAGE:
Acreage adjusted by the reduction factor.

ANALYSIS OF VARIANCE:
Statistical method for segregating from comparable groups of data the variance in the dependent variable traceable to specific sources.

AVERAGE RENT CHANGE:
Change in average of all rents per acre inclusive of whether or not movement has occurred.

CELL:
Compartment formed by the intersection of horizontal and vertical classifications in the Tables.

CHARITY:
Trustees or company whose income may be exempt from income tax liability under the Income Tax Acts.

COMPANIES:
Public and private joint stock companies exclusive of charities.

ESTATE:
Land owned and managed as a single unit.

FARM:
Interchangeable with "Holding".

HISTOGRAM:
Graphic representation of frequency distribution consisting of a series of rectangles, width proportional to the width of the class interval and area proportional to the quantities represented.

HOLDING:
A parcel of agricultural land of 15 acres or more let at a rack rent as a single unit.

HOMESTEAD:
Farmhouse with farm buildings.

INDEPENDENT VALUERS:
Valuers appointed to act between parties to avoid dispute.

MEDIATORIAL PROCEDURE:
Determination of rent by an arbitrator or an independent valuer.

NATIONAL AVERAGE RENT:
Average rent per acre for England and Wales.

OPEN MARKET RENT:
Rent negotiated with prospective tenants who are unrelated to landlord or other tenants of his when the rent asked had been previously specified.

OPEN TENDER RENTS:
Rent negotiated after inviting prospective tenants to offer bids other than by auction, and no rent had been previously specified.

OWNERSHIP PERSONALITY:
The character of an estate governed by the legal constitutional form of the estate owner.

POPULATION:
See "Universe".

RAISED SAMPLE:
Survey sample weighted to conform to a national pattern; e.g. national distribution of let holdings in size-groups.

REDUCTION FACTOR:
Ratio of 6 to 1 equating areas of rough grazings with cultivated land.

RENT:
Yearly rack rent reserved under a lease or tenancy agreement plus additional payments consequent on landlord's improvements.

RENT DETERMINATION PROCEDURE:
Method by which the rent of a holding is arrived at.

SOCIAL CONTRIBUTIONS:
The total yearly remuneration received from agriculture by the landowner, the farmer and the agricultural worker.

SPECIFIC RENT CHANGE:
Change in average of all rents per acre where rent movement has occurred.

TRUSTS:
Real persons and bodies corporate expressly appointed as trustees, exclusive of charities.

UNIVERSE:
A total or aggregate of all possible items of the class under consideration; the entire group of items from which the sample is taken; also called "population".

SUMMARY OF PRINCIPAL RESULTS

page of first
reference

16. Repair and maintenance obligations and incidence
of occupiers' rates and owners' drainage rate do not
appear to influence farm rent. 98-100

17. Open market rents are on average 13.5% higher
than rents awarded by arbitrators and independent
valuers. 105

18. Rents negotiated with sitting tenants are on average
3% higher than rents awarded by arbitrators and
independent valuers. 105

19. Rents of mixed livestock holdings, both lowland and
upland, negotiated with sitting tenants or awarded
by arbitrators and independent valuers are near or
above open market rents. 113

20. Rents on the largest farms (500 acres and over) both
lowland and upland negotiated with sitting tenants
or awarded by arbitrators and independent valuers
are near or above open market rents. 117

21. Open market negotiations resulted on average in a
rent increase of 64%, but rents awarded by
arbitrators and independent valuers resulted on
average in an increase of 37%. 124

22. General rent review is the most frequently occurring
cause of rent change. 125

23. Rents have remained unaltered for 12 years or more
on 10% of the holdings. 127

24. Landlords' improvements on average have advanced
farm rents 5%. 130

25. Farm rent per acre remains closely related to estate
size: the larger the estate the lower the rent per
acre. 134

26. Rents increased most on estates of 2,000 to 4,000
acres from 1945-1958 with an average increase of
73.2%. 140

27. Rents increased least on estates less than 1,000 acres
from 1945-1958 with an average increase of 59%. 140

28. Rents of farms owned by Charities averaged £2 6s.
7d. per acre in 1957 and were the highest of the
ownership personality classes. 143

*page of first
reference*

CHAPTER ONE

GENERAL FEATURES

Precedent and purpose.

Surveys, enquiries and Royal Commissions have provided information on farm rents since 1870[1]. Until 1941 these surveys and other sources of information, with the exception of an enquiry made by the Ministry of Agriculture in 1938, were not extensive. The Ministry's enquiry of 1938 extended over 1.6m. acres and was the first enquiry to cover more than one million acres. In area the sample equalled 8% of the country's cultivated land under tenancies and the official report refers to it as "the largest sample ever obtained in a rent enquiry in this country". The National Farm Survey of England and Wales followed in 1941-43. This survey among much else attempted to obtain figures for farm rents representative of the country at large and in this respect was unique. Other extensive surveys of farm rents were made in the period 1947-52 by the Country Landowners' Association conjointly with the Ministry of Agriculture and Fisheries; but these valuable contributions were not designed to match the unique achievement of the National Farm Survey of 1941-43.

Development of extensive rent surveys since 1938, especially during and after World War II, was not fortuitous. It was a step in the march of events from the early 1930's along the road to a protected and subsidised agriculture. Subsidies, controlled prices and the guaranteed markets of post-war years have led to systematic scrutiny of the national farming budget. Rent, whatever it may be in economic theory, in the account books of a tenant farmer is an item of expenditure and together with wages, machinery, maintenance, fertilizers and much else appears as a cost item on the debit side of the profit and loss account. To the landlord who provides land and buildings essential for a tenant's farming enterprise, rent is revenue, indeed the only monetary revenue earned by the capital wealth invested in the land and buildings. Farm rents are of paramount importance to owners, tenants and a Government committed to promote a stable and prosperous agriculture, prosperous alike to tenant and landlord.

[1] cf. *The Rent of Agricultural Land in England and Wales* 1870-1946. Country Landowners' Association, 1949.

In this country each year the Ministry of Agriculture, Fisheries and Food makes an estimate of the total rental value of agricultural land. This estimate is one of the costs included in the official figure for aggregate farming income, the national farm being treated as a rented farm for this purpose. The year to year movements in this item of expense are based on a sample of farm accounts and on information provided by professionally competent opinion. The various rent surveys which have been undertaken from time to time since 1938 have provided useful additional information against which to check the official estimates. The survey which is the subject and substance of this book was promoted and designed to a similar purpose, and, since the National Farm Survey of 1941-1943, is the first wherein the sample of rents selected has been planned to be statistically representative of the national picture.

Like previous surveys, the present survey sought information which would enable current rent to be compared with the rent of previous years; and the rent of holdings alike in form and circumstances to be compared with the rent of holdings differing in these respects. Although between the present and past surveys there is this similarity of purpose and principle, the depth of detail of the present survey is a distinctive mark and, it is believed, a general improvement.

In addition the survey has a novel purpose arising from the post-war land tenure policy. Farm rents have never suffered rent restriction. But by restricting the landlord's contractual power to terminate the tenancy of an agricultural holding, the Agriculture Act 1947[1] forced landlords to negotiate alterations in rent with sitting tenants who, but for the security of tenure thus provided, would have had to quit their holdings or compete successfully on the open market to retain them. Where a tenant thus secured in his holding could not agree a revised rent with his landlord, the dispute had to be referred to arbitration. Consequently the opinion of arbitrators influenced farm rents. The influence it would seem, was both direct upon the actual rents awarded and to a great extent indirect[2]. All this would have been of little moment but for a provision in the Agriculture Act 1947, later embodied in the Agricultural Holdings Act 1948, which required arbitrators to award rent "properly payable". This phrase and its counterpart in the corresponding measure for Scotland[3] have proved ambiguous

---

[1] Section 31 (re-enacted as Section 24, *Agricultural Holdings Act* 1948).

[2] cf. *Estate Capital* by D. R. Denman. pp. 100, 101.

[3] *Agricultural Holdings (Scotland) Act*, 1949: Section 11.

to the minds of arbitrators and others required to construe them[1].
Here and there landlords were occasionally in a position to relet
farms and a general impression was gained that rents awarded by
arbitrators were less than what the market for let farms was
prepared to offer, as expressed by the level of rents for the new
tenancies. One of the purposes of the present farm rent survey is
to obtain national information about rent determined by arbitration and by the market and to show the difference if any, between
them. It should be emphasised that these early statutes unlike the
recent Agriculture Act 1958, gave no guidance to the arbitrator:
it is a cogent argument that rent negotiated by a landlord with a
tenant upon taking a new tenancy is not the same thing as rent
"properly payable" envisaged by statute law. Hence, any difference
between what may be called the "market rent" and the rent of
arbitrators' awards does not in any way cast a reflection upon the
professional competence of arbitrators. The matter is simply factual.

Origin.

The beginning of the survey must be traced back to the summer
of 1955 when farm rent, a subject seldom widely discussed but
never far below the surface of things, became a topic of lively
public interest, mainly as a result of a provocative and searching
paper[2] prepared for the Country Landowners' Association in the
spring of the year. By the autumn the Land Agents' Society, whose
council throughout the summer had been reviewing all available
information on farm rents and radically debating the subject,
considered the thorough investigation of farm rents to be a primary
and pressing need, in the interests of British agriculture and the
landlord and tenant system of landownership. The investigation
in their opinion should be independent of Governmental control,
without interference by institutions which in the public eye might
have a vested interest in the outcome and should receive the
willing support of landlords, farmers, professional bodies and the
Government.

Prompted by these considerations the Land Agents' Society
approached the University of Cambridge. The Society stressed the
desirability of a unanimous backing by all interested parties and
suggested a meeting of representatives convened by the Ministry
of Agriculture, Fisheries and Food. The University readily agreed

[1] *Farm Rents* by R. C. Walmsley. Chartered Surveyor, 1956. Vol. 88, pp. 502-
508.
[2] *Farm Rents* by Lt. Col. R. B. Verdin, O.B.E., T.D., at the C.L.A. Estate Management Course, Ampleforth. April 1955. Country Landowner 1955, Vol. 6, pp.
283-298.

to participate in the proposal, provided the Ministry convened
the meeting of representatives. The Ministry concurred and in
November 1955 a committee was set up representing the Royal
Institution of Chartered Surveyors, the Land Agents' Society, the
Chartered Auctioneers' and Estate Agents' Institute, the Country
Landowners' Association, the National Farmers' Union, the
Department of Agriculture for Scotland, the Ministry of Agricul-
ture, Fisheries and Food and the Department of Estate Manage-
ment, University of Cambridge.

At their first meeting the committee unanimously endorsed the
conclusions of the Land Agents' Society and followed up the lead
given by discussing the scope, conduct and finance of the proposed
enquiry. A technical sub-committee was appointed to work out
the details. Progress was slow. Over a number of meetings the time,
basis and range of the survey and other fundamental points were
deliberated and settled. Ways and means of financing the work,
procedure and the format of questionnaires prolonged the dis-
cussions into the summer of 1956. Preliminaries were completed
by August, and on September 1, 1956 the survey was officially
launched by a circular letter over the joint signatures of the
presidents of the Royal Institution of Chartered Surveyors, the
Land Agents' Society, and the Chartered Auctioneers' and Estate
Agents' Institute, who were fully supported by the Country
Landowners' Association and the National Farmers' Union.

Procedure.

Although the survey was based upon holdings and not upon
estates, the range of information sought went beyond what would
usually be available to a tenant farmer. Consequently not the
tenants, but landowners and their agents were approached for
information. An attempt was made directly or through agents to
gain the co-operation of every landlord of agricultural land. Professional bodies represented on the sponsoring committee supplied
to Cambridge the names of their members managing agricultural
estates. The Country Landowners' Association circularised all
its members. Names of landowners not represented by professional
agents and not members of the country Landowners' Association
were provided where possible by the county agricultural executive
committees.

Each landlord, or his agent, was asked to make a "preliminary"
return[1] to Cambridge, giving no more than the size of each let
holding on his estate and the parish in which the holding was

------

[1] cf. Preliminary questionnaire p. 207 post.

situated. This initial information made it possible to introduce an element of random selection when the sample for the main survey was chosen.

A pilot survey preceded the main survey. One holding in each size-group in each county was selected. Owners were sent questionnaires in draft and asked to complete and comment upon them. In the pilot survey 218 landowners were approached and 79% responded to the invitation. Comments were most favourable. Here and there modifications to the questionnaire were desirable. In the main what had been submitted stood up well to the test of the pilot survey, and the questionnaire as modified was sent to the owners and agents of the holdings in the selected sample.

Completed questionnaires were asked for by 11 November, 1956. Response was slow and the date of return had to be postponed until 25 March, 1957. Many stragglers, happy to stay the course but hampered by want of time or by some other obstacle, did not send in their returns even by the postponed date; and not a few of the completed questionnaires were incomplete or unsatisfactory in some other way. Contingencies of this kind had been foreseen and the professional bodies represented on the sponsoring committee and the Country Landowners' Association had volunteered to organize a net-work of local honorary helpers to assist when necessary with anomalies, contradictions and other queries. The large number of late returns, the need for uniformity of treatment and the fact that most visits to landowners had to be made to give assistance in the completion of questionnaires and not to answer queries arising from them, caused the work envisaged for the honorary assistants, in the event, to be undertaken by the staff of the Department of Estate Management. Landlords and agents were systematically visited and this operation occupied twelve months from the summer of 1957 to the summer of 1958.

Questionnaires for half the sample had been completed, checked and the information analysed and tabulated by February, 1958. On this information an interim report was prepared at that time which showed the trend of results and made recommendations to the sponsoring committee on the format and content of the final report.

The Sample.

Response to the preliminary questionnaire represents an area of 6½m. acres. This figure is the sum of the acreage of the estates on which the holdings are situated. Some of the land is " in hand" to the owners, other portions are woodland, and a small percentage is occupied by holdings of less than 15 acres. Disallowing these portions, the balance is 27.7% of the total let land of England and Wales, under crops, grass and rough grazings, exclusive of holdings less than 15 acres. Response has not been uniform. Of England alone the area represented is 28.2%, and of Wales 24.7%. Some counties have been far more responsive than others. In the lead is Radnorshire whose representation is 49.7%; at the tail lags Cardiganshire with a response of 8.5%.

From the 6½m. acres a sample of holdings was selected at random for the main survey. Method of sampling and other aspects of the sample are dealt with later[1]. The sample contains 12,661 holdings. This is 10.5% of the total number of wholly let[2] holdings in England and Wales, exclusive of those with less than 15 acres. In acreage the sample is 13.1% of the land in wholly let holdings in England and Wales under crops, grass and rough grazings, exclusive of holdings less than 15 acres.

Representation is not uniform either county by county or size-group by size-group. Counties most generously represented are Berkshire[3] (18%), Northumberland (18%), Radnor (18%) and Sussex (17%). Counties with the meanest representation are Middlesex (5.5%), Brecon (5%), Cardigan (5%) and Pembroke (4%). Representation in size-groups moves in almost perfect direct ratio with the size of farm, from 7% representation of holdings 15-49 acres to 14% representation of holdings over 500 acres. Here and there among the counties representation by size-group does not display this direct ratio: in Leicestershire, Warwickshire and Oxfordshire representation is nearly uniform, but nowhere except in Merioneth is an indirect ratio observed.

A fully answered questionnaire was returned for 10,413 holdings of the 12,661 sample. Full information was received for each of the remaining 2,248 holdings, but for information about the rent in 1945. All figures and estimates tabulated and commented upon in the pages that follow are based on the evidence of the larger sample, except where they refer to the rent in the year 1945 or compare this with the rent of later years.

Limitations.

Statistical requirements, the nature of the survey itself and the

---

[1] v. Appendix p. 188 post.

[2] i.e. exclusive of holdings partly let and partly owner-occupied.

[3] All percentages, unless otherwise stated, are percentages of the total county acreage of land in wholly let holdings under crops, grass and rough grazings, exclusive of holdings under 15 acres.

sources of evidence set limits to what was possible and influenced the choice of a basic unit, the size of the holdings to be surveyed, and the length to which investigation could be carried backwards into the past.

Holdings Basis. A survey of farm rents can be based upon the farm, technically spoken of as "the agricultural holding", or upon the unit of ownership or estate. An estate basis has much to commend it. A landlord's outgoings are usually in his records as estate totals only and a survey of farm rentals estate by estate, unlike a survey on a holdings basis, could easily be extended to landlord's outgoings. National figures for farm rents and estate outgoings would be invaluable and revealing at this time, and many who were interested in the present survey thought it should include outgoings. This ideal was not feasible for statistical reasons. As yet there is no knowledge of the distribution of estates by numbers and character type in the country. Hence it would have been difficult if not impossible to select a sample of estates representative of the whole country. Surveys of farm rents and estate outgoings have been made in the past, notably the surveys undertaken by the Country Landowners' Association in conjunction with the Ministry of Agriculture and Fisheries in 1947-1952, but these present tendencies within the limits of the samples only and are not designed to give figures representative of the national picture.

On the other hand, the National Farm Survey 1941-1943 and information collected for a World Census of Landownership in 1950 have provided the Ministry of Agriculture, Fisheries and Food with figures of the number of let farms in the country, in size-groups and counties. Here was an adequate picture of the "population" of let holdings against which the degree of representation of a sample of let farms could be gauged. A choice therefore had to be made when embarking upon the present survey between figures which would compare rental revenue and estate outgoings, but could not be nationally representative, and figures for farm rents which stood some chance of being nationally representative. Need for national statistics was considered to have prior claim and the survey was based upon the agricultural holding as the unit of investigation.

Minimum size of holding. No standard definition of farm exists although statute law attempts to define an allotment[1]. Popular usage knows no maximum size of farm. But holdings of small acreage move back and forth over an uncertain boundary line. A property of small acreage although used for husbandry purposes

---

[1] cf. *Allotment Act* 1922. Section 3(7).

may be more residential than agricultural, or have the character of an allotment, or be accommodation land merely, an auxiliary to a commercial or industrial enterprise. Farm, therefore, for the purpose of the survey is arbitrarily defined as an agricultural holding of 15 acres and above with no maximum size limit. Statistical considerations also influenced the choice of the arbitrary minimal size of 15 acres: to include the heterodox world of tiny holdings in the survey would have added to the burden of work and increased the difficulties of sampling.

Length of retrospect. Comparison of current rents and past rents has its limitations. As time passes the records of past figures are more difficult to obtain and the length of retrospect possible is shortened. It would have been ideal to gather comprehensive information year by year back from the present day to the pre-war years, but so long a retrospect would have complicated and prolonged the work. The Ministry of Agriculture's 8% sample of 1938 and the National Farm Survey 1941-1943 provide figures for the immediate pre-war years and the early years of the war. The present survey is set within the bounds of possible accomplishment by limiting its retrospect to the post-war years after 1945, and by not seeking comprehensive information year by year over that period but only for the year 1945 and the year immediately preceding the current year of survey.

Presentation of Results.

Presentation of the results in the chapters that follow is arranged in seven parts after the main purposes of the survey and with some secondary intentions in mind, thus:

(*a*) National farm rent levels:
(*b*) Character of holding and farm rent:
(*c*) County farm rent levels:
(*d*) Tenancy conditions and farm rent:
(*e*) Determination of rents and causes of rent change:
(*f*) Character of estate and farm rent:
(*g*) Comparisons with other surveys.

National farm rent levels. Farm rent in the survey is contractual rent, the amount of rent reserved by the terms of a lease. Arrears and abatements are ignored. Average current rent per acre for the country at large is given in two ways: one figure is based on the total area of let land including woodland and rough grazings; and the other on the same total acreage adjusted to make allowance for rough grazings and woodland. Rent per acre is calculated for each holding, and the holdings arranged in rent per acre groups to show the distribution of rent levels for the country at large. National rent per acre averages are also calculated for the years 1945, 1956 and 1958. Average rents per acre are compared and demonstrate how rents have moved since 1945 and 1956 and are forecast to move between 1957 and 1958. Distribution into rent per acre groups is also made for 1945, 1956 and 1958. Average rent per acre is taken as the index of national rent movements when comparing one year with another, but because actual rent changes are likely to be greater than changes in averages, the evidence is also arranged to show average specific rent changes.

Character of holding and farm rent. An agricultural holding can have many characteristics. Those in the survey, three in number, were chosen on the hypothesis that farm rent is influenced by them. Two are physical features of a holding: its size and its fixed equipment. The third is an economic factor: the type of farming practised.

Farming type classification is modelled upon the farming types used for the early Farm Management Surveys. These have a broad affinity with the farming type categories of the National Farm Survey 1941-1943 and the classification scheme used for the "Type of Farming" map published by the Ministry of Agriculture and Fisheries in 1939. Using these categories of farming type for this survey rather than those used at present for the Farm Management Surveys, makes it possible to compare the findings of the present survey and the figures of the National Farm Survey 1941-1943.

Farming types are classified in the following four principal groups:

(a) Grass;
(b) Intermediate;
(c) Arable;
(d) Specialist.

For each principal group and farming type are given the average current rent per acre, the distribution of holdings in rent per acre groups, and the movement of rent between 1945 and 1958.

Holdings are arranged according to size in six size-groups: 15-49 acres; 50-99 acres; 100-149 acres; 150-299 acres; 300-499 acres; and 500 acres and over. Any series of regular intervals would have done. This particular series was adopted for statistical reasons. The size-groups correspond to those used for classifying official statistics of the number of the farms in the country. By adopting a similar size-group series, it is possible to check the proportions of the numbers in the size-groups in the survey against those for the country at large and to adjust results if necessary by "raising" the

C

sample. Size of holding is always the area of land let in a particular tenancy and usually corresponds to the area of land in the tenant's farming enterprise. In rare cases this is not so; where, for instance, land is let by a landlord (who in the survey returns particulars of it as "a holding") to a tenant who combines the let land (the holding) with other land into a single farming enterprise. The relationship between size of holding and farm rent is shown by giving the average rent per acre of the holdings in each size-group, and the distribution in rent per acre groups of holdings in each size-group. The results also give rent movements since 1945 in each size-group and compare these with similar movements in other size-groups.

Categories of fixed equipment are broadly conceived as: farm-house, cottages, farm buildings, electricity and water supplies. Holdings are grouped so that the provision of farmhouse, buildings and electricity in each group is uniform. The results show the differences in average rent per acre of each group.

Water supply is similarly dealt with. Five types of supply in descending order of modernity and technical efficiency provide a scheme of classification. Average rent per acre for each class is given.

Cottages receive special treatment and the results show how average rent per acre varies according to the number of cottages per holding by farm size-group.

County farm rent levels. Results are also presented geographically to give an average current rent per acre figure for each county. County boundaries have no obvious connection with farm rents, although the evidence points to hidden forces tending to localise rent levels and give them county significance. Moreover, presentation of the results in this way facilitates comparison with the figures of the National Farm Survey 1941-1943.

Tenancy conditions and farm rent. Conditions of tenancy of which the survey takes cognizance are those which determine the incidence of repair and maintenance expenditure, rates and other annual charges.

Responsibility for repairs and maintenance is shared by land-lords and tenants in many ways. Working arrangements often disregard the letter of the law and these might influence rent levels. Work-a-day arrangements are imprecise and for this reason they are not recognised by the survey as evidence of the incidence of repair and maintenance liability. The survey is content to note the legal obligations, and holdings are classified accordingly. The principle of classification recognises the tenant's liabilities under the Agriculture (Maintenance, Repair and Insurance of Fixed Equipment) Regulations 1948 (S.I. 1948, No. 184) as a standard. Holdings where the tenant's liabilities at law are more or less similar to those of the Regulations are put into one class; holdings where the tenant's liabilities are substantially greater than this standard are put in another class; and those where the tenant's liabilities are substantially less comprise a third class. On some holdings even the legal liability is uncertain and these are bundled into a fourth or residual class. Comparisons are made of the average rent per acre for each class. The results also show the frequency with which each of these four conditions of tenancy occurs in the sample.

The survey assumes as normal the condition of tenancy which requires the tenant to pay occupier's rates of all kinds, and any other outgoings which although exceptional are, when they occur, looked upon as tenant's liabilities. The survey only records aberrations from this standard. Owners' drainage rates, on the other hand, are assumed to be paid by the landlord and the survey only records the exceptions. The abnormalities are recorded not for the purpose of comparing the rent levels of the normal and abnormal holdings, but to ascertain what adjustments, if any, should be made, to national averages and other figures to allow for these exceptions. *Determination of rents and causes of rent change.* The most outstanding novel contribution of this survey is the information it gives about the stability of rents, the causes of rent change and the procedures of rent determination.

By observing when the rent of each holding last changed, it has been possible to show the percentage of the holdings whose rent remained stable over specific periods, varying in duration, since 1945.

It would have been highly satisfactory if the survey had obtained information about the causes of all rent changes since 1945. This however was too exacting a task, and the survey goes no further than the last rent change. Even so the information is illuminating. Causes of last rent change reflect in their variety and frequency something of the pattern of all causes of rent change. The results show the varieties and frequencies for each year since 1945. Rent may change because a tenancy changes; or as a consèquence of a review of rents on an estate; or in consideration of an improvement made by the landlord; or because the terms of the lease or farm boundaries are modified; or as the consequence of a combination of two or more of these causes. The survey presupposes that either one or another, or a combination of two or more causes is responsible for the last change in rent and merely observes the frequency of the causes year by year. Once again there is a residual class into which are cast those holdings where the cause of the last rent change is unknown.

Procedures of rent determination fall into two broad groups: those where the landowner (or his agent) negotiates direct with the tenant; and those where the rent is determined by a third person, either arbitrator or valuer, acting mediatorially between the parties. Division can go further and distinguish rent negotiated with a sitting tenant from rent negotiated with a prospective tenant. Furthermore, a prospective tenant may be a relative of the land-lord, or of other tenants, or he may be a stranger in every way, and this difference of relationship divides the procedures of rent determination into smaller sub-groups. Even finer sub-division is possible as explained later[1]. The survey distinguishes different procedures of rent determination in this way and the results are presented to show how the procedure at the last rent change influences the level of rent; the figures give both the overall national picture and the results within farming type classes and farm size-groups. The information is also arranged to show, year by year since 1945, the frequency of the occasions when each of these procedures of rent determination has been followed at the last rent change. Cause of rent change may have some bearing upon procedure of rent determination; evidence is used to test this hypothesis by noting the frequency of each procedure associated with each cause of last rent change.

Character of estate and farm rent. Farm rent has two faces: the rent of a holding is invariably the rent of an estate; what is rendered by the one is received by the other. That the character of an estate, its size, mode of ownership and other traits, is likely to influence rent levels is a reasonable supposition. The survey investigates the influence of estate character upon rent levels and rent movements, but does not probe deeply and is content to consider estate size and "ownership personality" to the exclusion of other estate character traits.

Size of estate depends upon the definition of the word "estate"; whether it means all land within a single ownership, irrespective of shape, user, form of administration and other features, topo-graphical and abstract. The definition used in the survey is given later[2]. Subject to the definition, estates are classified by size into six estate size-groups: 0-999 acres; 1000-1,999 acres, 2,000-3,999 acres; 4,000-5,999 acres; 6,000-9,999 acres; and those of 10,000 acres and above. Average rent per acre in each size-group is

[1] v.p. 103 post.
[2] v.p. 132 post.

given for the years 1945 and 1956 to 1958, thus showing how estate size itself influences rent and what bearing it has had upon rent movement.

"Ownership personality" is not a phrase peculiar to this survey[1]. Estates differ in the form of their proprietorship. Among forms of proprietorship are those which depend upon the constitutional form of the proprietor, and it is these forms of proprietorship which impress distinctive ownership personality upon the estates owned. The survey recognises six such forms—charities, companies, trusts, real persons, local authorities and Government departments. The estates are classified according to these forms of ownership personality and the average rent per acre in each class is given for 1945 and 1956 to 1958, thus showing the influence of ownership personality upon rent level and rent movement.

Comparison with other surveys. The results of the survey are finally compared with those of other surveys. Differences of sample and scope limit the possibilities of comparison. No other survey is identical with the present survey in treatment and subject matter and such comparisons as are made require adjustment of the evidence. By linking results of the present survey with figures from the National Farm Survey 1941-1943 and the enquiry conducted by the Ministry of Agriculture and Fisheries in 1938, it has been possible to compute national figures of rent movements over the twenty years 1937-1957. These figures are compared with estimated movements over the same period of farm incomes, earnings of agricultural workers and building costs.

[1] cf. D. R. Denman. op. cit. p. 29.

CHAPTER TWO

NATIONAL RENT LEVELS

A tenancy year seldom coincides with a calendar year. Agricultural tenancies in England and Wales usually run either from Michaelmas (29th September) to Michaelmas, or Ladyday (25th March) to Ladyday. The survey regards current rent as the rent due for the tenancy year falling mainly in the calendar year 1957. Thus, rent due for the tenancy year Ladyday 1956 to Ladyday 1957 is not current rent, but rent due for the tenancy year Michaelmas 1956 to Michaelmas 1957 is.

What the survey records is the rent reserved by the lease or tenancy agreement—the contractual rent. Earlier surveys have dealt with contractual rent and with rent actually paid. In the years of depression between the wars, contractual rent often differed much from rent actually paid because landlords allowed rebates and permitted rent payments to fall into arrear. Rebates and rent arrears have not been common features of the agricultural scene since 1945, although doubtless here and there they have occurred. Contractual rent therefore was thought to be a satisfactory standard for the purpose of this survey. The term is used inclusively of the rent reserved by the lease at the time of the survey[1] plus additional rent consequent upon landlord's improvements.

National average rent per acre 1957: £1 18s. 9d.

Over England and Wales, exclusive of the Isle of Man and the Scilly Isles, the average current (1957) farm rent is £1.90—or, £1 18s. 0d. per acre. This is the straight verdict of the rents reserved upon all holdings in the sample, and is calculated by dividing the total yearly rent by the total acreage under crops, grass and rough grazings, inclusive of woodland[2]. Farm size distribution in the sample however does not correspond to the national pattern. When the sample is "raised" to conform to the national proportions[3], the national average current rent becomes

---

[1] A rent reserved by the original terms of a lease may differ from the rent reserved at the time of the survey.

[2] The total let acreage of woodland in the sample is insignificant, amounting to only 0.5%, and has been added to the rough grazing acreage.

[3] Figures of the national distribution of rented holdings in size-groups were supplied by the Ministry of Agriculture, Fisheries and Food from statistics of a census of Agricultural holdings prepared in 1950 for F.A.O.

£1.94—or, £1 18s. 9d. per acre. The difference is hardly significant but if a choice is made the slightly higher figure should be regarded as the more acceptable of the two.

Earlier surveys, notably the National Farm Survey 1941-1943, attempted to bring estimates of the national average rent closer to the average rent of typical fertile land by excluding the rent-depressing influence of rough grazings[1]. This adjustment was made by using a reduction factor. The magic of the reduction factor purports to turn rough grazing acreage into an equivalent of typical fertile land. The principle is not above suspicion. Nevertheless the formula is adopted by this survey from time to time when comparisons with earlier surveys or some other reason make it advisable to do so. Over the total acreage of the sample adjusted in this way, the national average current rent is £2.13—or, £2 2s. 7d. per acre.

Current rent per acre distribution.

Average rent per acre is obtained by dividing total rent by total acreage. The result is not necessarily the measure of the rent per acre common to rented holdings in England and Wales. Rents high and low at either end of a rent scale can be married up in an averaging process and give an average deceptively unrepresentative of the rents averaged.

The national average rent of £1 18s. od. has therefore been tested against the pattern of the distribution of rents in rent per acre groups along a rent per acre scale. The scale is graduated at intervals of 10s. per acre ; it starts at os.—9s. 11d.and rises to 110s. and over. Histogram B of Diagram I gives the results graphically. Each rent per acre group is represented separately except the last four groups at the higher end of the rent scale (i.e. 80s.—110s. and over) and these are amalgamated.

Distribution of holdings in the rent per acre groups supports the calculation of the national average current rent per acre of £1 18s. od. Over two fifths of the holdings are concentrated in the two consecutive rent per acre groups 30s.—39s. 11d. and 40s.—49s. 11d. The higher rent group has a fractional advantage over its lower rented neighbour in numerical numbers (20.66% as compared with 20.49%) but acreage percentages reverse the favours. Throughout England and Wales the farm rent per acre most frequently occurring in 1957 falls between £1 10s. and £2 9s. 11d. per acre. To either side of this modal range lie the other rents and more of them occupy the higher rent per acre groups than occupy

National Farm Survey of England and Wales, H.M.S.O. 1946, p. 24.

the lower: 34% of the total number are in the rent range 60s.—110s. and over, and 25% in the rent range 0s.—29s. 11d. Numbers decline regularly on either side of the peak groups. Only in the highest rent per acre grouping is there a deviation and the number of holdings is greater than the number in the lower rented group immediately next to it. The irregularity is of no consequence and is due solely to the unlimited range of the last grouping with its capacity to mop up all stragglers of £4 0s. per acre and above.

This frequency pattern shows the distribution of the average rent per acre of holdings over the country and should not be mistaken for a pattern of the distribution of field by field rental values. Rent per acre is the average rent of an acre of land on each holding. On a particular holding with land of high and low rental value, an average rent per acre somewhere between the two would be returned and it is an average rent of this kind that is grouped in the distribution pattern. Because 42% of the holdings of the sample have average rents which are within the rent range £1 10s. to £2 10s. per acre it does not follow that 42% of the rental values of England and Wales, or of the farm land of the sample, when valued field by field lie between these two rents.

Farm rent movements 1945-1958.

Average rent per acre 1945-1958. Movement in farm rent over a period of years can be measured as the change in national average rent per acre year by year. Ideally the sample of holdings selected should be constant over the period of measurement. Consistency of sample becomes more difficult to ensure as information is pursued into the past. A choice has to be made between a consistent sample with limits set by the year with the least information (usually the earliest year) and samples that disregard the ideal and differ in size and structure. Choice is usually governed by the information available in the least informative year. Fortunately in the present survey 82% of the holdings in the sample have returned information on rent and acreage for the years 1945, 1956, 1957 and 1958 and this smaller but consistent sample has been used in measuring rent change between these years.

Current average rent per acre (1957) calculated from the evidence of this reduced sample is £1.86—or, £1 17s. 2d: 10d. per acre below the national average returned by the larger sample. The returns of the smaller sample for 1956 show an average rent of £1.74—or, £1 14s. 9d. per acre; and for 1945 an average rent of £1.13—or, £1 2s. 7d. per acre. These figures allow for what was a fractional net increase in acreage (0.41 % of total acreage) from 1945 to 1957. So slight a change is sufficient indication of a constancy of numbers in farm size-groups over the years. Observed changes in rent level are not therefore a consequence of alteration in the numbers of holdings in the farm size-groups.

Percentage change in average rent 1945-1958. An index of farm rent per acre averages related to the 1945 average as a base is given in Table 1. Average farm rent in 1956 is 54 % higher than the average rent of 1945. By 1957 the increase over the 1945 level is 64.6%. It is estimated to go further in 1958 to 69.9%. Between 1956 and 1957 average rent jumps 6.9% and by 1958 there is prospect of a further increase of 3.2%. The census of rented holdings in England and Wales which supplied information of the national total of rented holdings used for raising the larger sample of current rents[1] was taken near enough to 1945 for this information to be used to raise the smaller sample for the years 1945, 1956 and 1957. When this is done the resultant averages are raised slightly over 3%, which is a shade higher than the degree by which the national current average of the larger sample is increased by raising that sample, but in Table 1 change in the indices of the average rents is so slight as to be of no significance whatsoever.

TABLE 1

AVERAGE RENT PER ACRE 1945-1958.

YEAR	INDEX 1945 = 100		AVERAGE RENT PER ACRE £			
	Sample (smaller)	Raised sample	Sample (smaller)	Raised sample	Sample (large)	Raised sample
1945	100.0	100.0	1.13	1.17		
1956	154.0	154.4	1.74	1.80		
1957	164.6	164.4	1.86	1.92	1.90	1.94
1958	169.9		1.92			
Holdings	10,413	163,500	10,413	163,500	12,661	163,500

Rent per acre distribution 1945-1958. Comparison is also made of rent per acre distribution patterns. Histograms of the distributions are given in Diagram I for 1945, 1957 and 1958. For 1945 the histogram resembles a spinning top in shape, broad in the upper segments and tapering sharply towards the base. Nearly three quarters of all holdings, 74.8%, lie between 10s. and 40s. per acre, with the highest concentration—one third of the sample—between

[1] v.n3.p. 38 ante.

20s. and 30s. The spinning top effect is gained by the rapid falling
away of numbers in all rent per acre groups above 50s. per acre.
The seven groups within the rent per acre range 50s.—110s. and
over, only hold 8% of the sample between them. By 1957 the
spinning top is no more. It is as if someone had squeezed it until
the broad upper part is squashed into the middle regions to
resemble a fairly symmetrical spindle bulging just above its mid-
point. This is the pattern described above with its over two-fifths
concentration between 30s. and 49s. 11d. per acre. An important
feature is the broadening of the lower sectors revealing a marked
growth in the higher rent per acre groups. By 1958 further change
is almost imperceptible and 40% of the distributed rents are still
lodged between 30s. and 49s. 11d. per acre.

These histograms show merely how rents per acre have been
shuffled over the years between the dates represented. At first sight
they might appear to tell something of the proportionate increases
in the rent of the holdings in the respective rent per acre groups.
It is forecast, for example, that no change will take place in the
number of holdings in the lowest rent per acre group (0s.—9s. 11d.
per acre) between 1957 and 1958, whereas higher rent per acre
groups will have parted with holdings into still higher rent per acre
groups. Does this not indicate a greater increase of rent in the
original relatively higher rent per acre groups and a corresponding
stagnation of the original lowest rents? Not at all. To move from the
lowest rent per acre group (0s.—9s. 11d. per acre) into the group
next above it (10s.—19s. 11d. per acre) requires an increase of
100%. As the rent per acre groups get progressively higher the
required proportionate jump to move from one group to the next
highest group becomes progressively less. There may have been
movements among the rents of the lowest rent per acre group (0s.
—9s. 11d. per acre) that are not apparent in the histograms: a
concentration of numbers in the higher levels of the limited rent
range of the group. It is not possible to tell how many of the new-
comers to the higher rent per acre groups have risen from much
lower groups and how many have made but a single hop from the
next lowest rent per acre group. In so far as the shape of the 1945
histogram loses much of its top width between 1945-1957, it is
indicative of greater rent increases in the original low-rented
holdings than in the original high-rented holdings; and this is
supported when rent movements in farming type classes, farming
size-groups and estate size-groups are compared[1].

Average specific rent increases 1945-1957. When the average rent

[1] cf. pp. 61, 72, 140 post.

DIAGRAM I

DISTRIBUTION OF HOLDINGS IN RENT PER ACRE GROUPS

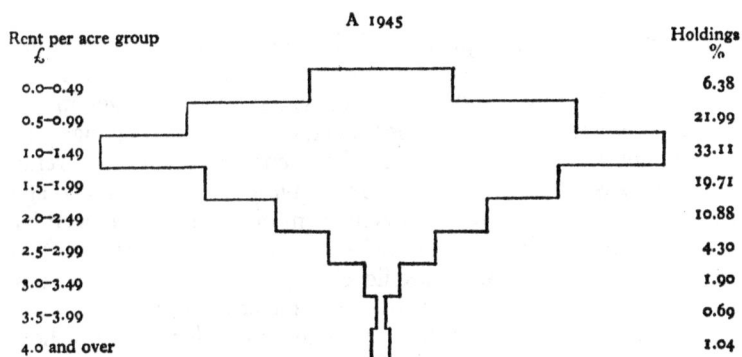

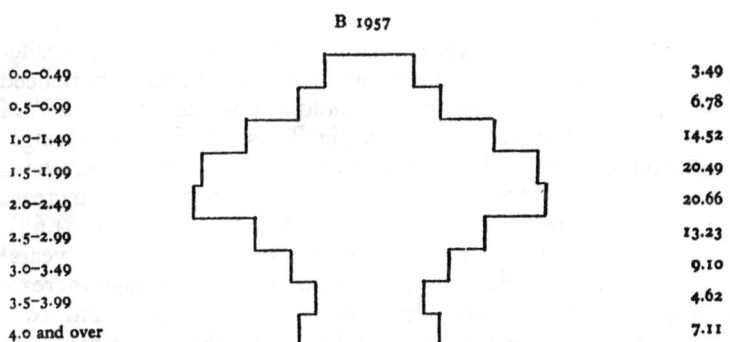

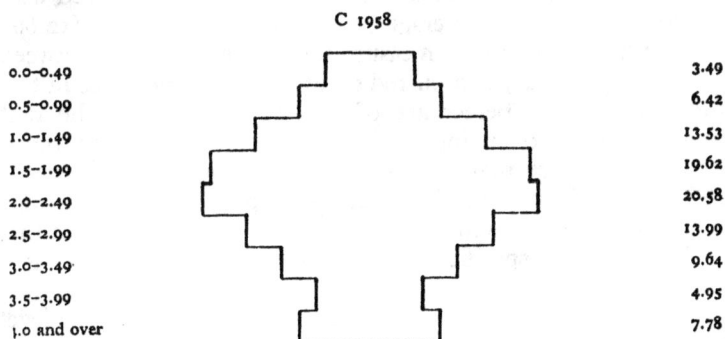

A 1945

Rent per acre group £		Holdings %
0.0–0.49		6.38
0.5–0.99		21.99
1.0–1.49		33.11
1.5–1.99		19.71
2.0–2.49		10.88
2.5–2.99		4.30
3.0–3.49		1.90
3.5–3.99		0.69
4.0 and over		1.04

B 1957

0.0–0.49		3.49
0.5–0.99		6.78
1.0–1.49		14.52
1.5–1.99		20.49
2.0–2.49		20.66
2.5–2.99		13.23
3.0–3.49		9.10
3.5–3.99		4.62
4.0 and over		7.11

C 1958

0.0–0.49		3.49
0.5–0.99		6.42
1.0–1.49		13.53
1.5–1.99		19.62
2.0–2.49		20.58
2.5–2.99		13.99
3.0–3.49		9.64
3.5–3.99		4.95
4.0 and over		7.78

of one year is compared with that of another year, the difference is not the measure by which specific rents have changed but the measure of change in total rent, inclusive of changed and static rents.

This is not always appreciated by landowners and tenants. Rent changes in their experience are always specific, often peculiar to their own holdings, and may differ widely from changes in the national average rent and other averages. Because changes in average rent are not distinguished from changes in specific rents false comparisons are made. Figures giving changes in average rent are not supported by the specific rent changes experienced by landowners and tenants and instead of realising the essential difference between average and specific changes, they are apt to view with suspicion the figures for changes in average rent. As a safeguard against confusion of this kind and in order to show how changes in average rent can differ from changes in specific rents, the specific rent changes recorded by the survey have been separately measured.

Between 1945 and 1957, 91.2% of the holdings in the smaller sample (10,413) used for measuring rent movement experienced a change of rent; in acreage these holdings account for 94.2% of the total acreage of the smaller sample. These specific rent changes in aggregate increase the rent of the holdings which experienced them 67.2%; this percentage should be compared with the increase in national average rent, over the corresponding period, of 64.6%. On the assumption of a rent change occurring once in four years[1] the sum of the specific rent changes points to an average increase of 22.4% at each specific rent change. Between 1945 and 1956 specific rent changes occurred on 88.7% of the holdings of the smaller sample; an acreage percentage of 91.7%. In sum they amount to an increase upon the 1945 rent of 57%, compared with an increase of 54% in average rent. The larger sample (12,661 holdings) has been used to measure specific rent changes between 1956 and 1957. Changes occurred on 25.8% of the holdings in this sample; an acreage percentage of 28.9%. In aggregate the rent changes amount to an increase of 25.7% over the 1956 rents. Increase in average rent between these years was 6.8%. Because 25.8% only of the holdings in this sample experienced a rent change the percentage increase in the average figure is much less than that of the sum of the specific increases and is guilty of obscuring it somewhat.

Yearly increase since 1945. Although information about the level

[1] cf. p. 127 post.

of farm rents on a national scale was sought only for the years 1945, 1956, 1957 and 1958, the survey is not altogether lacking in evidence concerning the relative level of rent in the years between. A chronology of the causes of the last rent change on the holdings of the sample is given later in Table 26. From certain figures of this Table it is clear that every year from 1945 to the current year of the survey (1957) was for certain specific holdings the year of the last rent change. By averaging for each year the rent per acre of those holdings which experienced a last rent change in that year, it is possible to provide a series of rent per acre figures year by year from 1946 to 1955. The figures are given in Table 26 as the average rent per acre for each year, adjusted for rough grazings. With one exception the figures show an increase in rent each year over the rent of the immediately previous year. The exception is 1949; in that year the average rent dropped 4.4% below the rent of the previous year, 1948; this exceptional decline probably reflects the delayed influence of the Agriculture Act 1947 with its novel strict security of tenure provisions and innovatory rental arbitration machinery. The rate of yearly increase is by no means uniform. The greatest pace is seen in 1950, the year of recovery from the impact of the recent legislation, when the average rent shows an increase of 9.2% from the average rent level of 1949. The smallest advance was 0.6% between 1945 and 1946. On average the yearly increment is 4%; a figure which becomes 4.75% if the decline of 1949 is omitted. These percentages agree closely with the calculated average yearly rent change of 4.5% between 1945 and 1956 given in Table 5. Even so, these calculations,[1] unlike the figures for Table 5, are based upon relatively small samples whose pattern and degree of representation are unknown and they must not be thought of as comparable in weight with the national average rent per acre figures already given for 1945, 1956, 1957 and 1958.

Variations from the national mean.

National levels of farm rent can only be expressed as averages of all rents extended between two extremes. In the sample used for the survey the majority of the rents concentrate in the rent per acre groups close to the average rent per acre and thus give significance to the national average figures. They are figures reflecting

---

[1] The analysis of variance by a single one-way test shows that these figures for yearly rent change are significant. The figures from the analysis of variance are as follows:

Degrees of Freedom {Between Classes. 11, Within Classes. 12, 644} Mean Squares {103. 1.38}

the majority trends. Even so the range in rent per acre is wide. Within the span of variations are differences in rent levels associated with the use, size, equipment and location of the rented holdings; with the terms of tenancy by which the rents are reserved to the landlords and the procedures which attended the determination of rent; and also with the character of the estates in which the holdings lie. The information behind the absolute averages and rent per acre distribution patterns is analysed in the chapters immediately following to show what these associations are and the significance of them as evidence of factors which have some bearing upon the level of farm rents.

CHAPTER THREE

CHARACTER OF HOLDING: FARMING TYPE

Physical and economic characteristics of holdings.

Physical and economic characteristics exert strong influences upon the agricultural productivity of holdings and also, it is reasonable to suppose, upon their rent. The present survey on this supposition examines the impact on farm rent of the three following physical and economic characteristics of holdings:—

> type of farming;
> size of farm;
> fixed equipment (*a*) farmhouse, cottages and buildings;
> (*b*) electricity and water supply .

The process is beset with difficulties of definition. Classification of holdings by type of farming, for example, meets with the obvious difficulty that a holding may be devoted to more than one type of farming. This classification problem had to be faced at the questionnaire stage of the survey. One solution aims at guiding the judgement of the participants by giving detailed instructions about completing the questionnaire forms, as was done by officials who visited each holding in the National Farm Survey 1941-43. Success in the present survey, however, depended upon the postal returns of many busy people and there was advantage in keeping instructions and the questionnaire form as simple as the need for adequate and accurate information would allow. A field to field survey of a heavy arable land holding might reveal small pockets of light sandy soil, but if the major proportion of the acreage were heavy arable land, this would determine the main farming type characteristic of the holding. Classification by farming type was approached in this practical manner. Fourteen farming type categories were chosen and it was left to those completing the questionnaires to judge into which category each holding best fitted.

Efficiency and the residential amenity of a holding are affected by the provision, condition, age and suitability of fixed equipment —farmhouse, cottages, buildings, electricity and water supply. The survey is concerned with the provision of fixed equipment but does not attempt to assess its condition, age and suitability. Even so, answers were not always obvious and in varying degree rested with the good judgement of those completing the questionnaires. They, for example, would have to decide whether dilapidated cottages were fit enough to rank as fixed equipment and whether buildings partly provided with electricity should be counted with the electrified buildings.

The three selected characteristics of holdings will be examined in detail. At first there is examined the influence on rent of each characteristic taken in isolation, and secondly the interaction of pairs of characteristics. No attempt is made to study the interaction of more than two characteristics; to do more would complicate the analysis and sift the cases under examination into groups too small to be significant.

Although the three characteristics chosen have an important bearing on farm productivity they are by no means the only common attributes of agricultural holdings to do so. Soil type and access to markets are among the important exclusions. The three chosen recommended themselves as probably significant and at the same time the least difficult to survey. It is realised also that less common characteristics may exceptionally influence productivity. Proneness to flooding or subsidence from mining operations must be reckoned with in some areas. In others, especially Wales and the northern parts of England, holdings are enhanced by grazing rights in common, excluded from the acreage of the holding. Several holdings in the survey are situated on the gathering grounds of reservoirs and are subject to stock movement restrictions. Occasionally, besides farming, holdings carry other enterprises such as riding schools, country hotels and agricultural contracting agencies. Productivity on others may be impaired by quarries, mineral workings and so on. Rents in these cases would usually be exceptional, either higher or lower than the normal level suggested by farm size, farming type and fixed equipment. Those completing questionnaires were asked to note exceptional characteristics like these. The results show only a handful of holdings with uncommon characteristics and the effect of them on the sum of the evidence is negligible. Subdivision of groups into cells with very small numbers might increase the danger of distortion from these uncommon factors. In the main, however, analysis is not taken thus far and the danger hardly exists.

Classification and representation of farming types.

Farming types in the survey are classified into four principal groups: Grass types, with two-thirds or more of cultivatable land under grass; Intermediate types, with between two-thirds and one-third of cultivatable land under grass; Arable types, with less than one-third under grass; and Specialist types, devoted to some form of specialist enterprise. These four principal groups are sub-divided into the fourteen farming types mentioned above, the criterion of identification being the main enterprises carried on on the holding.

The principal farming type groups are those used in the early Farm Management Surveys and in the National Farm Survey of 1941-43. The fourteen farming types are based upon the types of farming used in the Types of Farming Map, published by the Ministry of Agriculture and Fisheries[1], with the addition of poultry and pig holdings as types of specialist holdings, and correspond roughly with the classification used in these earlier surveys. The four principal groups with their constituent farming types are designated as follows:

1. *Grass:*
   mainly dairying;
   dairy and mixed;
   mixed livestock (upland) including hill farms and livestock farms;
   mixed livestock (lowland).

2. *Intermediate:*
   mixed farming with substantial dairying;
   general mixed farming;
   corn, sheep and dairying.

3. *Arable:*
   heavy arable land;
   light arable land;
   alluvial arable and mixed.

4. *Specialist:*
   market garden;
   mainly poultry;
   mainly pigs;
   other specialist types (hops, cherries, orchards, cress beds, etc.).

Over one half of the 12,661 holdings in the sample are in the Grass group, about one quarter in the Intermediate, rather less than a quarter in the Arable and a fiftieth only are Specialist. In terms of acreage, the Grass group forms a rather smaller proportion of the total than the proportion suggested by its numbers; the Intermediate group a larger proportion; and with the Arable and Specialist groups the proportions are unchanged. Numerically, the largest of the farming type classes are "mainly dairying"

---

[1] *Types of Farming Map* prepared by the Ministry of Agriculture and Fisheries, June 1939, printed by Director General, Ordnance Survey.

containing over a fifth of all holdings, "dairy and mixed" which
accounts for about a seventh and "general mixed farming" about
an eighth. By acreage the largest farming type class is "mixed
livestock upland" which covers 15% of the total acreage. Table
App. 1[1] shows the number of holdings and acreage in each farming
type class.

Current rent per acre of farming types.

Average current rent per acre (1957) for each farming type is
given in Table 2. Each figure has been calculated by dividing the
total rent bill for each type by the total acreage of crops, grass and
rough grazings. Allowance has not been made for the lower fertility
of rough grazings by using the reduction factor to adjust the acreage
of crops, grass and rough grazings. Average rent per acre figures
here and elsewhere are based on unadjusted acreages unless otherwise stated. Among most farming types rough grazings cover a
small fraction only of total acreage and adjustment has little effect
on rent per acre. An outstanding exception is the mixed livestock
upland type; over 60% of the total acreage of the farms of this type
is rough grazings compared with a corresponding figure of 4% of
the balance of the acreage surveyed. When mixed livestock upland
acreage is adjusted to allow for rough grazings rent per acre
doubles.

Specialists apart, the Arable group[2] has the highest average rent
of £2.14—or £2 2s. 9d. per acre. The Intermediate group has a
slightly lower rent, £2.01—or £2 0s. 2d. Rent of the Grass group
is lowest at £1.69—or £1 13s. 9d. per acre. The low rent of the
Grass group is due to the inclusion of mixed livestock upland
farms which have an average rent of only £0.6—or 12s. per acre.
When upland livestock farms are excluded, the average rent per
acre of the Grass group rises to £2.2—or £2 4s. 0d. per acre, an
average higher than that of any other principal group, including
the Specialists. Thus when the upland livestock farms are excluded
the maximum difference between the rents of groups is 3s. 10d.
per acre.

Rents of specific farming types within the principal groups
vary considerably. Highest rent is paid for market gardens, £3.46
—or £3 9s. 2d; then pig farms £2.61—or £2 12s. 2d; and mainly
dairying holdings, £2.5—or £2 10s. 0d. Each of these farming type
classes includes a high proportion of small holdings: two in three
of the market garden holdings, two in five of the mainly dairying

---

[1] v. Appendix p. 194 post.
[2] v. Table App. 1, Appendix p. 194.

holdings, and one in three of the pig holdings are under 50 acres. These high proportions of small holdings probably influence the average rent figures. The lowest average rent per acre is on mixed livestock upland farms with their extensive areas of poor land.

TABLE 2
AVERAGE CURRENT RENT PER ACRE FOR EACH FARMING
TYPE.

1957

FARMING TYPE	RENT PER ACRE	ABOVE (+) or BELOW (—) AVERAGE
	£	%
With rent above average		
Market garden	3.46	+82
Mainly pigs	2.61	+37
Mainly dairying	2.50	+32
Alluvial arable and mixed	2.33	+23
Heavy arable land	2.23	+17
Mixed with dairying	2.16	+14
Mainly poultry	2.15	+13
Dairy and mixed (Grass)	2.03	+ 7
Light arable land	2.01	+ 6
Average all farming types	1.90	—
With rent equal to or below average		
General mixed	1.90	—
Corn, sheep and dairying	1.82	— 4
Mixed livestock (lowland)	1.82	— 4
Other specialists	1.73	— 9
Mixed livestock (upland)	0.61	—68

Table 2 shows the average rent per acre for each farming type class in 1957, and compares it with the average rent of all farming types. A number of farming type rents diverge from the average rent for all types by more than twenty per cent. Market garden rent per acre at 82% above the average, and upland livestock rent at 68% below it, form the two extremes. Rent per acre for pig farms, mainly dairying farms and alluvial arable and mixed farms is in each case more than twenty per cent above the average. Rents per acre of other farming types cluster fairly close to the average; from 17% above for heavy arable land farms to 9% below for farms of the miscellaneous specialist type.

The apparent importance of farming type in determining rent level is confirmed by the analysis of variance[1] which shows a highly significant correlation between farming type and rent per acre.

Influence of size on farming type rents.

Table 2 presents a rent per acre pattern by farming type but does

[1] v. Single one-way classification, Appendix p. 191.

not show how, if at all, farm size affects the pattern. As will be seen in the next chapter, increase in farm size is associated with a decrease in rent per acre, due partly to the averaging out of the rent for the farmhouse, buildings and certain other fixed equipment over greater acreages. The rent per acre pattern by farming type is likely in part to reflect the influence of farm size, especially as farm size distribution in some farming types is exceptional.

Table 3 shows how the acreage of each farming type class is distributed among three broad size-groups. The middle size-group, 100-299 acres, contains the highest percentage of the total acreage surveyed. With the majority of farming types the weight of acreage also lies in this size-group; but corn, sheep and dairying, upland mixed livestock, alluvial arable and mixed and light land arable are farming types with a lower than average proportion of their acreage in the middle size-group, and the weight of it lying in the largest size-group. Heavy arable land farms have roughly equal

TABLE 3

AVERAGE SIZE OF HOLDING AND ACREAGE DISTRIBUTION
IN FARM SIZE-GROUPS FOR EACH FARMING TYPE.

1957

FARMING TYPE	AVERAGE SIZE OF HOLDING	DISTRIBUTION OF ACREAGE IN SIZE GROUPS		
		15-99 acres	100-299 acres	300 acres and over
	acres	%	%	%
Corn, sheep and dairying	274	4.9	36.3	58.8
Mixed livestock (upland)	243	9.5	25.4	65.1
Alluvial arable and mixed	198	9.3	41.5	49.2
Light land arable	190	11.5	35.9	52.6
Mixed with dairying	173	12.4	51.3	36.3
Heavy land arable	168	13.2	45.0	41.8
General mixed	168	13.1	50.8	36.6
Average all farming types	156	15.7	45.8	38.5
Dairy and mixed (Grass)	135	17.1	61.1	21.2
Mixed livestock (lowland)	116	21.6	46.0	31.4
Mainly dairying	98	31.9	57.2	10.9
Specialists (excluding miscellaneous)	64	46.7	36.6	16.7*

proportions in the two groups. Farm size distribution in these farming type classes may affect the average rent per acre by the overweight of farms in the largest size-group. Similarly, rents of farming types at the other end of the average farm size scale are likely to be influenced by relatively high percentages of farms between 15 and 99 acres. Differences in the average rent of farming types due solely to dissimilar distribution of farm sizes can be eliminated by comparing the rents of farms of similar size and differing farming type. Diagram 2 shows the patterns of rent per acre by farming types in farm size-groups.

Except for heavy arable land farms, all farming types show a rent per acre for farms of less than 100 acres appreciably higher than the average rent for all sizes within the particular farming type class. Heavy arable land farms of less than 100 acres are rented at £2.22 per acre and compare with an average figure of £2.23 per acre for heavy arable land farms of all sizes. The latter figure when compared with corresponding averages for other farming type classes shows the rent of holdings less than 100 acres of the heavy arable land type to be considerably depressed. Although the average rent of the heavy arable land farms is surpassed only by the average rents of Specialists, mainly dairying and alluvial arable and mixed farms, heavy arable land rent in this size-group is among the four lowest rents and is responsible for the surprising rearrangement of the pattern of rent per acre for farming type.

DIAGRAM 2.

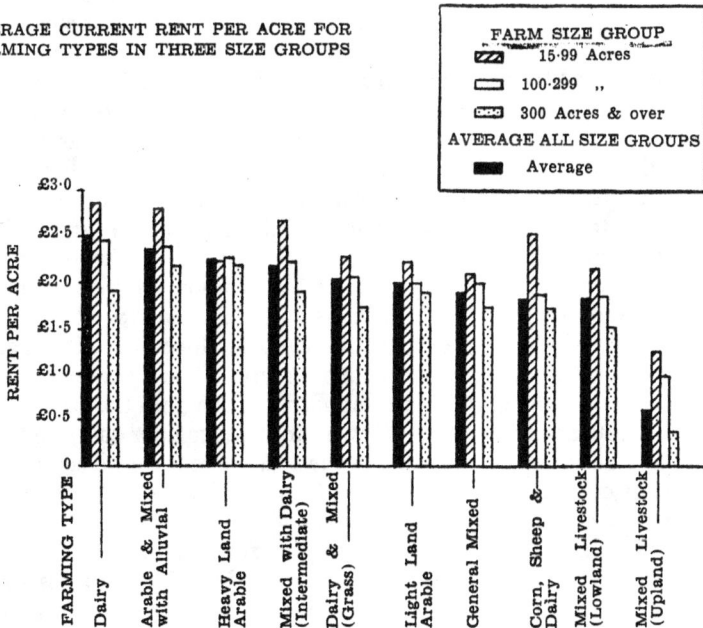

AVERAGE CURRENT RENT PER ACRE FOR FARMING TYPES IN THREE SIZE GROUPS

FARM SIZE GROUP
15·99 Acres
100-299 ,,
300 Acres & over
AVERAGE ALL SIZE GROUPS
Average

Another change is observed in the pattern of rents in the less than 100 acres size-group. In this group rent of the corn, sheep and dairying farms at £2.53 per acre is higher than the rents of holdings in the farming type classes, dairy and mixed, light arable land and general mixed farming. The average rent of all the corn, sheep and dairying farms is lower than the average rent of every other farming type except lowland and upland livestock, but of the less than 100 acres holdings, the rent of the corn, sheep and dairying farms is fourth highest on the rent scale. Over thirty per cent of the acreage of this farming type is in holdings of 300 acres and over with an average rent of £1.72 per acre and this depresses the average rent for all sizes of farms and conceals the relatively high rent of the smaller farms.

In each farming type, save one, rent per acre of farms in the middle size-group also slightly exceeds the average rent of farms of all sizes. Mainly dairying farms are the exception and in this size-group they first show signs of a relative rent decline. The rent per acre pattern by farming types for all sizes however holds good for the middle size-group and is not affected by the decline in the rent of mainly dairying farms. It is noticed, however, that the position of the rent of the dairy and mixed farms of the Grass group moves downwards to the level of the rent of light arable type farms.

The most startling re-arrangement of the normal rent per acre pattern by farming types occurs among farms of 300 acres and over. Here the heavy land arable types and the alluvial arable and mixed and light land arable types are highest rented, followed by mixed with dairying of the Intermediate group and the mainly dairying farms of the Grass group. Dairy and mixed farms of the Grass group are half way down the rent scale. All dairy farms of the Grass group forego the favourable position, familiar to them, in the rent scale of the smaller size-groups and of the general picture. Their position in this size-group produces a transformation in the rent per acre pattern by farming type. Eleven per cent only of the acreage of the mainly dairying farms falls within the size-group; in consequence the relatively low rent of the mainly dairying farms in this size-group is concealed in the average rent for all sizes which takes its cue from the high rent of farms under 100 acres that make up nearly a third of the total acreage.

This brief analysis shows that the rent per acre pattern by farming type, seen in Table 2, is not unaffected when farm size is taken into account. It is modified in the two extreme size-groups. In the smallest group, 15-99 acres, rent of corn, sheep and dairying farms has a higher place in the rent scale than is suggested by the rent per acre pattern for all farm sizes; while heavy and light arable land farms fall in the scale to share fourth lowest place. In the largest acreage group—300 acres and over—the dairy farms of the Grass group give place to the Arable types.

Clearly, therefore, the influence of farming type upon rent can be considerably modified by farm size, and it is impossible to assess accurately rent variations due to farming type without reference to the size of farm. In general, it is true to say that the smaller the farm the higher the rent per acre. But this does not hold for all types of farming. Some types of farming for one reason or another are more efficient on broad acres while others respond best to intensive methods. For this reason the margin between the high rent per acre of small farms and the low rent of large farms is greater with one farming type than with others. The figures of Table 8[1] clearly illustrate this. For example, the difference in rent per acre between the smallest and the largest mainly dairying farms is 48%; but the corresponding figure for heavy arable land farms is 2%. What appears to be a difference in rent due to farming type when rents of two holdings differing in farming type but of the same size are compared may on some occasions be accounted for by a difference in the optimum size of farm required for each farming type.

The analysis of variance[2] sheds considerable light on the relative importance of the two factors farming type and farm size. It is clear that farming type is by far the more important influence, when farming type and farm size are considered together.

Influence of fixed equipment on farming type rents.

Farming types differ much in the proportion of holdings equipped with farmhouse, buildings, cottages, and electricity and mains water supplies. Differences in average rent per acre apparently contingent upon farming type might in some measure be due to these differing proportions. Diagrams 3 and 4 show the patterns of rents per acre by farming type within groups of holdings, each group distinguished from the others by a difference in the provision of fixed equipment to its holdings.

The groups of Diagram 3 are three, as follows:

holdings with farmhouse and buildings
   and electricity supply to both;
holdings with farmhouse and buildings,
   but electricity to neither;
holdings of land only.

[1] v. p. 68.
[2] v. Appendix p. 192.

A small number of holdings with other combinations of equipment are excluded[1].

Among holdings with homestead and electricity supply the pattern of rent per acre by farming types is remarkably similar to the normal pattern. The only change is an improvement in the position of lowland mixed livestock rent. Although the average rent of all holdings of this farming type is 54% lower than the corresponding rent of corn, sheep and dairying farms, and 57% lower than the corresponding rent of general mixed farms, the rent of lowland mixed livestock holdings equipped with homestead and electricity supply is £2.03 per acre; a rent equal to the rent of general mixed farms similarly equipped, and 11% higher than the rent of similarly equipped corn, sheep and dairying farms.

DIAGRAM 3.

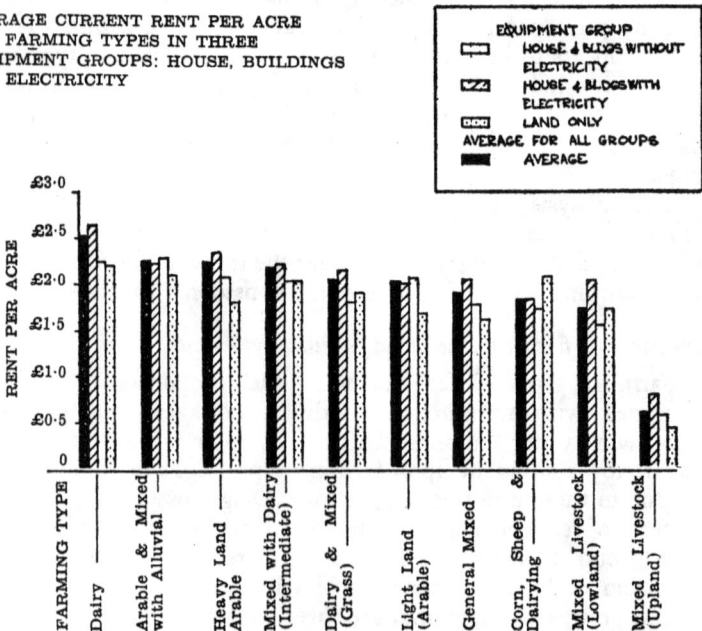

AVERAGE CURRENT RENT PER ACRE
FOR FARMING TYPES IN THREE
EQUIPMENT GROUPS: HOUSE, BUILDINGS
AND ELECTRICITY

EQUIPMENT GROUP
HOUSE & BLDGS WITHOUT ELECTRICITY
HOUSE & BLDGS WITH ELECTRICITY
LAND ONLY
AVERAGE FOR ALL GROUPS
AVERAGE

As might be expected, where no electricity is provided, the rent of the mainly dairying farms loses position. Mainly dairying farms in these circumstances have an average rent of £2.23 per acre and dairy and mixed farms of the Grass group an average rent of £1.79 per acre, and both fall one place in the rent scale. Mainly

[1] cf. 76 p.post.

dairying farms give place to alluvial arable amd mixed farms at £2.37 per acre rent, and the dairy and mixed farms of the Grass group give place to light arable land farms at £2.05 per acre rent. Rent of mixed and dairying farms of the Intermediate group, while not actually falling a place in the scale reduce their lead over the rent of light arable land to less than sixpence an acre, compared with an average figure of over three shillings an acre.

Roughly seventy-nine per cent of all holdings in the survey is in these first two fixed equipment groups. The third group, land only, includes eleven per cent of the total number of holdings. The pattern of rent per acre by farming types in this group departs considerably from the normal pattern. Admittedly the number of holdings in this group is relatively small and this sparsity in numbers may be partly the cause of the abnormality. The lowest rents per acre are those of the farming types, heavy and light arable, general mixed, and upland mixed livestock. Highest rents are those of the farming types, mainly dairying, mixed with dairy of the Intermediate group, corn, sheep and dairying and alluvial arable and mixed.

The groups of Diagram 4 differ according to the mode of water supply as follows:

piped mains water;

DIAGRAM 4.

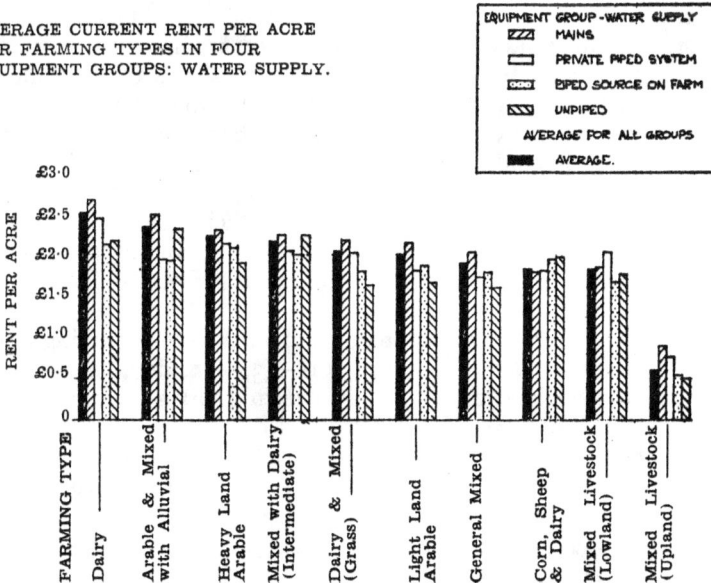

AVERAGE CURRENT RENT PER ACRE
FOR FARMING TYPES IN FOUR
EQUIPMENT GROUPS: WATER SUPPLY.

EQUIPMENT GROUP - WATER SUPPLY
MAINS
PRIVATE PIPED SYSTEM
PIPED SOURCE ON FARM
UNPIPED
AVERAGE FOR ALL GROUPS
AVERAGE.

piped estate water system;
piped supply from a source on the farm;
no piped supply or no water supply at all

The pattern of rent by farming types among farms with piped mains water supply conforms fairly closely to the normal pattern. Although for each farming type all rents per acre in this group are higher than the average rent for all groups, the relative position of the average rent of each farming type remains unchanged in the rent scale. The other three water supply groups show several departures from the normal pattern. The most outstanding and sustained trend being the progressive decline of the normally superior rent of dairy holdings as the type of water supply becomes technically less efficient.

Farming type and rent per acre distribution.

The rent per acre figures for each farming type examined so far in this chapter are average figures and may or may not conceal wide variations. The range of variation is shown in Table 4 which gives for each farming type the percentage distribution of holdings in five rent per acre groups[1].

Nearly 70% of the holdings in the survey lie in the two rent per acre groups, £1—£2 and £2—£3. About 10% are in the group with rent below £1 per acre. And the remaining 20% or so of the holdings are in the rent per acre groups, £3—£4 and £4 and over. Examination of the distribution of holdings of particular farming types in the rent per acre groups shows that within all farming types, except two, the distribution pattern conforms more or less to the pattern of the overall distribution: half to three quarters of all holdings are in the rent per acre range £1—£3. The two exceptions are market gardens and mixed upland livestock farms. Market gardens have the bulk of their holdings (68%) in the rent groups £3 per acre and over. Mixed upland livestock holdings cluster at the other extreme with most of their number (54%) in the under £1 per acre group.

Although the bulk of the holdings in all the other farming types lie in the rent per acre range £1—£3, considerable variation occurs in the percentages. Mainly dairying farms have 60%, the the lowest percentage. Corn, sheep and dairying farms have 86%, the highest. Variation in the centre causes variation at the extremities. Several farming types, including all the Specialist group, have a higher percentage than then average in the rent per acre groups

---

[1] v. Table App. 2. Appendix p. 195 for the acreage and number of holdings in each rent in per acre group.

£3 and over, and are sparsely represented at the other extremity of the rent per acre scale. Obviously market gardens belong to those of this pattern, with 68% of all holdings in the high-rented groups. The other farming types that make up the company are mainly dairying farms with 37% in these groups; pig farms with 34%; alluvial arable and mixed with 27%; mainly poultry with 24%; and mixed with dairying of the Intermediate type with 23%. Unlike other farming types poultry farms have at either extreme a higher than average proportion of holdings; there is little significance in this exception as there are only eighteen poultry farms in the sample.

TABLE 4
DISTRIBUTION OF HOLDINGS OF EACH FARMING TYPE
IN RENT PER ACRE GROUPS.

1957

FARMING TYPE	RENT PER ACRE	PERCENTAGE OF HOLDINGS IN EACH RENT PER ACRE GROUP				
		Under £1	£1–£2	£2–£3	£3–£4	£4 and over
	£	%	%	%	%	%
Market gardens	3.46	1*	4*	27	28	40
Mainly pigs	2.61	—	20*	46*	7*	27*
Mainly dairying	2.50	3	24	36	23	14
Alluvial arable and mixed	2.33	3	29	41	15	12
Heavy arable land	2.23	4	38	40	13	5
Mixed with dairying	2.16	3	33	41	17	6
Mainly poultry	2.15	13*	13*	50	16*	8*
Dairy and mixed (Grass)	2.03	9	38	35	13	5
Light arable land	2.01	6	43	36	10	5
General mixed	1.90	8	46	34	9	3
Corn, sheep and dairying	1.82	5*	47	39	6*	3*
Mixed livestock (lowland)	1.82	10	41	36	9	4
Mixed livestock (upland)	0.61	54	34	9	2	1
All farming types	1.90	10	35	34	14	7

Farming types with a higher than average percentage of holdings in rent per acre groups £3 an acre and over, are in the main those with the highest average rent per acre. Market gardens, pig farms, mainly dairying and alluvial arable and mixed types have the four highest average rents per acre, and have the four highest percentages of holdings in the rent per acre range £3 and over. Mixed with dairying of the Intermediate group and poultry holdings, have the sixth and seventh highest average rents per acre, but are next to the highest four in the percentage of holdings in the rent per acre groups mentioned. Heavy arable land holdings with the fifth highest average rent per acre do not conform. Although the average rent of heavy arable land holdings is not very different from the average rent of alluvial arable and mixed holdings, the rent per acre distribution patterns of the two are entirely different. Heavy arable land rents are mainly in the £1—£3 rent per acre range and comparatively few are in the higher rent per acre levels; while the alluvial arable and mixed farms have a higher than average percentage of holdings in the rent per acre range £2 and upwards. Lowest rents per acre are mainly the preserve of upland livestock farms which make up 45% of all holdings with rents under £1 per acre. Apart from poultry farms, no other farming type has more than the average percentage of holdings in this rent per acre group.

Each farming type shows a wide range of rents, with some holdings at either end of the rent per acre scale. Generally, however, a generous percentage in the highest rent per acre groups is the distribution pattern of mainly dairying farms, alluvial arable and mixed, mixed farming with dairying of the Intermediate group, market gardens and specialist pig farms. Although other types of farming may have average rents approximating to the average rents of these farming types and may have some holdings with high rents per acre among them, it is normal for the rents per acre of these other farming types to cluster near the average and to vary within the confines of £1 and £3 per acre.

Farming type rent movements 1945-1958.

As already intimated, a record of the 1945 rent is not available for all the farms in the survey and the figures of rent movements given here are based upon the smaller sample of 10,413 holdings[1]. As was done when calculating the rent movement of the national average, allowance is made for changes in the acreage of holdings between 1945 and 1957, and between 1956 and 1957. Where in any one case very large acreage changes had fundamentally altered the character of a holding the holding was not included. All 1958 figures are exclusive of farms where an acreage change took place between 1957 and 1958 and no allowance in this instance is required.

As might be expected, the Arable group shows an overall net increase in acreage over the period 1945-1958, particularly in the case of heavy land arable farms whose acreage increased by 1.6%. The Grass group shows a slight net decline in acreage, mainly due to a fall in the acreage of livestock farms; upland mixed livestock farms fell in acreage by 3.6%; both types of dairy farm in the group increased slightly in acreage. Intermediate and Specialist types declined slightly in overall acreage. Changes between 1956

[1] p.p. 40, 44 ante.

and 1957 suggest that on average the yearly alteration in total acreage in recent years is very small for all types.

The average increase in the rents of all farming types between 1945 and 1958 as already shown was 69.9%[1]. Of the four principal groups, the Arable group shows the highest increase with a rise of 77.9%; the Intermediate group the next highest with a rise of 73.5%; then the Grass group with a rise of 62.3%; and finally the Specialist group with a rise of 52.1%.

Among the fourteen farming types, the highest rent increase occurs on the corn, sheep and dairying farms of the Intermediate group where rent rose 91.8%. The Arable group provides the next two highest increases: for heavy arable land farms an increase of 82.9%, and for light arable land farms an increase of 80.7%. The lowest rent increases during the thirteen years are in the Specialist group: 46% for poultry farms and 50.4% for market gardens. Other farming types with low rent increases are the upland and lowland livestock farms with increases of 52.9% and 56.1% respectively.

The farming types which enjoyed the higher rent increases between 1945 and 1958 were among the low or moderately low rented types in 1945 whose rents at that time were below or just above the national average rent. Farming types paying the highest rents per acre in 1945, namely pig farms, market gardens, mainly dairying, alluvial arable and mixed, and dairy and mixed, increased their rents by less than the average increase of 70%[2] in the period 1945-1958 and yet are still relatively high rented. They appear however to be marking time, while the demand strengthens for farms of a general Arable and Intermediate type.

Rent increases between 1956 and 1957, and between 1957 and 1958 are presented separately in Table 5. This Table also gives the average annual increases over the twelve years 1945-1956.

The Table compares the figures for each farming type with the overall figures for all types. Movements in the overall averages show an increase of 6.9% between 1956 and 1957, and an additional 3.2%[3] by 1958. The average annual increase over the period 1945-1956 was 4.5%. The increase between 1956 and 1957 might well be a peak achievement; certainly what is forecast for 1958 appears to be a levelling off of the rate of increase.

In keeping with the overall averages, the rate of rent increase of all farming types, but three, was higher between 1956 and 1957

[1] v.p. 41 and Table App. 3, Appendix p. 196.
[2] rounded from 69.9%.
[3] cf. p. 41.

than the average annual increase for the preceeding twelve years. The exceptions were among the Specialist group, namely, pig farms, market gardens and poultry holdings. Rents of Arable and Intermediate farming types between 1956 and 1957, as in the previous years, strove to catch up with those of other farming types by increasing faster. Highest rent increase is recorded on light and heavy land arable farms which increased their rent 10% in the year 1956-57. Three Intermediate farming types challenge these two Arable types with rent increases higher than the average: corn, sheep and dairying farms achieve a 7.8% increase in rent, mixed with dairying 7.6%, and general mixed 7.5%.

Rents of farms of the Grass group rose by less than the average increase for all types and consistently have the lowest average rate of increase of the principal farming type groups, except the Specialist farms. No farming types of the Grass group between 1956 and 1957 achieve increases above the average. Rate of increase on mainly dairying farms appears to be fairly steady, with an average yearly increase of 5.25% between 1945 and 1956 rising to only 5.4% in the following year.

TABLE 5

AVERAGE ANNUAL RENT CHANGE FOR EACH FARMING TYPE
1945–1956, 1956–57 and 1957–58.

FARMING TYPE	AVERAGE ANNUAL RENT CHANGE 1945–56	AVERAGE RENT CHANGE	
		1956–57	1957–58
	%	%	%
GRASS			
Mainly dairying	5.25	5.40	2.00
Dairy and mixed	4.03	5.80	2.55
Mixed livestock (upland)	3.86	5.00	1.63
Mixed livestock (lowland)	3.31	6.51	2.76
Total Grass	4.09	6.31	2.40
INTERMEDIATE			
Mixed with dairying	5.02	7.62	3.20
General mixed	4.32	7.51	2.14
Corn, sheep and dairying	6.02	7.78	3.34
Total Intermediate	4.78	7.06	3.03
ARABLE			
Heavy land	4.88	9.78	5.11
Light land	4.83	10.00	4.03
Alluvial and mixed	3.99	6.22	5.47
Total Arable	4.54	8.99	4.83
SPECIALIST			
Market garden	3.42	3.04	3.51
Mainly poultry	3.33	3.21	1.04
Mainly pigs	5.42	− 0.78	0.79
Other types	3.71	3.81	0.61
Total Specialist	3.70	3.39	1.88
All farming types	4.50	6.88	3.22

Outstanding exceptions to these tendencies of the 1945-56 and 1956-57 yearly rent changes are the rents of pig farms and of lowland livestock farms. Pig farms show an average yearly rate of increase between 1945 and 1956 of 5.4%, but in 1956-57 a reversal occurs and a sudden fall reduces the rent by about 1%; pig farms are the only farming type in the survey to show a fall in rent over the period. Lowland livestock farms are exceptional for the contrary reason; compared with the rent increases of the Grass types the rent of these farms shows a remarkable improvement in the rate of increase after 1956; the yearly increase in the period 1945-56 is nearly doubled in the year 1956-57.

Too much weight should not be given to the figures for 1957-58 as they are based on incomplete information of specific rent changes in that year. Rent changes proposed but not settled when survey forms were completed are not recorded; in addition it was not practicable to include rent changes associated with or caused by alteration in acreage. Thus only a proportion of the changes between 1957 and 1958 are known and the degree and variation of change among farming type rents shown may not be entirely reliable. Future changes as recorded in the survey are probably most frequently those occasioned by the addition to existing rents of interest payments on landlord's improvements and as such would be smaller increases to total rent than would result from revision of total rents by comprehensive rental reviews. It seems probable therefore that the available information of proposed rent changes between 1957 and 1958 somewhat understates the true movements.

Similar caution need not be exercised towards the relative rates of increase of the average rents of the farming types. Table 5 shows for all farming types a rent increase of 3.2% between 1957 and 1958; half only of the previous year's achievement. The Arable group still shows the greatest vigour with just under 5% increase and the three Arable farming types taken separately show a higher increase than any other farming type. Rents of the Intermediate group increased on average 3%; and the Grass group 2.4%; Specialists have the lowest increase with less than 2%. Some farming types have moved on the scale of relative rent increases in 1957-58: rent of alluvial arable and mixed farms, for example, increased by 5.5% between 1957 and 1958 compared with 6% the previous year and rose from sixth place in order of increase to the highest.

CHAPTER FOUR

CHARACTER OF HOLDING: FARM SIZE

Distribution of holdings in farm size-groups.

The survey excludes holdings of less than 15 acres, as many of these holdings are either not wholly agricultural or are simply parcels of accommodation land. No upward size limit is imposed and the range of farm size is thus very wide. For the purpose of analysis, the survey classifies farms in six size-groups:

      15-49 acres;
      50-99 acres;
      100-149 acres;
      150-299 acres;
      300-499 acres;
      500 acres and over.

The proportions of the holdings surveyed in each size-group differ from the national proportions. The survey has a lower proportion of holdings in the smaller size-groups and a higher proportion in the larger size-groups. Table 6 shows the percentage of the holdings and acreage of the sample in each size-group and compares this distribution with the corresponding percentages for the whole of England and Wales as given by the figures prepared by the Ministry of Agriculture for the 1950 Census[1].

TABLE 6
DISTRIBUTION OF RENTED HOLDINGS IN FARM SIZE-GROUPS.

FARM SIZE-GROUP	ACREAGE		HOLDINGS	
	Present survey	1950 Census	Present survey	1950 Census
acres	%	%	%	%
15-49	4.8	8.3	24.3	33.9
50-99	10.9	15.3	23.3	26.3
100-149	15.0	14.6	18.1	14.8
150-299	30.8	29.1	22.8	17.4
300-499	19.0	15.6	8.0	5.1
500 and over	19.5	17.1	3.5	2.5
All size-groups	100.0	100.0	100.0	100.0

The Table shows the survey sample to be weighted in favour of the larger size-groups, with 34.3 % of its holdings in size-groups

[1] cf. n. (3) p. 38 ante.

from 150 acres upwards, against 25% in the national census. Percentages in the size-group 15-49 acres, show the greatest difference between the survey and the national census. The survey has about one quarter of its holdings in this size-group, compared with one third in the national distribution. The percentage of acreage in the survey is 4.8% compared with 8.3% of the national distribution, that is, a 58% conformity. Conformity is not uniform throughout all counties. In Oxfordshire for example, the 15-49 acre holdings in the survey have a 67% conformity while the corresponding percentage in Cornwall is 19%. This irregular proportionate representation among counties might bias the rent per acre average of the size-groups. A county with exceptionally high-rented small farms, well represented in the smallest size-group and a county with exceptionally low-rented small farms poorly represented in this group contributing to a national average rent for 15-49 acre holdings, will together contribute too high a figure. Adjustment of county contributions to allow for unrepresentative distribution of farm size-groups has been made. The resulting rents per acre do not change much. All that is noticeable is a rather wider margin between rents in the largest size-groups and rents in the smallest size-groups (£2.77 per acre for farms of 15-49 acres, compared with £1.26 per acre for farms 500 acres and over). The figures in Table 7 and elsewhere in this chapter are not adjusted in this way.

Average current rent per acre in farm size-groups.

Average current rent per acre falls distinctly and consistently as farm size increases. Although farms in the larger size-groups tend to have higher than average proportions of rough grazings, this is no explanation of the farm size and farm rent inverse ratio. When adjustment[1] is made for rough grazings on holdings of 500 acres and over, average rent per acre is raised from £1.17 to £1.70, but the higher figure is still the lowest average rent of all the size-groups. Holdings of 300-499 acres, when acreages are adjusted for rough grazings, rise in rent from £1.82 to £1.98 per acre and this adjusted rent is not less than the adjusted rent of the larger holdings. And so it is when adjustment is made for rough grazings in other size-groups. The general picture remains one of falling rent per acre as farm size increases, although the margins between the rents of the size-groups tend to be less when the acreages are adjusted.

Average current rent per acre for each size-group is given in

[1] v. Table App. 4, Appendix p. 197.

E

Table 7 and the percentage of its divergence from the overall average current rent per acre.

TABLE 7

AVERAGE CURRENT RENT PER ACRE FOR EACH FARM SIZE-GROUP.

1957

FARM SIZE-GROUP	RENT PER ACRE	ABOVE (+) OR BELOW (—) AVERAGE
acres	£	%
With rent above average		
15–49	2.62	+38
50–99	2.27	+19
100–149	2.13	+12
150–299	2.05	+ 8
Average rent all size-groups	1.90	—
With rent below average		
300–499	1.82	— 4
500 and over	1.17	—38

The positive deviation of rent in the 15-49 acres size-group exactly equals the negative deviation of rent in the largest size-group, 500 acres and over.

As in the case of farming type, the apparent relationship is confirmed by the test of the analysis of variance,[1] which shows farm size to be a significant factor in determining rent level, although relatively less significant than farming type when the two are considered together.

Farming type, farm size and rent per acre.

The inverse ratio between farm size and rent per acre evident in the figures of Table 7 does not hold good for all farming types. Heavy and light arable land, and corn, sheep and dairying farms sometimes have on the larger farms a higher rent per acre than on the smaller farms. Such exceptions to the general rule and the effect they have upon the relationship between rents of some farming types has already been described[2]. Here attention is focused upon farm size and from that point of view the exceptions are examined.

Rents of heavy arable land farms are the most outstanding exception. On farms between 50 and 149 acres rents are lower than on the larger farms. Light arable farms tend to follow suit and have rents slightly higher on farms between 150-299 acres than on the

[1] v. Appendix p. 191.
[2] cf. p. 54 ante.

100-149 acre holdings. Similar departures from the general rule are found with corn, sheep and dairying farms; with them, farms of 100-149 acres only have lower rents per acre than the larger farms. In every farming type, however, the farms in the smallest size-group, 15-49 acres, have the highest rents per acre, although the margins between the rent of small farms and the rent of large farms vary much with farming type.

Table 8 shows these variations; rents are given by farm size and farming type. Widest variation of rent is found among the upland mixed livestock farms. Rent of holdings 15-49 acres is almost two and a half times the average rent for the farming type and five times the rent of the largest holdings, 500 acres and over. Rent for this farming type is affected by extensive acreages of rough grazings and adjusted rents are not so extreme; on the smallest farms, rent is almost twice the average rent and exactly twice the rent of the largest farms.

Variation is least apparent in the rent of the heavy arable land farms. Average rent per acre varies from £2.15 to £2.36, about an overall average for all farm sizes of £2.23 per acre. Such variation is slight compared with the vicissitudes of the rents of upland livestock farms, which range from £0.30 to £1.52 per acre, about an average of £0.61 per acre.

Influence of fixed equipment on rent of farm size-groups.

Small farms tend to have a higher rent per acre than large farms for an identical provision of fixed equipment, farmhouse, buildings, cottages and services. The capital represented by the equipment is more highly concentrated per acre unit on a small farm. This implies that the rent per acre for fixed equipment is exactly proportional inversely to the size of farm. But farms of one size might for the privilege of certain fixed equipment pay a rent disproportionately higher than the corresponding rent on farms of another size. Something of the kind was seen when farming types identically provided with fixed equipment were considered separately[1]; mainly dairying farms were paying more rent than other farming types for similar equipment. Diagrams 5 and 6 illustrate how the pattern of rents by farm size is influenced by the provision of fixed equipment.

Diagram 5 shows that no matter what combination of farmhouse, buildings and electricity is provided, rent per acre increases as farm size decreases. On holdings with farmhouse, buildings and electricity, average rent ranges from £3.26 on farms of 15-49 acres

[1] cf. p. 56 ante.

TABLE 8

AVERAGE CURRENT RENT PER ACRE FOR EACH FARM SIZE-GROUP BY FARMING TYPE.

1957

FARM SIZE-GROUP	RENT PER ACRE BY FARMING TYPE									
	GRASS				INTERMEDIATE			ARABLE		
	Mainly dairying	Dairy and mixed	Mixed livestock (upland)	Mixed livestock (lowland)	Mixed with dairying	General mixed	Corn, sheep and dairying	Heavy land	Light land	Alluvial and mixed
acres	£	£	£	£	£	£	£	£	£	£
15–49	3.13	2.44	1.52	2.25	3.03	2.38	2.69*	2.36	2.39	2.93
50–99	2.67	2.23	1.13	2.07	2.59	2.01	2.51	2.15	2.15	2.75
100–149	2.52	2.14	1.08	1.91	2.30	1.95	1.82	2.15	2.05	2.33
150–299	2.38	2.03	0.94	1.83	2.19	1.99	1.91	2.30	2.10	2.41
300–499	2.00	1.79	0.64	1.71	1.98	1.78	1.89	2.19	2.06	2.22
500 and over	1.62*	1.59	0.30	1.19	1.76	1.62	1.62	2.17	1.77	2.14
All size-groups	2.50	2.03	0.61	1.82	2.16	1.90	1.82	2.23	2.01	2.33

to £1.55 on farms of 500 acres and over. The average for all farm sizes is £2.12 per acre; rent on the smallest farms is 54% above this and on the largest farms 17% below it. On holdings with farmhouse and buildings but no electricity, average rent ranges from £0.5 per acre for farms of 500 acres and over, to £2.42 for the smallest farms; rent on the largest holdings is 66% below £1.50, the average rent for all sizes, and on the smallest holdings 66%

DIAGRAM 5.

AVERAGE CURRENT RENT PER ACRE
FOR FARM SIZE GROUPS IN THREE
FIXED EQUIPMENT GROUPS

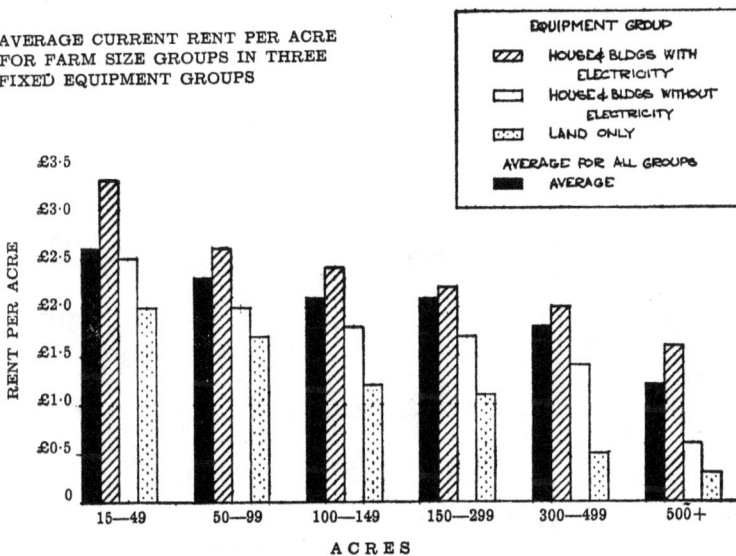

above this figure. Due in part to the influence of rough grazings, the rent of the largest unequipped farms (land only) is further below the average rent for all sizes than usual. Average rent for all unequipped holdings is £1.51 per acre. Rent of holdings 15-49 acres is only 33% above this figure; the rents of holdings 300-499 acres, and 500 acres and over are below it by 69% and 77% respectively.

Diagram 6 shows that in general, whatever the water supply may be, rents tend to decrease as farm size increases. But there are one or two exceptions which call for comment. Where water is supplied from private estate systems, holdings of 15-49 acres have the highest rent at £2.85 per acre, 55% above the all-sizes average; and holdings of 500 acres and over have a rent of £1.17

per acre, 36% below the all-sizes average. Between these two extremes are one or two exceptions; holdings of 50-99 acres are rented at £1.29 per acre only, a rent which is lower than the rent of every other size-group except the very largest, and holdings of 100-149 acres show a slight decline in rent instead of an increase

DIAGRAM 6.

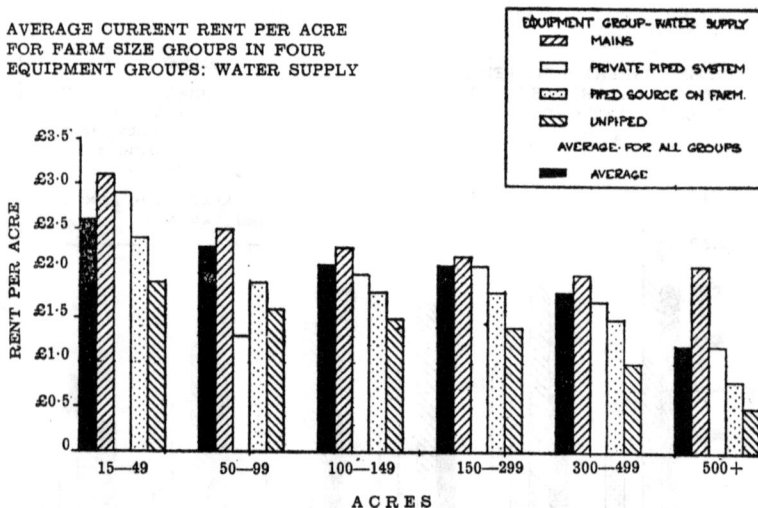

AVERAGE CURRENT RENT PER ACRE
FOR FARM SIZE GROUPS IN FOUR
EQUIPMENT GROUPS: WATER SUPPLY

relative to rent of the holdings of the next size-group, 150-299 acres. An exception also occurs among holdings with piped mains water supply. Rent of holdings 500 acres and over is higher than the rent of holdings 300-499 acres; the difference in rent being about 2s. 2d. per acre.

These exceptions apart, the normal inverse ratio between farm size and farm rent per acre is unaffected by the manner of water supply although there are variations in the ratio. Variation is widest among the farms with a piped water supply from a source on the farm; rent of the 15-49 acre holdings is £2.42 per acre, or 70% above the all-sizes average, while rent of the largest farms is £0.75 per acre, 47% below the average. Variation is least among the farms with piped mains water. Rent on holdings 15-49 acres is £3.06 per acre or 38% above the all-sizes average figure, and on holdings of 500 acres or over, £2.13 per acre or 4% below the average.

Farm size and rent per acre distribution.

When the holdings of each farm size-group are arranged in the five rent per acre groups as in Table 9, they confirm the trend in rents previously observed. A considerably higher than average percentage of the farms of 300 acres and over is in the under £1 rent per acre group; those 500 acres and over are outstanding exceptions, with 33% of holdings in the lowest rent per acre group. But these larger farms are poorly represented in the higher rent per acre groups, and have less than 2% of all their holdings in the £4 and over rent per

TABLE 9
DISTRIBUTION OF HOLDINGS WITHIN EACH FARM
SIZE-GROUP IN RENT PER ACRE GROUPS.

1957

FARM SIZE-GROUP	PERCENTAGE OF HOLDINGS IN EACH RENT PER ACRE GROUP				
	Under £1	£1–£2	£2–£3	£3–£4	£4 and over
acres	%	%	%	%	%
15–49	8	27	30	19	16
50–99	9	32	36	17	7
100–149	10	38	35	13	5
150–299	9	40	38	10	2
300–499	14	45	33	6	2
500 and over	33	42	19	3	2*
All size-groups	10	35	34	14	7

acre group, in sharp contrast to the 16% of farms under 50 acres and the 7% of farms between 50 and 99 acres. Farms 100-299 acres have percentages less than average in the two extreme rent per acre groups, but percentages somewhat above average in the rent range £1 to £3 per acre. The smallest farms have percentages of less than average at under £2 per acre but are exceptionally well represented in the highest rent per acre groups; in particular, farms under 50 acres have percentages twice the average in the rent per acre group £4 and over.

Farm size and rent movement 1945-1958.

The percentage distribution of holdings in size-groups of the sample of 10,413 holdings whose rent movements from 1945 to 1958 are known is very similar to that of the larger sample. A slight difference is noticeable between the size-groups 100-149 and 150-299 acres: in the larger sample, 15% of all holdings are in the 100-149 acres group and 31% in the 150-299 acres group, and in the smaller sample the respective proportions are 13% and 33%. In the smaller sample the current rent of the smallest holdings (£2.65 per acre) is 143% above the rent of the largest holdings

(£1.09 per acre): and in the larger sample the corresponding difference between the rent of the smallest holdings (£2.62) and the rent of the largest holdings (£1.17) is 124%. The overall net decrease in acreage between 1945 and 1957 of less than 0.5% was mostly with the smallest farms: the total acreage of farms 15-49 acres fell 12%; farms of 50-99 acres 0.3%; 100-300 acres 0.03%. Total acreage of the largest farms like the last mentioned was almost static, increasing very slightly by 0.5%.

Between 1945 and 1958 the average rent per acre for the sample increased 70%. Higher increases are recorded for the average rents per acre of the three largest size-groups, broadly covering all farms over 155 acres, the average size of farm in the survey. The larger the size of the holding, the greater the percentage of rent increase[1]. Rent on the largest farms, 500 acres and over, rose from £0.62 per acre in 1945 to £1.13 in 1958, an increase of 82.3%; on farms between 300 and 499 acres rent rose from £1.03 to £1.82, or 76.7%; and on farms between 150 and 299 acres from £1.19 to £2.06, or 73.1%. The increase in the average rent of each of the three smaller size-groups was less than the increase in the overall average. Least change occurred in rents of the smallest farms, a rent of £1.72 rose to £2.72 per acre, or 58%; of farms 50-99 acres, rent rose from £1.41 to £2.34, or 66%; and of the 100-149 acre farms from £1.3 to £2.16, or 66%. Although the rents of the three smaller size-groups will by the forecasts be the highest per acre in 1958, the rents of the larger size-groups will be gaining upon them. This faster rental increase of the largest farms is narrowing the margin between the rents per acre of small and large farms. In 1945 the rent of the smallest farms was 177% higher than the rent of the largest and by 1958 this difference will have shrunk to 140%.

The progressive gain in rent by the larger farms provides a close parallel to the rent increase of the Arable and Intermediate farming types[2]. In 1945 holdings of these farming types were, like the larger farms, relatively low-rented and it is these low-rented holdings which by 1958 will have achieved the greatest rent gains. The per-centages of the farming types in each farm size-group, indicate a probable relationship between the two movements. Over forty per cent (41%) of the total acreage of farms below 150 acres is either mainly dairying or dairying and mixed farms while only 20% of the acreage of holdings 150 acres and over is of these farming types. Conversely the farming types, corn, sheep and dairying, heavy land arable, light land arable, and mixed with dairying of the

[1] cf. Table App. 5, Appendix p. 197.
[2] cf. p. 61 ante.

Intermediate group cover 36% of the total acreage of farms 150 acres and above, and 26% of the total acreage of the holdings below 150 acres.

Rents of the larger holdings are clearly seen to be more rapidly advancing than the rents of the smaller holdings when the yearly rates of increase are compared as in Table 10.

TABLE 10
AVERAGE ANNUAL RENT CHANGE FOR EACH FARM SIZE-GROUP
1945–1956, 1956–57 and 1957–58.

FARM SIZE-GROUP	AVERAGE ANNUAL RENT CHANGE 1945–56	AVERAGE RENT CHANGE	
		1956–57	1957–58
acres	%	%	%
15–49	3.9	5.2	2.6
50–99	4.5	3.7	3.5
100–149	4.3	6.1	3.3
150–299	4.6	7.6	3.5
300–499	4.8	7.4	3.5
500 and over	5.1	9.0	3.7
All size-groups	4.5	6.9	3.2

Between 1945 and 1956, farms in the three largest size-groups enjoyed average yearly rent increases greater than the average yearly increase for all holdings, of about 4.5%. The yearly rise on farms of 500 acres and over was 5.1%; on farms 300-499 acres 4.8%; and on farms 150-299 acres 4.6%. On farms in the three lowest size-groups, the yearly increase was average or less; 4.3% on farms of 100-149 acres, 4.5% on farms between 50 and 99 acres and 3.9% on the smallest farms. A slight reversal in the pronounced trend for yearly average increments to rise with acreage occurs between the yearly increment in the rent of the 50-99 acre farms and the yearly increment in the rent of the 100-149 acre farms. The rate of increase for 1956-57 is on average 6.9% and is distinctly higher than the yearly average over the eleven years of the previous period. Again, the three size-groups over 150 acres achieve a rent increase considerably higher than average: a 9% increase on farms of 500 acres and over, a 7.4% increase on 300-499 acre farms, and a 7.6% increase on 150-299 acre farms. In the three lowest size-groups increases are less than average: ranging from 5.2% on 15-49 acre farms to 6.1% on 100-149 acre farms. In this period the rent of the 50-99 acre group appears to be suffering from over-strain and increases by only 3.7%, the lowest rate of increase of all size-groups. The 50-99 acre group of farms also is the only size-group to show in 1956-1957 a lower rate of increase than the yearly average rate for the previous period.

In accordance with the movements in the national average rents, all size-groups show the lowest rates of increase in the year 1957-1958. As in previous years, the three largest size-groups achieve the highest increases, surpassing those of the smallest size-groups with the exception of the 50-99 acres group. The rent of this group recovers its former energy and surpasses the rent increase of the next higher size-group and so revives the reversal in trend noticed in 1945-56.

CHAPTER FIVE

CHARACTER OF HOLDING: FIXED EQUIPMENT

Holdings hitherto have been grouped according to the provision of fixed equipment as an incidental step in the analysis of information about farming type rents and the rents of farm size-groups. The incidental grouping has hinted more than once of a probable relationship between the level of rent and the provision of fixed equipment and the evidence for this relationship must now be considered.

The analysis of variance[1] shows that buildings and electricity combined have a significant effect on rent per acre. The following paragraphs examine their separate effects on rent.

The survey information refers only to fixed equipment provided by the landlord as part of the demised holding for which the tenant pays rent. The definition of fixed equipment does not recognise tenant's fixtures; where for example a tenant has installed his own generating plant, the holding, for the purposes of the survey, is "without electricity". Sometimes cottages on a particular farm may be independently hired by the farmer under a separate tenancy agreement. Adventitious provision in this way is outside the relationship of fixed equipment and farm rent.

Rent per acre and standards of fixed equipment.

Farmhouse and buildings. A homestead—farmhouse and farm buildings—is provided on 84% of the holdings in the survey, representing 91% of the total acreage. Either farmhouse or buildings are provided on 5% of the holdings, representing about the same

TABLE 11
AVERAGE CURRENT RENT PER ACRE AND FIXED EQUIPMENT.
1957

FIXED EQUIPMENT	RENT PER ACRE	PERCENTAGE OF TOTAL	
		Acreage	Holdings
	£	%	%
Farmhouse and buildings	1.92	91.4	83.7
Farmhouse only	1.89	0.2	0.4
Buildings only	1.82	4.4	4.7
Land only	1.51	4.0	11.2

[1] v. Single one-way classification. Appendix p. 191.

percentage of the acreage. Holdings of bare land without home-steads make up 11% of the total number and 4% of the total acreage. Holdings are classified according to these four standards of provision of fixed equipment. Table 11 gives the average rent per acre in each class.

Rents per acre unadjusted for rough grazings rise distinctly and regularly as the standard of fixed equipment improves from bare land to a full homestead. Rent of holdings with house and buildings averages £1.92 per acre. This is approximately 8s. per acre higher than the £1.51 per acre rent of land only; 2/- higher than the £1.82 rent of holdings with farm buildings only; and only 6d. per acre higher than the £1.89 per acre rent of holdings where only a farm-house is provided. A farmhouse without buildings is unusual and in the survey only 56 holdings are so equipped.

Electricity supply. When the first three classes of Table 11 are subdivided according to whether electricity is provided either to farmhouse or to buildings or to both, the rent per acre relationship is disturbed. Holdings with farmhouse and buildings, when elect-ricity is provided to one or the other, have somewhat lower rents than holdings with a farmhouse only and holdings with farm buildings only, when these have electricity. Moreover, when holdings with electricity are excluded from the others, the rent of the holdings with homesteads is no longer the highest; the rent of each class tends to be equal. Table 12 gives the figures.

TABLE 12

AVERAGE CURRENT RENT PER ACRE AND FIXED EQUIPMENT
WITH AND WITHOUT ELECTRICITY.

1957

FIXED EQUIPMENT	WITH ELECTRICITY TO:						NO ELEC-TRICITY	
	House and buildings		House only		Buildings only			
	Rent per acre	Average size of holding	Rent per acre	Average size of holding	Rent per acre	Average size of holding	Rent per acre	Average size of holding
	£	acres	£	acres	£	acres	£	acres
Farmhouse and buildings	2.12	182	1.83	121	1.23	248	1.50	155
Farmhouse only	—	—	2.14	61	—	—	1.53	61
Buildings only	—	—	—	—	2.23	183	1.51	128

While in the subdivisions the regular relationship between rent per acre and the provision of farmhouse and buildings is not apparent, regular relationship is displayed between rent per acre and the standard of electricity supply. On holdings where the provision of farmhouse and buildings is uniform, the provision of electricity is invariably accompanied by higher rent. Where there is a homestead and electricity is supplied both to house and buildings the average rent per acre is £2.12; with electricity only to house the rent is £1.83; and to buildings only, £1.23: without electricity, the rent is £1.5 per acre. While the provision of electricity appears to make a difference of 12/- per acre between the extremes, its provision to farmbuildings only of a homestead has apparently no influence upon rent; this lack of response to the supply of electricity is the only exception to the regular relationship otherwise displayed between rent and electricity supply. The farms without electricity, however, have four times as much rough grazing land as the farms with electricity. Adjustment for rough grazings raises the rents per acre; the highest becomes £2.24 and the lowest £1.87, reducing the difference between extremes to about 7/6d. per acre. But the regular relationship between rent per acre and the standard of electricity supply displayed by the unadjusted rents is not disturbed.

Of all holdings with a farmhouse and buildings, sixty-two per cent have electricity provided to both, and this substantial percentage helps to keep high the average rent of all holdings with a homestead whatever their electricity supply. The percentage of the homestead holdings otherwise provided with electricity is quite low: five per cent have it to the farmhouse only, and less than one per cent to the buildings only. Holdings with homestead and no electricity are thus thirty-two per cent of the total.

Where a farmhouse only is provided, farms with electricity show a difference of 8/- rent per acre, even when the figures are adjusted for rough grazings. These holdings have 59% of their number supplied with electricity; a percentage substantial enough to boost the average rent of all holdings with farmhouse only and keep it close to the average rent of the holdings with homesteads. Where buildings only are provided, farms with electricity show a difference of 6/6 rent per adjusted acre. Of these holdings, 35% have electricity, a relatively low percentage, but in keeping with the average rent of all holdings of this type.

Provision of electricity is patently associated with higher rent per acre, on average an additional 6/6 to 8/- per adjusted acre. The evidence strongly suggests that the apparent relationship between the provision of farmhouse and buildings and rent per acre is illusory and in fact is the consequence of differences in the extent to which the holdings of these categories are supplied with electricity. Without electricity the average rent of the holdings in each of the three fixed equipment categories of Table 12 is not only approximately equal but is equal also to the average rent of the wholly unequipped holdings of Table 11. This apparent indifference of rent to the provision of farmhouse and buildings is partly explained by the size of the holdings which comprise the "farmhouse only" and "land only" categories. From the average size of holding figures given in Table 12 it is evident that the level of the average rent of the "farmland only" holdings is higher than it would have been if the holdings in this category had been similar in average size to those in the other categories. Comparison of the average size of holding figures for the electrified holdings with their counterparts for the non-electrified holdings shows clearly that the higher average rents of the electrified holdings are not the consequence of telling differences in the average size of holding among the categories, and supports the presence or absence of electricity supply as an influential determinant of farm rent.

Rough grazings acreage is invariably greater on the holdings without electricity, suggesting that the rent differences between the "haves" and "have nots" may to some extent be due to the influence of farming type. It is significant, for example, that one third of the total acreage of the holdings with farmhouse and buildings and no electricity lies in upland mixed livestock holdings where rents are the lowest of all farming types[1]. To eliminate the influence of farming types from the comparison of the rents of electrified and non-electrified holdings, these rents are compared within each farming type. The figures are given in Table 13. Holdings with homesteads and electricity to buildings only, and holdings with farmhouse and no buildings, are too few for this analysis and are therefore excluded.

Although sixty-two per cent of all farms in the survey with farmhouse and buildings have electricity to both, widely different percentages are found among the various farming types. Each of the four farming types which in Table 13 display the least difference in rent between the "haves" and "have nots" have a higher than average number of holdings with electricity—from 69% of all alluvial arable and mixed farms to 78% of all corn, sheep and dairying farms. All the other farming types with their greater differences in rent between electrified and non-electrified holdings, Specialists and the two dairying types of the Grass group excepted, have a lower than average number of holdings with electricity. Apart then from specialist holdings and dairying farms, the greatest rent differences are associated with farming types relatively badly off

[1] cf. p. 51 ante.

for electricity supply. Doubtless to some extent this association spells scarcity value: the scarcity of these types of farms with electricity enhances their rental value above that of the farms without electricity. But the possibility that electricity has gone to the better type of holding must not be overlooked as a partial cause of the association. With the specialists and dairying farms, the greater rent difference consequent upon electricity cannot be due to scarcity, as these types are better provided with electricity than the average. Whatever the explanation may be, the important fact here is the difference in rent between the electrified and non-electrified.

The general verdict of analysis supports what has been previously observed. Rents of most farming types are higher where electricity is provided, on average by nearly eight shillings per acre. Apart from specialists with a rent difference of nearly £1 an acre, lowland mixed livestock farms and dairying farms are the most sensitive, with a rent difference averaging about eight shillings per acre. Upland mixed livestock farms, general mixed farms and dairy and mixed farms of the Grass group are moderately sensitive and increase their rent by about six shillings per acre. Also responsive are the heavy arable land farms with a rent difference of five shillings per acre, and mixed with dairying of the Intermediate group with a rent difference of about three shillings per acre. There are three exceptions to this sensitivity. Alluvial arable and mixed farms and light arable land farms without electricity are about 1/- and 1/6d. per acre higher rented than the electrified holdings. Corn, sheep and dairying holdings appear to be fairly indifferent to electricity; the rent difference is about 1/6d. per acre where electricity is provided.

When on holdings with homesteads the farmhouse only has electricity, the provision of electricity is associated with a rent difference of about 4/6d. per acre. Specialist holdings exert a strong influence upon this difference. Amongst most of the other farming types, the rent differences are remarkably uniform, varying between 2/- and 3/- per acre. The exceptions are alluvial arable and mixed farms, dairying and mixed farms (Grass group) and upland mixed livestock farms; electricity makes no positive difference to the rent of the electrified holdings, on the contrary, they are lower by two shillings, four shillings and about one shilling per acre respectively.

The tendency of the rent differences of holdings with buildings only is almost the reverse of what has hitherto been observed. The specialists, alluvial arable and mixed farms and light arable land farms are the most sensitive to electricity, its provision being

TABLE 13

DIFFERENCE IN AVERAGE CURRENT RENT PER ACRE(i) ON PROVISION OF ELECTRICITY BY FARMING TYPE.

1957

FARMING TYPE	RENT PER ACRE DIFFERENCE ON PROVISION OF ELECTRICITY		
	TO HOLDINGS WITH HOMESTEADS		TO HOLDINGS WITH BUILDINGS ONLY
	House and buildings £	House only £	£
Specialists	.06	1.68	.98
Mixed livestock (lowland)	.42	.10	—.03
Mainly dairying	.37	.13	.05
Mixed livestock (upland)	.31	—.06	.67*
General mixed	.30	.14	.29
Dairy and mixed (Grass)	.28	—.20	.13
Heavy arable land	.25	.11	—.12
Mixed with dairying	.16	.11	.25
Corn, sheep and dairying	.08	—.66*	—.44*
Alluvial arable and mixed	—.06	—.10	.38
Light arable land	—.08	.11	.33
All farming types	.37	.22	.32

(i) Adjusted for rough grazings.

associated with differences of rent of nearly £1, about seven shillings and sixpence, and six shillings and sixpence per acre respectively. The rent of heavy land arable farms, on the other hand, is lower where the holdings are electrified than where they are not, by five shillings per acre. Lowland mixed livestock farms and the dairying farms, show the smallest differences of all types: with one, the rent of electrified holdings is lower by about 6d. per acre, and with the other higher by a 1/- per acre. On general mixed farms with electricity rents are higher by about six shillings per acre; and on mixed with dairying farms by five shillings per acre. On dairying and mixed farms of the Grass group, electricity makes little difference to the rents, no more than an additional two and sixpence per acre.

Having looked at the provision of electricity by farming type, it will complete the picture to look at this aspect of fixed equipment by farm size-groups. Table 14 sets out the evidence. The rent differences between electrified and non-electrified holdings shown in the Table, with one exception, are positive. Here is consistent evidence of the provision of electricity making for higher rents.

Capital per acre invested in fixed equipment, it has been pointed out before, will tend to be less on large than on small farms. By this principle the rent difference per acre due to the provision of electricity should diminish as farm size increases. This tendency, somewhat obscured by other factors, can be traced in the rent differences of Table 14. Farms of the two smallest size-groups invariably display the highest rent difference, and on the 15-49 acre holdings the rent difference is higher than on the 50-99 acre holdings.

In all the categories of fixed equipment and electricity the tendency is patent. Among the holdings with a homestead, the difference in rent when electricity is supplied to the entire homestead falls regularly as the size of holding increases, except with the largest holdings: on the smallest holdings the difference is about fifteen shillings and sixpence per acre; on 50-99 acre farms about eleven shillings and sixpence per acre; on 100-149 acre farms about nine shillings; and on 150-299 acre and 300-499 acre farms about eight shillings. But with the largest farms, 500 acres and over, the tendency to fall is reversed and the rent difference shoots up to about eleven shillings per acre. Although there is clearly a tendency for the extra rent per acre associated with electricity to diminish as acreage rises, the fall is less than proportionate to the rise in acreage. Other factors exert a cross-influence, especially differences in representation of farming types in the size-groups. With some farming types, as previously observed, the rent

F

TABLE 14

DIFFERENCE IN AVERAGE CURRENT RENT PER ACRE(i) ON PROVISION OF ELECTRICITY
BY FARM SIZE-GROUPS.

1957

FARM SIZE-GROUP	RENT PER ACRE DIFFERENCE ON PROVISION OF ELECTRICITY			
	TO HOLDINGS WITH HOMESTEADS		TO HOLDINGS WITH BUILDINGS ONLY
	House and buildings	House only	
acres	£	£	£
15–49	.77	.35	.90
50–99	.58	.25	.51
100–149	.44	—.06	.38
150–299	.40	.11	.29
300–499	.37	.23	.49
500 and over	.54	.25*	.33*
ALL SIZES	.37	.22	.32

(i) adjusted for rough grazings.

difference consequent upon electricity is greater than with others. Differences of farming type representation also impair somewhat the comparison of the rents of the electrified holdings and those of the non-electrified; this is especially so with the larger farms.

Water supply. Water supply, a further feature of the fixed equipment of holdings included in the survey is considered by grouping the holdings into five groups, those with

piped mains;
piped estate supply;
piped supply from source on the farm;
supply not piped;
no supply.

Just over half the number of holdings, 54%, have piped mains; 13% have a private piped estate supply; 17% have piped water from a source on the farm; 11% have a supply of water but not piped; and 5% have no supply at all. Private piped supplies are more frequent on the larger farms. In terms of acreage therefore the percentages are higher for holdings with piped estate supply, and for those with piped farm supply; conversely, holdings with no piped supply and those without a supply represent only 7% and 2% respectively of total acreage.

Average rent per acre for each of the five water supply groups is given in Table 15.

TABLE 15
AVERAGE CURRENT RENT PER ACRE AND WATER SUPPLY.
1957

WATER SUPPLY	RENT PER ACRE		PERCENTAGE OF TOTAL	
	adjusted	unadjusted	acreage	holdings
	£	£	%	%
Piped mains	2.30	2.22	52.2	53.6
Private estate	2.05	1.84	15.0	12.7
Source on farm	1.84	1.42	23.5	17.4
Not piped	1.81	1.39	7.1	10.8
No supply	1.78	1.40	2.2	5.5

Technical efficiency of water supply clearly has a direct bearing upon rent per acre. This is confirmed by the analysis of variance[1] which shows that water supply exerts a highly significant influence on rent per acre. Table 15 shows holdings with piped mains as the highest rented, with a rent of £2.3 per acre (adjusted). This average rent exceeds by five shillings per acre the next highest average, the rent of holdings with a private piped estate supply;

[1] v. Single one-way classification, Appendix p. 191.

and is about ten shillings and sixpence above the lowest rent of all, on farms without water supply.

The rent of holdings with a private piped estate supply is £2.05 per acre (adjusted), and exceeds by about four shillings per acre the next highest rent, that of holdings with a piped supply from a farm source. The margins of rental difference between the three other groups are very narrow. Rent of the holdings with a piped supply from a farm source exceeds the rents of the two lowest rental groups, holdings with no piped supply and those without a supply, by no more than about sixpence and a shilling per acre respectively.

When the rents of farming types are compared[1], the principle of highest rent associated with piped mains is characteristic of all farming types save three. Two of the exceptions are corn, sheep and dairying farms[2], where the highest rent is found on farms with no piped water supply; and lowland mixed livestock farms where the highest rent is found on holdings supplied by a private estate system. The third exception is dairy and mixed farms of the Intermediate group where the rent of holdings with piped mains water equals the rent of holdings with an unpiped supply. Throughout all farming types, apart from the two main exceptions mentioned above, holdings with piped mains have rents at least a shilling an acre higher than average. As would be expected, the rents of the the first two exceptions just mentioned are very near the average, mixed lowland livestock less than sixpence above it and corn, sheep and dairying about sixpence below. The rent of the holdings with mains water of the other farming types rises above the average by varying amounts: six shillings on upland livestock farms; about three and six on the dairying farms; two and six to three shillings on light arable land farms, dairying and mixed farms, alluvial arable and mixed and general mixed farms; and barely over one and sixpence on heavy arable land farms and mixed with dairying farms.

Rents of holdings in the other water supply categories are less inclined in each farming type to follow the normal pattern. Holdings with private estate water systems tend, as with the normal pattern, to attract higher rents per acre than the holdings supplied from a source on the farm: for example, mixed lowland livestock farms have a rent advantage of about seven shillings and sixpence per acre; the dairying farms about six shillings; the upland mixed live-

---

[1] No table is given for rents associated with forms of water supply and farming type, but the number of holdings in each combination of these categories to which reference is made in this section of the text is in each case more than ten unless specifically referred to by footnotes as being less.

[2] Seven holdings of the corn, sheep and dairying class have no water supply; nine have a water supply but not piped.

stock farms about four shillings and sixpence; and the dairying and mixed farms of the Grass group also about four shillings and sixpence. On the contrary, corn, sheep and dairying farms have rents which are about three shillings per acre higher and light arable and general mixed farms have rents about one shilling higher where the water supply is from a source on the farm, than where it is supplied by a private estate water system. Rents of heavy arable land farms and mixed with dairying farms of the Intermediate group and alluvial arable and mixed are indifferent to whether the water supply comes from an estate system or a piped farm supply, with a margin of difference between one shilling and one and sixpence per acre. Rents of holdings where the water is unpiped and those with no supply at all, as with the normal pattern, tend on average to be lowest of all. But there are weighty exceptions. In three farming types, the rent of these holdings is higher than the rent of holdings where water is piped either from a private estate system or from a source on the farm: the three farming types are alluvial arable and mixed, mixed with dairying of the Intermediate group, and corn, sheep and dairying. These exceptionally high rents are probably associated in some way with the extraordinarily high rents of these farming types on holdings without buildings[1]. Rents of the dairying farms and mixed lowland livestock farms behave somewhat similarly. On holdings with un-piped water supply and on those with no supply at all, rents are higher than on holdings with a piped supply from a source on the farm.

Farm Cottages. Farm cottages, unlike homesteads, are a form of fixed equipment which by its very nature tends to increase proportionately in quantity with the size of farm. The number of farm cottages on a holding is likely to bear proportionate resemblance to the number of acres. The level of fixed equipment, in this case, on which the level of rent might depend is best expressed as the number of cottages per acre, or per holding of a uniform size. An attempt is made in Table 16 to show how rent per acre is related to the number of cottages per unit of area. The evidence is arranged in farm size-groups and by density of cottages per holding; these categories run from no cottages at all to six cottages or more per holding.

The evidence of Table 16 shows a remarkably regular relationship between rent per acre and the number of cottages per unit area. The figures in each farm size-group show rent per acre rising as the density of cottages per holding increases. Here and

[1] cf. p. 57 ante.

there are slight aberrations from this general trend. On the whole, however, the evidence is so consistent that these aberrations do not call for particular attention and finer analysis. It is noteworthy that the difference in rent between holdings with no cottages and those with the highest density of cottages tends to increase with farm size; lack of cottages on a small holding is a less serious matter for farm rent than lack of cottages on a larger one although this is to some extent dependent on type of farming also.

TABLE 16
RENT PER ACRE AND COTTAGES BY FARM SIZE-GROUPS.
1957

FARM SIZE-GROUP	RENT PER ACRE	NUMBER OF COTTAGES						
		None	one	two	three	four	five	six or more
		Rent per acre	Rent per acre	Rent per acre	Rent per acre	Rent per acre	Rent per acre	Rent per acre
acres	£	£	£	£	£	£	£	£
15–49	2.62	2.58	2.96	4.42	5.35*	2.43*	1.42*	2.70*
50–99	2.27	2.18	2.58	2.85	2.70	2.78*	—	1.61*
100–149	2.13	1.88	2.34	2.51	2.73	2.93	2.18*	4.00*
150–299	2.05	1.56	1.99	2.23	2.46	2.40	2.76	2.93
300–499	1.82	0.93	1.49	1.85	2.05	1.98	2.17	2.31
500 and over	1.17	0.29	0.40	0.66	1.01	1.61	1.51	1.84
All sizes	1.90	1.69	1.95	2.00	2.13	2.08	2.08	2.03

The analysis of variance[1] shows that when farm size and provision of cottages are considered together the two factors interact significantly but it is cottages which exert the dominant influence on rent and not size of farm.

[1] v. Appendix pp. 192, 193.

CHAPTER SIX

COUNTY RENT LEVELS

A county boundary of itself has no obvious logical connection with farm rent, but, as stated earlier, the evidence from the survey points to the existence of forces which tend to localize rent levels within county boundaries and hence to give significance to county average rents. This presentation of the evidence would be incomplete if no reference were made to the county averages and their relationship with each other and the national average farm rent.

County average farm rents provide a simple geography of rent levels, simple because it is not deliberately linked with the location of farming types or any similar complication. The geography of current rent levels as county averages is cartographically depicted on the accompanying map. County average rents have been calculated from the raised sample[1] of holdings in each county corresponding to the county totals of rented holdings[2]. Figures used for the map are given in Table 17. These figures, reliable guides to farm rent in general within each county, have nevertheless in their make-up rent figures from all sorts and conditions of farming. In a county of many-sided farming they might, therefore, obscure a variation in rent level peculiar to a particular farming type. The county rent levels of the map should therefore be compared with the finer analysis of Table 17 which gives for each county the average rent per acre by principal farming types and throws light upon what may be obscured by the simple county averages. The analysis of variance[3] indicates that county location exerts, in general, a strong influence upon farm rent per acre.

High and low rented counties. The peak of the simple geography of rent levels occurs in the county of Cheshire. Here current farm rent averages £3.19—or, £3 3s. 9d. per acre and lies in the highest rent stratum of the map. Counties with an average rent somewhere between £2. 10s. and £2 19s. 11d. per acre, the next highest stratum, are near neighbours to Cheshire: Lancashire

---

[1] v.p. 38.
[2] County average rents based on an unraised sample differ only slightly from those of the raised sample; cf. Table App. 6 Appendix p. 198.
[3] v. Single one-way classification, Appendix   p. 191.

to the north, Shropshire and Staffordshire to the south and the Flint appendage in the west. These counties and Cheshire form a large pocket of highly rented farm land. Only two other counties approach so exalted a rent range: Kent in the south east and Somerset in the Wessex peninsula.

Averages up to 12s. per acre above the national average of £1 18s. 9d. are found in a great horseshoe area: the western Midlands from Derbyshire in the north to Wiltshire in the south form the western limb of the horseshoe; Nottinghamshire is an arch spanning Derbyshire and Lincolnshire, the northern-most county of the eastern limb; the eastern limb, greater in length than the western, reaches the south coast at Sussex, via East Anglia and Surrey. But for the high rent of Somerset the western limb of the horseshoe would have reached the Channel, for the average rent of Devonshire lies within the rent range of the horse-shoe counties.

County averages within the range £1 10s.—£1 19s. 11d. per acre and thus running up to the national average, are characteristic of the counties in the horseshoe centre, from Northamptonshire to Dorset. Averages within the same rent range touch the outer rim of the horseshoe: Yorkshire crowns the north, Norfolk flanks the east, and the border counties of Denbigh and Monmouth lie to the west. In this range of averages is also the peninsular county of Cornwall.

The deepest depression of this geography of rent levels corresponds with the highlands of physical geography. All is not deepest gloom—there are degrees of depression. Northumberland, Durham, Cumberland and Westmorland are among the better off counties with average rents in the range £1—£1 9s. 11d. per acre. Assoc-iated with these in this rent range are the southern counties of Wales, the border county of Montgomery and the Isle of Anglesey. The sea-board counties of mid-Wales and Radnorshire inland have the lowest average rents of all; and among them the average rent of Merioneth is the nadir of the depression.

Influence of farming type. County average rent, it was observed just now, might obscure variations in rent level, peculiar to a particular farming type which, if the variations were patent, could in themselves place a county differently in the scale of county average rents. This would happen as a consequence of an uneven distribution of farming types in a county, if the relationship of overall county average rents to each other were peculiar to those averages and were not found also among the county average rents of all holdings of specific farming types. The evidence of Table 17

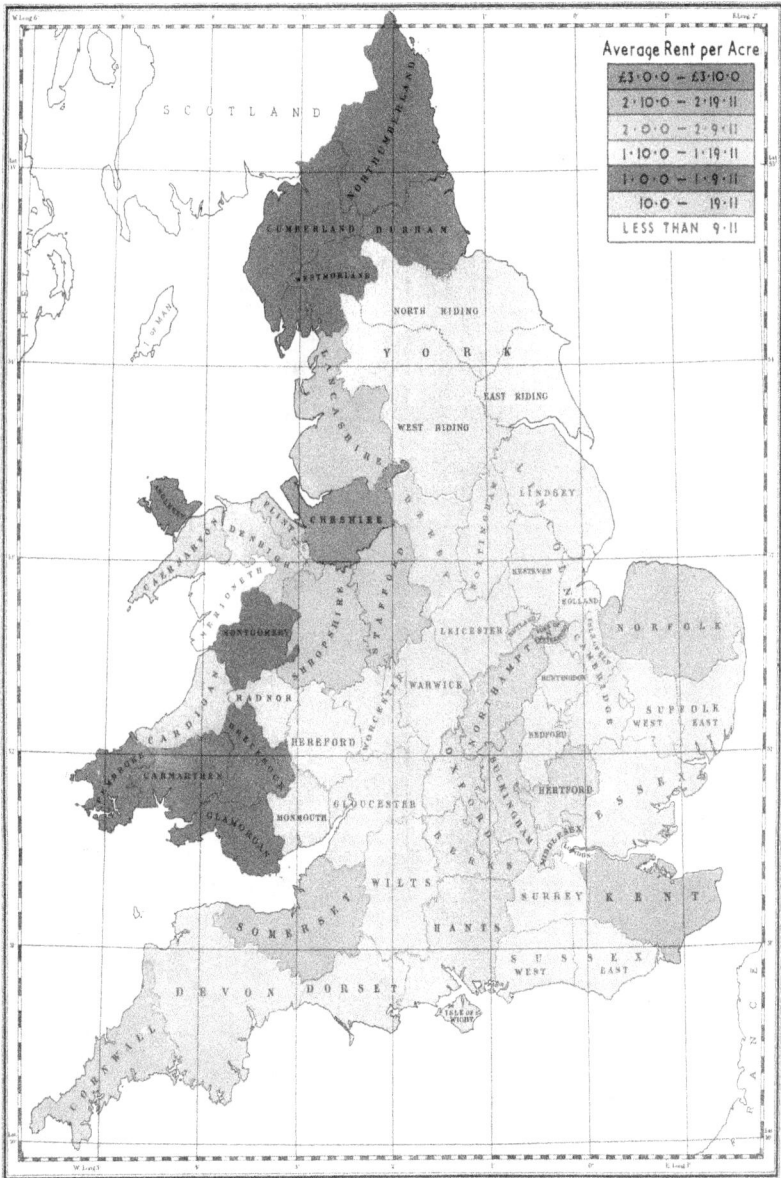

Average Rent per Acre
£3·0·0 — £3·10·0
2·10·0 — 2·19·11
2·0·0 — 2·9·11
1·10·0 — 1·19·11
1·0·0 — 1·9·11
10·0 — 19·11
LESS THAN 9·11

Farm Rent, 1957. Distribution by County Averages.

indicates that, in the main, the relationship of the overall county average rents to each other is reflected in the relationship of county average rents of holdings of specific farming types.

Cheshire for example has a higher overall average county rent than Leicestershire. Cheshire's superiority over Leicestershire, however, is not entirely due to a higher percentage of dairy acreage and a correspondingly lower percentage of Intermediate and Arable type acreage. The key to Cheshire's high position is the relatively high rent of dairy holdings and Intermediate and Arable holdings in the county; without exception, their rents are higher than the corresponding rents in Leicestershire. Cheshire indeed boasts the highest county average rent among all holdings of the larger sample given to dairy farming, lowland livestock farming and farming of all Intermediate and Arable types and is among the first ten highest rented counties in the Specialist class. Cheshire's high farming type rents are responsible for the high overall county average rent.

On the evidence of Cheshire, it appears that the relationship of overall county rents to each other is in some measure independent of the acreage distribution of particular farming types in the respective counties. This is borne out by looking at the position of county average rents within the five principal farming type classes. Table 17 sets out the five series. Of the ten counties with the highest overall county average rents, six are among the ten highest-rented counties in the dairy and lowland livestock type and in the Intermediate and Arable groups; seven are among the foremost ten of the dairy and lowland livestock rents and of the Intermediate group, and eight are among the foremost ten of the Intermediate group. On this showing, the relative position of the overall county average rents is a consequence of locality and not of farm type distribution.

The tendency for counties with the highest farming type county average rents to correspond to the counties with the highest overall county average rent is not apparent in the rents of upland livestock holdings. Of the ten counties with the highest overall county averages, Kent only finds a place among the ten counties with the highest upland livestock rents. The exception does not weaken the general principle that high overall county averages are not mainly the consequence of dominant percentages of particular farming types. Upland livestock holdings are the lowest rented of the farming types[1] and a dominant acreage of them in a county would not lift the overall county average rent to the highest position on

[1] cf. p. 94 post.

TABLE 17 (Part I)
CURRENT AVERAGE RENT PER ACRE FOR EACH COUNTY OVERALL, AND BY PRINCIPAL FARMING TYPES.

RENT PER ACRE AND ACREAGE

COUNTY (with overall rent above national average)	OVERALL		PRINCIPAL FARMING TYPES										
			GRASS				INTERMEDIATE		ARABLE		SPECIALISTS	
	£(i)	acres(ii)	Excluding mixed livestock (upland)		Mixed livestock (upland)							
			£	acreage %	£	acreage %	£	acreage %	£	acreage %	£	acreage %
Cheshire	3.19	42,286	3.40	69.39	0.90*	3.41	3.18	23.98	3.24	2.87	4.50*	0.35
Somerset	2.68	49,998	3.04	60.45	0.85	15.93	2.53	20.11	2.65	3.18	3.86*	0.33
Shropshire	2.64	58,247	2.70	59.65	1.06	6.10	2.61	22.45	2.13	7.26	2.11	4.54
Lancashire	2.62	55,513	2.25	47.42	0.57	26.02	3.01	10.62	3.01	14.92	2.80*	1.02
Stafford	2.55	34,941	2.56	49.24	1.24	3.34	2.57	40.87	2.33	6.36	3.58*	0.19
Flint	2.53	9,308	2.61	75.89	1.02*	11.07	2.37	13.04	—	—	—	—
Kent	2.52	36,881	1.85	23.63	1.33*	0.86	2.42	33.28	2.59	26.31	3.47	15.92
Essex	2.43	47,052	2.45	9.88	—	—	2.42	19.74	2.42	67.07	3.33	3.31
Cambridge	2.43	33,784	2.75	1.98	—	—	1.69	8.11	2.43	87.98	3.04*	1.93
Huntingdon	2.40	14,117	2.01*	1.01	—	—	2.16	26.93	2.23	71.93	1.32*	0.13
Lincoln	2.33	120,510	2.02	4.64	2.91*	0.23	1.85	23.36	2.42	71.08	4.17	0.69
Hereford	2.29	32,337	2.39	52.13	1.63	9.71	2.28	34.47	2.47*	2.87	3.58*	0.82
Warwick	2.26	27,998	2.29	33.20	1.61*	0.33	2.18	53.60	2.32	12.31	3.08*	0.56
Devon	2.25	54,722	2.45	50.73	0.95	15.92	2.08	31.50	2.62*	1.17	3.01*	0.68
Wiltshire	2.24	54,142	2.62	37.07	—	—	2.08	39.33	1.70	22.60	5.43*	0.10
Rutland	2.23	5,936	2.22	34.57	—	—	1.81	39.34	2.68*	26.09	—	—
Worcester	2.19	21,384	2.16	35.86	1.60*	5.77	2.34	36.12	1.99	17.91	2.23*	4.34
Leicester	2.17	30,682	2.22	58.79	1.06*	0.40	2.14	30.55	2.17	8.97	1.46*	1.29
Derby	2.12	36,800	2.28	58.09	1.62	18.18	2.19	22.11	2.42*	1.33	4.82*	0.29
Suffolk	2.08	48,753	1.86	3.79	—	—	1.90	25.61	2.18	70.23	2.48*	0.37
Nottingham	2.05	32,883	2.24	10.08	1.27*	0.29	2.06	34.82	1.97	54.82	4.57*	0.09
Sussex	2.05	54,670	2.01	37.98	1.01	1.32	2.02	53.30	2.39	6.37	3.73*	1.03
Bedford	2.03	15,461	2.07	8.87	—	—	1.85	34.54	1.98	42.95	2.09	13.64
Gloucester	2.00	45,075	2.44	40.80	1.08	1.87	1.71	37.65	1.62	18.51	2.95*	1.17
Surrey	2.00	11,882	1.98	45.49	1.50*	0.22	1.82	29.08	2.18	23.18	3.07*	2.03
Middlesex	1.97	1,285	2.68*	4.13	2.00*	1.32	2.10*	94.55	—	—	—	—
Oxford	1.97	34,669	2.00	30.31	0.67*	3.10	2.31	44.15	1.92	22.07	0.95*	0.37
Hertford	1.95	25,859	1.88	10.75	—	—	2.09	30.89	1.88	55.61	2.93*	2.75

(i) Raised sample. (ii) In sample.

TABLE 17 (Part II)

RENT PER ACRE AND ACREAGE

COUNTY (with overall rent at or below national average)	OVERALL		PRINCIPAL FARMING TYPES									
			GRASS				INTERMEDIATE		ARABLE		SPECIALISTS	
			Excluding mixed livestock (upland)		Mixed livestock (upland)							
	£(i)	acres(ii)	£	acreage %	£	acreage %	£	acreage %	£	acreage %	£	acreage %
Berkshire	1.94	20,762	2.23	15.75	—	—	1.81	50.84	1.65	22.76	2.14*	1.65
Buckingham	1.94	32,387	2.03	42.30	0.16*	0.96	1.87	35.48	1.90	20.50	1.76*	0.71
Hampshire	1.94	53,248	2.07	32.37	1.14*	1.64	1.89	37.51	1.78	26.94	2.88	1.54
Northampton	1.94	30,724	1.96	37.18	—	—	1.93	47.68	1.98	15.14	1.81*	0.23
Dorset	1.93	59,543	2.01	57.71	1.23	4.42	1.80	30.05	1.75	7.59	2.07*	0.36
Norfolk	1.93	77,706	1.95	2.26	2.67*	0.04	1.86	16.99	1.92	80.35	4.31	1.28
Cornwall	1.87	34,709	1.81	50.84	0.84	11.84	1.73	33.13	1.59*	2.91	3.26*	0.10
Denbigh	1.81	21,720	2.27	64.32	1.03	31.79	2.68*	3.79	—	—	3.80*	0.39
Yorkshire	1.71	184,186	1.75	18.71	0.63	13.50	1.84	35.53	1.06	31.81	—	—
Monmouth	1.54	10,927	1.80	62.20	0.93	20.95	1.60	10.85	—	—	—	—
Anglesey	1.49	9,610	1.52	87.70	—	—	1.15	12.30	—	—	1.25*	1.27
Durham	1.48	26,383	1.50	30.86	0.55	18.02	1.49	39.46	1.93	10.39	—	—
Pembroke	1.42	7,720	1.41	78.85	0.92*	3.88	1.14*	17.27	—	—	—	—
Westmorland	1.35	20,655	1.56	40.57	0.69	32.07	1.56	27.36	—	—	1.82*	0.03
Cumberland	1.30	85,644	1.90	27.51	0.33	56.65	1.87	15.31	2.86*	0.50	4.09*	0.09
Northumberland	1.17	108,006	1.68	19.35	0.52	51.13	1.70	18.62	1.93	10.81	0.05*	0.13
Glamorgan	1.17	16,773	1.74	48.48	0.30	22.35	1.31	28.16	0.68*	0.88	—	—
Brecon	1.11	7,022	2.23	24.14	0.75	68.78	1.17*	7.08	—	—	—	—
Montgomery	1.09	19,026	2.25	22.20	0.51	62.49	1.73	13.52	1.34*	1.79	—	—
Carmarthen	1.06	14,596	1.32	81.28	0.46	17.68	1.43*	0.77	0.75*	0.27	0.06	35.87
Radnor	0.80	22,789	1.75	7.06	0.64	47.34	1.56	9.73	—	—	—	—
Caernarvon	0.75	11,495	1.23	40.78	0.45	56.15	2.02*	2.04	1.36*	1.03	—	—
Cardigan	0.73	8,958	1.26	28.54	0.15	63.54	0.68*	7.92	—	—	—	—
Merioneth	0.48	17,270	1.03	13.57	0.42	84.24	1.05*	2.19	—	—	—	—

(i) Raised sample. (ii) In sample.

the county rent scale: on the contrary, a dominant acreage of this type would tend to depress it.

Low overall county average rents tend also to be reflected in county farming type averages. Counties with the lowest overall averages are elevated and mountainous. Obviously a high percentage of their farm holdings are upland livestock holdings. Rent in these counties cannot avoid the rent-depressing influence of this low-rented farming type. But, as the evidence of Table 17 shows, the lowest average county rents of this and other farming types, with the exception of Arable and Specialist types, are also found in these counties. Six of the ten counties with the lowest overall county average rents are among the ten lowest-rented counties of the dairy, lowland livestock, upland livestock and Intermediate farming type classes; and eight of the ten are among the ten lowest-rented counties of the upland livestock class. Four of the ten are among the ten counties with the lowest average rents in the Arable classes; and four of the other six counties have no rented Arable holdings in the sample.

High or low or in between, overall county average rents as a general rule are reliable indicators of the relative levels of county rents for all farming types. There are exceptions. Cumberland provides an example. This county is one of the ten with the lowest overall average county rents and yet the average rent of its Arable type holdings places it in the ten upper counties of the Arable farming type county averages. The high rent of Cumberland's arable land is obscured by the very low overall county average rent. An exceptionally high percentage of the county acreage is under upland livestock farming, and this is partly to blame for the very low overall county average. This high acreage must not take the whole blame, for the rent of Cumberland's upland livestock holdings is among the lowest for that farming type. Arable type holdings in the county only occupy 0.5%[1] of the county area. In counties like this, where the acreage is very low of farming types whose rents are out of step with the overall county average rent, what is obscured by the overall county average is of little consequence and the overall county average should be accepted as an index of the relative level of farm rents of the county. Exceptions to the general rule that overall county average rents are reliable indicators of local rent levels are, like Cumberland's Arable types, insignificant. Even the evidence for Yorkshire supports the general

---

[1] This percentage is not the percentage of all arable land in the county. It pertains only to those holdings of the Arable farming types and is taken from the evidence of the sample and not from the *National Farm Survey 1941-43*.

rule. The overall county average rent is of a low order. It would be reasonable to accuse the upland livestock acreage of the West and North Ridings of being the cause of this. In fact, the overall county average rent is remarkably in step with the average rents of all the farming types in the county: all are well below average and veer towards the lowest levels. Ironically, only the rent of the upland livestock holdings is above the average for its farming type.

Distribution of farming types within a county does not, as a general rule, obscure the true relative level of the farm rents of the county. Counties low in overall county average rent are likely to be low-rented in all farming types. Land use in a county can however affect the absolute level of the overall county average rent. Caernarvon, for instance, would not be in the second lowest rent stratum if all its holdings were Arable types. If that could be so it would move into the next higher stratum. What is significant in this make-believe is not the move itself but the fact that conversion to an Arable type county would lift the average rent level no further than the next rent stratum and leave the county still among the lowest-rented. This is further evidence indicative of the reliable testimony of overall county average rents to the relative rent levels of the counties.

Influence of farm size. Because of the relationship of rent per acre and size of holding[1], an overall county average tends to reflect the average rent of the most extensively (not necessarily numerically) represented farm size-group in the county. The relation to the average rent of the dominant size-groups of the counties where such occur is not a true picture of the standing of county rents, unless the average rent of a dominant size-group is accepted as the criterion of the county position. The verdict of the dominant size-group is not unreasonable and has already been accepted in principle when dealing with the distribution of Arable types in Cumberland.

A decision on this point need not be made because, as with farming types, the counties with the highest and lowest overall county rents tend to occupy the same positions when county average rents are compared in size-groups. The degree of correspondence is very close among leading counties in the three size-groups, 50-99 acres, 100-149 acres and 150-299 acres: eight of the ten leading counties in each size-group are among the ten counties with the highest overall county averages. Six of the foremost ten counties of the size-group 15-49 acres are among the ten leading counties of the overall county averages. In the size-groups 300-499

[1] cf. p. 65 ante.

acres and 500 acres and over, the corresponding figures are five and
four respectively. With counties of low overall county average rent
the degree of similarity is as close as it is with the leading counties
and is more uniform throughout the size-groups. In the two size-
groups 50-99 acres and 300-499 acres, eight of the ten hindmost
counties are among the ten counties with the lowest overall county
averages. In each of the remaining three size-groups the corresponding figure is seven.

So close a similarity allays the fear that because of dominant
size-groups in the counties the relationship of overall county
average rents to each other misrepresents the true picture of county
rents. Admittedly among the leading ten counties in the 500 acres
and over size-group there are six which do not appear with the
ten leaders of the overall county averages. But there is little danger
of a dominant acreage of holdings, 500 acres and over, in any one of
these counties influencing and misrepresenting the position of the
overall county average rent by placing it higher in the list of comparison than the rents of other areas of the county would warrant,
for, as with the upland livestock holdings, a dominant acreage of
the largest holdings would as a general rule depress the overall
county average rent, and not raise it[1] since the largest holdings
tend to have the lowest rent per acre[2]. One slight exception to this
rule is the rent per acre of holdings of the heavy arable land farming
type. The only counties with an acreage of this farming type above
10% of the total county acreage are Essex, Huntingdonshire,
Cambridgeshire and Suffolk. A high proportion of holdings, of
500 acres and over, has not caused these counties to be erronously
placed among the ten with the highest overall county average rents,
because Essex and Cambridgeshire are two of the ten counties
with the highest average county rent in the 500 acres and over size-
group; Suffolk is neither in the upper ten of the overall averages,
nor in the upper ten of the 500 acres and over size-group; and
Huntingdonshire has less than 10% of its area in heavy arable land
holdings of 500 acres and over.

Influence of water supplies and fixed equipment. High rent is associated with mains water supply[3]. It is possible therefore that the
high overall county average rents may be accounted for by high
percentages of acreage with mains water supply in those counties.
Analysis of the figures, however, does not clearly support the possibility. Only five of the ten counties with the highest percentages

---

[1] cf. p. 89 ante.
[2] v.p. 65 ante.
[3] cf. p. 83 ante.

of acreage supplied with mains water are also among the ten counties with the highest overall county average rents. Somerset, Shropshire and Flint of the ten counties with the highest overall county average rents have mains water supply percentages equal to or below the average percentage. This dissimilarity among the leading counties is not apparent among the lowest-rented counties. Seven of the ten counties with the lowest overall county average rents are among the ten counties with the lowest mains water supply percentages. Probably geographical features play a not insignificant role in this. Lack of mains water, and high uplands, inaccessible, unprofitable and low-rented, go together. Overall county average rents are not significantly affected by water mains as a single factor. Glamorgan, Westmorland and Durham illustrate this in another way. Each one has a very low overall county average rent, but each is blessed with a high percentage of acreage connected to main water supplies; high mains water percentages have not lifted these counties from the lowest ranks of the overall county average rents.

Provision of other forms of fixed equipment, even more obviously is not the key to the level of county overall average rents. Holdings with farmhouse and buildings connected to main electricity supplies tend to be higher rented[1] than holdings similarly equipped with buildings but without electricity. High overall county average rents might, therefore, be accounted for by abnormally high concentrations of holdings having farmhouse, buildings and mains electricity. But the counties with the highest overall county average rents are not those with the highest percentages of acreage equipped in this way. One only of the ten counties with the highest equipment percentages is among the ten counties with the highest overall county average rents.

[1] cf. p. 77 ante.

CHAPTER SEVEN

TENANCY CONDITIONS

Conditions of a contract of tenancy may impose upon the landlord burdens which reduce net rental income. On the contrary, burdens may be placed on the tenant which add to his financial commitments. However the incidence of these burdens may fall, it is reasonable to suppose it will affect the rent reserved by the lease. The survey assumes certain responsibilities for these burdens as normal. Deviations are recorded and an attempt made to trace the effect of their abnormality upon farm rent. The aim is not to gain information about the effects of abnormality for its own sake, but to discover to what extent, if at all, the national average rent per acre and other averages should be adjusted to allow for the influence of abnormal tenancy conditions. The burdens dealt with are repair and maintenance obligations, and rates of various kinds.

Repair and maintenance obligations.

Before 1947 it would have been difficult to find standard conditions of tenancy covering repair and maintenance. Terms of written leases varied a good deal. Common law settled the matter when the tenancy agreement was oral; but liability at common law is imprecise and would not have provided a satisfactory standard or norm. Fortunately, since 1947 the law has altered and a ready-made standard has been provided by the Agricultural Holdings Act, 1948[1]. The Act prescribes terms that are read into all leases of agricultural holdings where there are no express provisions. The terms themselves are set out in detail in the Agriculture (Maintenance, Repair and Insurance of Fixed Equipment) Regulations, 1948[2]. The survey adopts these terms as a standard. Repair obligations in leases whether express or implied are often honoured in the breach rather than the observance. But if vague work-a-day arrangements between landlords and tenants had been recognised by the survey, it would have been difficult to relate them to a standard and the work would have overtaxed the time available, and would probably have been impossible, even after allowing liberal margins for error. The survey is content therefore to record

[1] Section 6.
[2] S.I. 184, 1948.

the contractual obligations of tenancy. On some holdings these are not known and answers to this effect have been returned.

On a high percentage of the holdings, 80%, as shown in Table 18, the tenant is bound by repair terms similar to those of Statutory Instrument 184, 1948. Similarity does not mean the Instrument itself is operative. A written lease worded in identical terms or incorporating by express reference the terms of the Instrument may be the legal authority governing the tenant's repair and maintenance responsibilities. Deviations from the standard one way in favour of the tenant and another in favour of the landlord are few in number: on 7% of the holdings the tenant's obligations are greater than those prescribed by the Instrument, and on 11% they are less. These percentages of abnormality are low but not insignificant and if abnormality has a marked influence upon rent, their presence in the sample could have a bearing upon the national average rent per acre and other figures.

TABLE 18

AVERAGE CURRENT RENT PER ACRE AND TENANT'S REPAIR AND MAINTENANCE OBLIGATIONS.

1957

TENANT'S OBLIGATIONS	RENT PER ACRE		PERCENTAGE OF TOTAL	
(*STANDARD:* as under S.I. 184, 1948)	unadjusted	adjusted	acreage	holdings
	£	£	%	%
As *Standard*	1.90	2.14	79.3	80.1
Greater than *Standard*	1.90	2.10	8.8	7.2
Less than *Standard*	1.90	2.08	10.7	11.2
Uncertain	1.81	2.18	1.2	1.5

On average, as Table 18 shows, the rent per acre of holdings where repair obligations follow the terms of the Instrument is exactly the same as the average rent per acre of the "greater" and "less" abnormalities. The averages are calculated on acreages unadjusted for rough grazings. Adjustment alters the figures slightly. Where the tenant's liability is greater than standard, the average rent drops by 9d. per acre below the average for standard conditions. This is logical. But the logic is not followed by the average rent per acre where the tenant's liability is less than standard. On these holdings the average rent per acre is 1/2d. below the average of the standard holdings and 5d. below the average where the tenant's liabilities are greatest. The analysis of variance[1] indicates that the rent per

[1] v. Single one-way classification, Appendix p. 191.

G

acre figures of Table 18 are statistically significant, but the degree of their significance is the lowest among all the constant factors surveyed.

The differences between the adjusted and unadjusted rents suggest that the figures are slightly influenced by the representation of farming type among the three tenancy conditions groups; but so far as this analysis goes terms of tenancy touching repair and maintenance obligations do not in general appear to influence the amount of rent reserved by the lease.

Occupier's rates and farm rent.

Farm rent in England and Wales is usually exclusive of all rates except owner's drainage rate. The survey adopts this normal form as a standard. General and special rates on farmhouse and cottages, water rate and occupier's drainage rate are assumed to be the liability of the tenant; and to this list is added a rag-bag of miscellaneous outgoings which common usage regards as tenant's burdens. The evidence of the survey tests and overwhelmingly supports the surmise behind the adopted standard. From among the 12,661 holdings in the sample, only 505 (4%) are abnormal; should the landlord on some of the holdings meet two or more of these outgoings, the figure of total abnormal holdings would be less.

TABLE 19

AVERAGE CURRENT RENT PER ACRE AND TENANT'S OBLIGATIONS FOR OCCUPIER'S RATES AND OTHER CHARGES.
1957

TENANT'S OBLIGATIONS	RENT PER ACRE		RATES, etc. PER ACRE		HOLDINGS
	unadjusted	adjusted			
	£	£	£	% of rent	No.
Exclusive of:					
Water rates;	2.02	2.17	.10	4.8	76
Rates on farmhouse;	1.85	2.15	.12	6.3	181
Rates on cottages;	2.11	2.17	.12	5.6	66
Drainage rate;	2.08	2.10	.13	6.1	123
Other charges	1.41	1.72	.13	8.9	59
Average	1.91	2.09	.12	6.2	505
Inclusive of all occupier's rates and charges	1.90	2.14	—	—	12,156

Distribution of the 505 holdings among the five classes of outgoings is shown in Table 18. Rates on the farmhouse are responsible for 181 abnormal holdings, the greatest number; next in numbers comes drainage rate on 123 holdings; then water rate on 76; followed up by rates on cottages and miscellaneous charges. The amount of one burden per acre is remarkably similar to the amount of another and never exceeds 2s. 7d. or drops below 2s. The average current rent per acre over the unadjusted acreage of these holdings is £1 18s. 3d., a figure almost equal to the rent of £1 18s. per acre of the holdings where the conditions are standard and the outgoings are paid by the tenant. The slight difference leans in the expected direction, but is insufficient to support the hypothesis that the incidence of these burdens affects farm rent.

There is little point in making an analysis of the evidence to discover how far, if at all, distribution of farming type and other features of a holding's character influence the figures, because wherever the truth lies the sum of the burdens is too exiguous to affect the findings of the survey. All the abnormal charges together only amount to £0.004 per acre over the whole sample, and 0.24% of the total rental revenue. Each burden, on average, deprives the landlord of 6% of his inclusive rent. The figures of Table 18 fail to show the number of holdings on which landlords discharge more than one of these burdens and incur a correspondingly greater rent reduction; whatever this number may be, it is of little consequence as it can never be higher than 123 holdings (the second highest number of holdings in the classes of outgoings) or 1% of the total number of holdings.

Owner's drainage rate and farm rent.

Owner's drainage rate is not common in England and Wales and on 84.4% of the holdings in the sample it is not levied. Where it is levied the landlord, as a rule, pays it. The survey assumes this practice to be normal.

Throughout the whole sample, only 275 holdings have any abnormal arrangements, and on these the tenants pay the owner's drainage rate. The average rent per acre, somewhat surprisingly, is 11.9% higher than the average rent of the normal holdings. The higher average rent might be due to a preponderance of holdings whose character attracts a relatively high rent. Had the number of abnormal holdings been larger the significance of their rent levels would have given point to a detailed presentation of the distribution amongst them of farming types, farm sizes and other categories of a holding's character. As it is, a brief consideration of the distribution of farming types is adequate and substantially conclusive. Amongst the abnormal holdings the farming types most prominent, both numerically and by acreage, are heavy land arable, light land arable, alluvial arable and mixed, mainly dairying, dairy and mixed and general mixed. The high-rented farming types

among these are the heavy land arable, the alluvial arable and mixed
and the mainly dairying holdings. Each one of these three farming
types has a lesser share of the holdings and acreage where tenancy
conditions are normal. On this evidence it can be argued that the
high average rent of the abnormal holdings is the consequence of
farming type distribution and is not indicative of the indifference
of farm rent to the incidence of owner's drainage rate. But the
argument will not stand because taken in isolation the abnormal
holdings of heavy arable land type have higher rents than their
counterparts among the normal holdings; and so it is with the
mainly dairying holdings and with all the prominently represented
farming types, except the alluvial arable and mixed holdings. These
comparisons of farming type rents in isolation, like the comparison
of the average rents of all abnormal and normal holdings, indicate
that farm rent is indifferent to the incidence of owner's drainage
rate.

CHAPTER EIGHT

RENT DETERMINATION PROCEDURES

Classification of procedures.

Farm rents since 1945, unlike house rents, have not been directly restricted by legislative control. Landlord and tenant have been free to negotiate whatever rent they can agree upon. Legislation[1] during and since World War II, however, gave tenants of agricultural holdings security of tenure which could hamper the free negotiation of farm rent and impose an indirect rental control. Before 1947 as a general rule a landlord legally empowered to terminate a tenancy by giving the tenant notice to quit, could act in this way if when seeking a revised rent he was unable to agree a figure with his tenant. After 1947 a notice to quit an agricultural holding given by the landlord was subjected conditionally to the sanction of the Minister of Agriculture, Fisheries and Food. This sanction gave tenants security of tenure and indirectly controlled farm rents. A landlord who could not oust a tenant with whom he had a difference of opinion over rent was obliged either to negotiate with him as a sitting tenant or to refer the dispute to the jurisdiction of an arbitrator.

All rent changes since 1947 have not been rent revisions of statutory secured tenancies. Sometimes tenants have left their farms of their own fancy; notices to quit by landlords have for one cause or another been effective; and holdings "in hand" after some years have been offered on the market to let. Hence over the years 1945-1957 farm rents have been arranged either with prospective tenants or with sitting tenants.

Rents arranged with prospective tenants from the nature of the case are the outcome of free negotiation between the parties, and the appointment of professional valuers to act for either party does not cause the procedure to be other than this. A landlord fortunate in having vacant possession to offer could go about the business of finding a suitable tenant in more than one way. Farms to let in post-war years were hard to come by and other tenants of his might recommend their relatives to him; or the landlord himself would look no further afield than his own kith and kin. Tenants, strangers

---

[1] cf. *Defence General Regulations*, 1939: Reg. 62(4a): *Agriculture Act 1947:* and *Agricultural Holdings Act, 1948.*

alike to tenantry and the landlord, would at other times be sought either through professional agencies or by advertising in the press. When this happened the landlord would have some notion of the rent he wanted for the holding, and having this figure in mind would negotiate with prospective tenants. The market however was strong and in very short supply and here and there a landlord uncertain of its mood would test it by soliciting tenders.

Absence of rent restriction allows negotiation with a sitting tenant also to be a perfectly free procedure; the parties are free to agree upon what rent they please. There is however a difference, in the issue at stake, and this makes it necessary to recognise negotiation with a sitting tenant as a procedure distinct from negotiation with a prospective tenant. For a prospective tenant failure to agree a rent means failure to secure possession of the holding. For a sitting tenant the direst consequence of disagreement is facing an arbitrator whose award may be more in favour of the landlord than himself.

Between negotiation and arbitration is a procedure known as reference to an independent valuer. Both the freedom of negotiation and the detachment of arbitration go to its make-up, although it tends to be more akin to arbitration. To avoid dispute, the landlord and tenant agree to refer the question of rent to the decision of a surveyor or valuer acting between them and hence independent of a peculiar obligation to either. An independent valuer makes an award much as an arbitrator does, but unlike the arbitrator he does not act judicially between the parties. His award becomes a corporate part of the contract in which the parties, to avoid dispute, agree to accept his decision. The mediatorial detachment with which the valuer hears evidence gives him the guise of an arbitrator and makes an important distinction between this procedure and the procedure where two valuers act, each for a particular client—a procedure which is as much free negotiation as direct negotiation between landlord and tenant.

Arbitration is a procedure enforced upon the parties by law[1] in the event of dispute. An arbitrator takes evidence and conducts the reference in a judicial manner. He publishes his award which by special process of law is enforceable upon the parties. Although the law requires disputes over the rent of agricultural holdings to be referred to arbitration, it leaves the parties free in the first instance to decide upon the person of the arbitrator. Where the parties are at loggerheads, even on this point, the Minister of Agriculture,

---

[1] cf. *Agricultural Holdings Act, 1948.* Sections 5-9.

Fisheries and Food appoints an arbitrator on the application of either party[1].

These procedures for determining farm rent are common form. There are rare exceptions, where, for example, farms to let are auctioned and the rent determined by the fall of the hammer. For the purpose of the survey procedures are classified, according to the common form, as:

A. Prospective tenant procedures:
  (i) open tender;
  (ii) negotiation with—
      (a) stranger;
      (b) relative of tenant;
      (c) relative of landlord:
B. Sitting tenant procedures:
  (i) negotiation;
  (ii) mediatorial—
      (a) arbitration by agreed arbitrator;
      (b) arbitration by Minister-appointed arbitrator;
      (c) independent valuer:
and in addition as:
C. Other procedures.
D. Procedure unknown.

Open market and other rents.

The average rent per acre determined by each procedure has been calculated from the survey evidence for unadjusted and adjusted acreages. Table 20 gives the result. Adjustment of acreage makes a noticeable difference to the figures. Those based on adjusted acreages are the more reliable because holdings in the class "negotiation with a stranger" have only 16.4% rough grazings, while those in the class "open tender" have 32.6% rough grazing, and those in the class "Minister-appointed arbitrator" have 22.6%[2], and differences in the rents might be due to these differences in rough grazings and not to differences of rent determination procedures.

The average rent per acre determined by negotiation with a prospective tenant, not related either to the landlord or his tenants, is taken as a basic figure, or standard, against which figures in the other classes are measured. Such a standard has been adopted because this procedure of rent determination, among those recognised by the survey, comes nearest to expressing the consensus

[1] cf. loc. cit. 6th Schedule para. 1(1).
[2] cf. Table App. 7, Appendix p. 199.

of opinion of an unbiased market between landlords and tenants; rents determined by open tender might conceivably have about them an element of the supposed premium payment made to obtain possession of a holding. And negotiation with relatives, either of landlord or tenantry, can hardly escape some taint of bias. In sum, it can be said that the figures of Table 20 measure rents determined by other procedures against rents negotiated in an "open market".

Rents negotiated with prospective tenants who are not related either to the landlord or to other tenants of his—the "open market" standard—average £2.34 per acre (adjusted acreage)[1]. Only rents determined by open tendering are higher than this: open tender rents average £2.72 per acre and are 16% higher than open market rent. Open market rent almost equals rent negotiated with prospective tenants related to established tenants of the landlord.

TABLE 20

AVERAGE CURRENT RENT PER ACRE
AND RENT DETERMINATION PROCEDURES.

1957

PROCEDURE	RENT PER ACRE		INDEX
	unadjusted	adjusted	adjusted rent
Prospective tenant procedures:			
open tender;	1.97	2.72	116
negotiation with—			
stranger;	2.01	2.34	100
relative of tenant;	1.97	2.30	98
relative of landlord	1.15	1.94	83
Sitting tenant procedures:			
negotiation;	1.93	2.12	91
mediatorial—			
agreed arbitrator;	1.92	2.02	86
Minister-appointed arbitrator;	1.74	2.15	92
independent valuer;	1.93	2.04	87
Other Procedures	1.54	2.13	91
Procedure unkown	1.19	1.54	66

Open market rent, however, exceeds all the others: it is 9% in advance of rent determined by arbitrators appointed by the Minister of Agriculture; 10% above negotiated sitting tenant rent; 15% above rent determined by independent valuers; 16% above other arbitrator rent; and 21% above rent negotiated with prospective tenants who are related to the landlord.

Open tender rent being 16% above open market rent is correspondingly in advance of every one of the others: 26% above rent determined by arbitrators appointed by the Minister of Agriculture; 28% above negotiated sitting tenant rent; 33% above rent determined by independent valuers; and 35% above other arbitrator rent.

---

[1] All other figures cited in this chapter are related to adjusted acreage, unless expressly stated otherwise.

Prospective and sitting tenant rents.

All rents in the prospective tenant classes inclusive of open tender rent average £2.35 per acre; and rents in the sitting tenant classes inclusive of rents determined by arbitrators and independent valuers average £2.11 per acre. By setting the evidence in a broad focus in this way, it is seen that to have vacant possession to offer has meant, in a general way, the negotiation of farm rents 11% higher than rents negotiated with sitting tenants, or awarded by arbitrators and independent valuers mediating between sitting tenants and landlords.

Mediatorial rent.

Rents awarded by arbitrators and independent valuers average £2.06 per acre and as a class are the lowest of all, disregarding rent where procedures of rent determination are unknown. Open market rent is 13.5% above this mediatorial average. Rent negotiated with sitting tenants is higher than mediatorial rent, but only by 3%. Running slightly ahead of mediatorial rent in this way, the rent negotiated with sitting tenants appears to be the bargain of landlords whose eyes are cast over the shoulder to see what arbitrators and valuers are doing, and of tenants self-conscious of the protection security of tenure gives them against the vigorous demands of the open market. Or, perhaps it is the arbitrators whose eyes are over the shoulder, curious to know what rent landlords are agreeing with their sitting tenants—after all the number of rents negotiated with sitting tenants is greater than the number of all others put together, and for every mediatorial rent there are twenty-six rents negotiated with sitting tenants[1]. It is not possible to say whether mediatorial rents have influenced sitting tenant negotiations or vice versa. The evidence however points somewhat conclusively to an affinity between the two, a mutual interaction, which is not evident between open market and open tender rent on the one hand and mediatorial rent on the other.

There is an element of difference in the nature of open market rent and mediatorial rent that could account in some measure for the former being higher than the latter. Arbitrators when determining the rent of a holding are required by Statute[2] to disallow the effect of tenants' improvements upon rent; independent valuers it may be assumed would do likewise. Tenants' improvements in some cases attract compensation from the land-

---

[1] v. Table App. 7, Appendix p. 199.
[2] Section 8, *Agricultural Holdings Act, 1948.*

lord at the termination of the tenancy, and when the holding is
re-let the landlord increases the rent to allow for interest on the
capital invested by him in the outgoing tenant's compensation.
The open market rent in such a case would therefore be higher
than the rent which the arbitrator would correctly have awarded
if the tenant who had made the improvement had remained the
sitting tenant. How far the influence of tenants' improvements
is a cause of the disparity between the average open market rent
and the average mediatorial rent of the holdings in this survey is
not known. The influence is probably slight. Evidence from the
investigation into estate finances, previously referred to, indicates
that over the period 1945 to 1955 tenants had not readily undertaken
improvements of a kind that would affect the rental value of a
holding, and of those who did so the majority have a special
affinity with the landlords[1] which would prevent rent disputes
and ensuing arbitrations. Returns for application of assistance
under the recent (1957) Farm Improvements Scheme show the
number of tenants applying for assistance to be almost equal to
the number of landlords doing the same, but it does not follow
that the improvements proposed by the tenants are such as would
increase the rental value, and if they were the influence of them
would be too late to be reflected in the figures of this survey.

Adjustment for farm size, farming type and equipment.

The holdings classified in determination of rent classes in Table
20 differ in character among themselves, and the number with a
particular characteristic in one class is not precisely proportionate
to the corresponding number in other classes. Averages could be
biased therefore one way or another by holdings of similar type
and rent level differing in number. Adjustments to effect a balance
have been made by weighting the averages according to the number
of each type in the open market or standard class.

When adjusted to allow for disparity in the numbers of holdings
of similar size range, the figures for rents negotiated with prospective tenants do not alter much; the most noticeable change
is a slight closing up of the figure for open tender rent towards
the open market rent, by a drop in the average open tender rent
from £2.72 per acre to £2.68 per acre. Among the mediatorial
rents, however, change is more clearly marked. There is a distinct
move upwards towards the open market rent, especially by rents
determined by Minister-appointed arbitrators and by independent
valuers; the arbitrator rent jumps from an average of £2.15 per

[1] v. D. R. Denman, op. cit. p. 59.

acre to £2.27 per acre, and the independent valuer rent from an average of £2.04 per acre to £2.12 per acre. These rises lift the average for all mediatorial rents until it equals the average sitting tenant rent. Holdings below 50 acres and above 500 acres are very short in number among the arbitrator and independent valuer classes, and raising the representation in this way redresses the balance and accounts in part for the alteration in figures. But it would be unwise to read a general verdict here and suppose that mediatorial rent is in general closer to open market rent than the figures of Table 20 allow. The explanation of the closing up of the figures must be found primarily and principally in the relatively high rents awarded by arbitrators and independent valuers for holdings at either end of the size range,[1] and the relatively low mediatorial rents of the intermediate size ranges.

When adjustments are made to balance the numbers of holdings of similar farming type, the most marked alteration is again an improvement in mediatorial rent, an increase wholly due to the influence of holdings where the rent at the last rent change was determined by award of a Minister-appointed arbitrator. Compared with the open market class, this class is short of mainly dairy farms, a farming type that attracts relatively high rents[2], and doubly strong in the number of upland mixed livestock farms, a farming type running to very low rents[3]. Hence the weighting process tends to advance the average rent per acre of rents awarded by Minister-appointed arbitrators. Minister-appointed arbitrator rent jumps from £2.15 per acre to £2.24 per acre; and the mediatorial average from £2.06 per acre to £2.14 per acre.

Here the adjusted figures can be accepted as a reliable modification of the general figures of Table 20. Admittedly, mediatorial rent is inclined to run above the open market rent for upland mixed livestock holdings[4], but the number of holdings of this farming type among the mediatorial classes does not differ greatly from the corresponding number in the standard class, and adjusting the balance of numbers does not increase the proportionate representation of upland mixed livestock holdings. The adjusted figures only alter slightly the relative levels of the average rents of Table 20. Negotiated sitting tenant rent loses its advance over mediatorial rent, but solely through the influence of rents awarded by Minister-appointed arbitrators. The adjusted figures in general draw negotiated sitting tenant rent closer to mediatorial rent and

[1] v.p. 117 post.
[2] v.p. 50 ante.
[3] v.p. 51 ante.
[4] cf. p. 113 post.

heighten the impression of an affinity between them. The adjusted figures also lift the average of open tender rents; from £2.72 per acre it is raised to £2.81 per acre. This is because balancing the numbers of holdings of similar farming type increases the proportionate representation of mixed farms with dairying of the Intermediate group and of the light land arable farms, and for these two types of farming open tender rent is higher than open market rent by double the advance shown in the general findings of Table 20. Alteration of the proportional representation of farming types *per se* does not therefore account for the increased open tender rent. The increase is due to a high open tender rent peculiar to the two farming types and consequently there is no cause to amend the general findings.

Chronology of procedures 1945-1957.

The national figures of farm rent movements show a definite upward trend from 1945. With this in mind, it might be conjectured that the relatively low level of mediatorial rent was due to a preponderance of arbitrations and independent valuations in the earlier years when rents were low, and to more prospective tenant negotiations in the later years, when rents had begun to rise, than in the earlier years. This conjecture is not supported by the survey. An arrangement of the evidence given in Table 21 shows, year by year, the number of occasions on which each procedure of rent determination was followed at the last rent change. The number in each procedural group is expressed as a percentage of the total number of occasions in the year; and as a percentage of the total number of occasions in all the years covered by the survey.

The procedures are broadly grouped as—prospective tenant, sitting tenant and mediatorial. Understandably the percentages of the occasions for all three procedural groups are higher in the later years, which were the years of last rent change for the greater proportion of the holdings in the sample. The percentages of mediatorial procedures are no exception, but in the later years they are higher than the corresponding percentages of the sitting tenant and prospective tenant groups: in 1946 only .3% of their total is recorded, in 1950 2.3%, and in 1956/57 38.1%; the corresponding percentages of the prospective tenant procedures are 1.6%, 4.7% and 24.2%. The relatively low rents associated with arbitrations and independent valuations are consequently not to be explained on the ground of priority of occurence. Indeed since arbitration and independent valuation percentages increase in the later years more rapidly than do the percentages of the prospective tenant procedures, the difference between mediatorial rent and open market rent is the more significant and implies that during the later years the gap between the two has been wider than the averages of Table 20 indicate.

The chronologies of Table 21 show in 1948 a high immediate rise, sheer as a cliff face, in the percentage of total yearly procedures which were sitting tenant negotiations. From that year onwards the percentage tends to increase, but far less steeply. Percentages of prospective tenant negotiations fall correspondingly. The pronounced increase in 1948 of sitting tenant negotiations and the definite increase since then are the outcome of the policy of tenurial security introduced in 1947 by the Agriculture Act. A sharp change in 1948 was to be expected. Less understandable is the definite increase in sitting tenant procedures after that date. Together with the increase in arbitrations and independent valuations, it is probably due to the time-lag between the passing of an Act of Parliament and the full effective working of its provisions. A feature of less consequence[1], but nonetheless of interest, is a relatively high percentage of "unknown" procedures in the indeterminate period "1945 and earlier"; indeed 91% of all the unknown procedures is in that period. Because the cloud of ignorance settles so decidedly over 1945 and the years beyond, 95% of the known evidence belongs to the period 1946-1957.

Influence of farming type.

Information from the survey is sufficient to show how rent per acre related to determination procedure appears when the holdings are arranged according to type of farming, exclusive of specialist farms. There are only two gaps in this evidence: rents awarded by Minister-appointed arbitrators for corn, sheep and dairying farms of the Intermediate group and arable and mixed farms among the Arable types. Prospective tenant rent sitting tenant rent negotiated with tenants and mediatorial rent, are compared with open market rent. The results are given in graphic form in Diagram 8 and tabulated as Table 22. The Diagram shows the percentage deviation of the rents of the determination procedures from the open market rent. The Table makes comparisons by following the principle already adopted and uses open market rent as the base of a series of indices.

Farming type appears to influence the consequence of rent determination procedure. Four main trends are traceable through

[1] Not shown in Table 21.

TABLE 21 (Part I)
FREQUENCY OF RENT DETERMINATION PROCEDURES AS AT LAST RENT CHANGE, 1945–1957.

PROCEDURES	FREQUENCY OF RENT DETERMINATION PROCEDURES BY HOLDINGS FOR EACH YEAR											
	1945 and earlier		1946		1947		1948		1949		1950	
	%	%	%	%	%	%	%	%	%	%	%	%
Prospective tenant: % of all procedures	48.0		39.3		47.6		23.5		18.2		22.6	
% of all years		12.0		1.6		2.8		3.7		2.8		4.7
Sitting tenant: % of all procedures	51.3		59.6		50.8		75.9		80.9		75.6	
% of all years		3.0		0.6		0.7		2.8		2.9		3.7
Mediatorial: % of all procedures	0.7*		1.1*		1.6*		0.6*		0.9*		1.8*	
% of all years		1.1*		0.3*		0.6*		0.6*		0.9*		2.3
	100.0		100.0		100.0		100.0		100.0		100.0	
Total number of holdings:	538		89		126		341		330		452	

TABLE 21 (Part II)

FREQUENCY OF RENT DETERMINATION PROCEDURES AS AT LAST RENT CHANGE, 1945–1957.

FREQUENCY OF RENT DETERMINATION PROCEDURES BY HOLDINGS FOR EACH YEAR

PROCEDURES	1951		1952		1953		1954		1955		1956 and 1957		All years		
	%	%	%	%	%	%	%	%	%	%	%	%	%	%	No.
% of all procedures	17.2		18.1		14.7		14.6		20.4		14.0		18.4		2,157
Prospective tenant: % of all years		5.0		7.7		9.2		10.0		16.3		24.2		100.0	
% of all procedures	80.5		78.3		83.0		81.5		76.1		82.5		78.6		9,207
Sitting tenant: % of all years		5.4		7.9		12.1		13.1		14.2		33.6		100.0	
% of all procedures	2.3		3.6		2.3		3.9		3.5		3.5		3.0		349
Mediatorial: % of all years		4.0		9.4		8.9		16.6		17.2		38.1		100.0	
	100.0		100.0		100.0		100.0		100.0		100.0		100.0		
Total number of holdings:	622		924		1,347		1,480		1,718		3,746		11,713		
Other procedures and unknown procedures													948		
Holdings in the Sample													12,661		

DIAGRAM 8

RELATIONSHIP OF OPEN MARKET RENT TO RENTS DETERMINED BY OTHER PROCEDURES WITHIN FARMING TYPES.

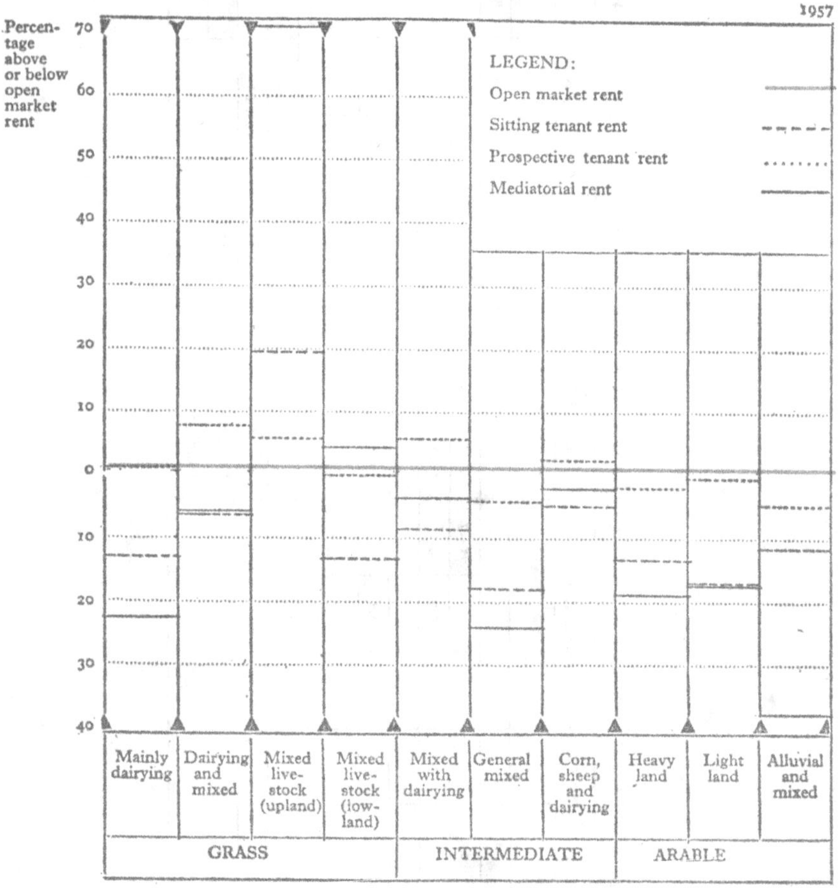
1957
Percentage above or below open market rent
70
60
50
40
30
20
10
0
10
20
30
40
LEGEND:
Open market rent
Sitting tenant rent
Prospective tenant rent
Mediatorial rent
Mainly dairying
Dairying and mixed
Mixed live-stock (upland)
Mixed live-stock (low-land)
Mixed with dairying
General mixed
Corn, sheep and dairying
Heavy land
Light land
Alluvial and mixed
GRASS
INTERMEDIATE
ARABLE

minor deviations to left and right. On some farms, sitting tenant rent and rent awarded by arbitrators and independent valuers contrary to the general findings of the survey are near or above open market rent. This tendency is seen among the mixed livestock holdings and to a remarkable degree among the upland mixed livestock holdings. The sitting tenant rent of the latter is 20% above open market rent; and the mediatorial rent 69% above open market rent. Mediatorial rent is greatly influenced by the exceptionally high rents awarded by Minister-appointed arbitrators; on the upland mixed livestock holdings this arbitrator rent is 85% above open market rent.

In an opposite direction and characteristic of general mixed farms of the Intermediate group, and the alluvial arable and mixed farms open market rent soars high above mediatorial rent to a distance outstretching the height that lifts open market rent above mediatorial rent in the general findings. Among the general mixed farms of the Intermediate group, open market rent is 31% above mediatorial rent; and among the alluvial arable and mixed farms it is 60.5% above mediatorial rent. Rents of the mainly dairying farms show a similar trend with open market rent 28% above mediatorial rent.

The third of the four main trends in the evidence is an upward movement in mediatorial rent and sitting tenant rent and this takes them much nearer to the open market level than the general findings allow. In this movement are the dairying and mixed holdings of the Grass group, and the mixed with dairying holdings and the corn, sheep and dairying holdings of the Intermediate group.

The fourth main trend is observable among the heavy land and light land arable farms where the indices run more or less parallel with those of the general findings.

The general findings point to mediatorial rent out of sympathy with open market rent and failing to reach its level. Sorting the evidence out into farming type shows how the general findings can obscure, on the one hand, a certain degree of agreement between open market rents and the awards of arbitrators and independent valuers and, on the other, opinions which require of sitting tenants, both by negotiation and award, a rent well above the level of the market.

Obscured also by the combination of open tender rent and other rents negotiated with prospective tenants, is a distinct tendency among open tender rents of mixed dairy farms of the Intermediate group and light arable farms to move towards a level twice as far above open market rent as the corresponding distance revealed

H

TABLE 22 INDEX OF AVERAGE CURRENT RENT BY RENT DETERMINATION PROCEDURES AND FARMING TYPE.

(Open Market Rent = 100).

FARMING TYPE

PROCEDURE	ALL TYPES		GRASS								INTERMEDIATE						ARABLE					
			Mainly dairying		Dairy and mixed		Mixed livestock (upland)		Mixed livestock (lowland)		Mixed with dairying		General mixed		Corn, sheep and dairying		Heavy land		Light land		Alluvial and mixed	
	Index	Hold-ings %	Index	Hold-ings %	Index	Hold-ings %	Index	Hold-ings %	Index	Hold-ings %	Index	Hold-ings %	Index	Hold-ings %	Index	Hold-ings %	Index	Hold-ings %	Index	Hold-ings %	Index	Hold-ings %
Prospective tenant	101	18.5	100	20.1	108	18.5	105	24.1	100	22.2	105	15.2	96	16.7	102	13.1	98	17.7	99	16.2	96	15.8
Sitting tenant	90	78.5	87	77.5	93	78.5	120	72.4	86	75.6	91	81.3	82	78.9	95	82.5	86	78.8	83	81.0	88	83.4
Mediatorial	88	3.0	78	2.4	94	3.0	168	3.5	104	2.2	96	3.5	76	4.4	98	4.4*	81	3.5	83	2.8	62	0.8*
Number of holdings		11,478		2,493		1,793		1,018		742		1,328		1,493		137		815		1,171		488

by the general findings of Table 20. This open tender rent is in consequence further in advance by the measure indicated of sitting tenant rent and mediatorial rent.

The so-called mixed upland livestock holdings comprise the most heterogeneous class among the farming types. What in Sussex would be called an upland farm, may be less elevated than a general mixed farm in Cumberland growing wheat along the 700 ft. contour. Bleak acres, stretches of water-logged peat about the Cheviot, steep, crag-broken ascents whose best crops are nardus and molinia grass, are properly returned as upland livestock holdings, but they find company in this title with the higher lands of Wiltshire, Worcestershire and Dorset, thin flinty lands, yet healthy and profitable, the natural home of fescues and upland bents. The low open market rent of an upland livestock holding and the exceptionally high mediatorial rent may have a geographical explanation. The rents from the awards of arbitrators and independent valuers may pertain to upland holdings in the relatively fertile southern and midland counties, and the open market quotations may come from the foothills of Snowdonia and the "in byes" of the Cumberland fells.

It this were so, the comparison of the rents of different rent determination procedures of holdings of the upland livestock type made in Table 22 and its attendant Diagram would be misleading. The evidence, therefore, has been analysed geographically. Open market rent is compared with rents of other rent determination procedures in three distinct areas: the Welsh counties; Northumberland, Durham, Cumberland, Westmorland; and other counties who returned information about upland livestock holdings. The result of this geographical analysis is set out in Table 23[1]. Evidence from each geographical region reflects fairly faithfully the pattern of relative rent levels drawn by the composite evidence for this farming type class. In Northumbria and Cumbria, mediatorial rent is 88% above the open market rent; in Wales 76% in advance; and elsewhere it over-reaches open market rent by 54%. In general this finer analysis can be said to have confirmed the impression first given of open market rent

---

[1] In the open market averages of Table 23 are contributions from two upland farms whose exceptionally extensive acreage brings a somewhat disproportionate contribution to this procedural class of relatively few holdings. One of the two giants belongs to Northumbria, the other to Wales. When they are excluded the essentiality of the rents pattern does not alter. Mediatorial rent approaches open market rent, but is still far ahead of it by 59%.

TABLE 23
INDEX OF AVERAGE CURRENT RENT FOR UPLAND LIVESTOCK HOLDINGS BY RENT
DETERMINATION PROCEDURES IN THREE REGIONS.
(Open Market Rent = 100).

1957

PROCEDURE	ALL REGIONS		WALES		NORTHUMBERLAND DURHAM, CUMBERLAND, WESTMORLAND		ELSEWHERE	
	Index	Acreage (adjusted) %	Rent Index	Acreage (adjusted) %	Index	Acreage (adjusted) %	Index	Acreage (adjusted) %
Prospective tenant	105	23.1	107	26.5	93	23.8	112	20.2
Sitting tenant	120	73.6	103	68.9	116	74.4	124	75.9
Mediatorial	169	3.3	176	4.6	188	1.8*	154	3.9
Total Acreage adjusted	128,075		33,262		46,026		48,787	
Total Acreage unadjusted	265,757		61,168		128,869		75,720	

far below mediatorial rent and, in lesser measure, below sitting tenant rent.

The analysis of variance[1] bears out the above observations. Both farming type and the method of rent determination are significant influences upon farm rent per acre. Of the two, the method of rent determination is the stronger. This may be put another way by saying that whether a landlord has vacant possession of a farm or not is of greater consequence for the level of rent per acre than the type of farm. On the other hand the interaction between farming type and method of rent determination while significant is not impressive, thereby indicating as observed above that the relationship of farm rent per acre and method of rent determination seen in the general findings of Table 20 is not followed in the rents of every particular farming type.

Influence of farm size.

Farm size, like farming type, has a bearing upon the consequence of rent determination procedure for farm rent. Average rent per acre in rent determination classes within farm size-groups is expressed as an index related to open market rent in Table 24 and graphically represented by Diagram 9.

Mediatorial rent, thanks to the influence of rents awarded by Minister-appointed arbitrators, rises close to open market rent on the smallest farms, 15-49 acres. On the largest farms of all, those 500 and over acres, it is 11% above open market rent. On holdings between 100 and 149 acres and between 300 and 499 acres it falls below open market rent more seriously than in the general findings of Table 20; with the former open market rent is 20% above mediatorial, and with the latter 23% above it. On holdings from 50-99 acres and 150-299 acres, mediatorial rent conforms closely with the general findings. The exceptional advance of mediatorial rent over open market rent on the largest farms is probably due in part to the high proportion of upland mixed livestock holdings among holdings of this size and to the propensity of mediatorial rent on these holdings to out-distance open market rent.

Rent negotiated with sitting tenants is close to open market rent on the smaller farms, 15-99 acres; and on the largest of all, those 500 acres and over. At these extremities sitting tenant rent falls clearly below mediatorial rent; on the smallest farms the difference is 3% and on the largest it is 11%. On farms of the middle ranges from 100-499 acres sitting tenant rent honours the general

[1] v. Appendix pp. 191-193.

TABLE 24
INDEX OF AVERAGE CURRENT RENT PER ACRE BY RENT DETERMINATION PROCEDURES AND FARM SIZE-GROUPS.
(Open Market Rent = 100).

1957

PROCEDURE	FARM SIZE-GROUP (acres)													
	All sizes		15–49		50–99		100–149		150–299		300–499		500 and over	
	Index	Holdings %	Index	Holdings %	Index	Holdings %	Index	Holdings %	Index	Holdings %	Index	Holdings %	Index	Holdings %
Prospective tenant	101	18.4	104	23.6	108	19.9	101	18.3	99	15.1	101	11.9	93	14.9
Sitting tenant	91	78.6	96	75.1	100	77.4	90	78.5	90	80.6	91	84.5	99	81.5
Mediatorial	88	3.0	99	1.3	92	2.7	84	3.2	90	4.3	82	3.6	111	3.6
Total holdings		11,713		2,670		2,731		1,977		2,938		975		422

trend by being above mediatorial rent, but the degree of its advance is greater.

A salient feature is the behaviour of open tender rent. On farms from 15-299 acres it is above open market rent to a degree far greater than the measure of its superiority in the general findings of Table 20. But on the larger farms, 300-500 acres and over, there is a complete change round and open tender rent drops below open market rent. This erratic behaviour of open tender rent is obscured by the figures of Table 24 which compress the evidence into the three procedure classes—prospective tenant, sitting tenant and mediatorial. The buoyancy of open tender rent on all but the largest farms keeps prospective tenant rent near open market rent. Prospective tenant rent is depressed on the largest farms because of the depressed open tender rent, and on account of a precipitous decline in rent negotiated with prospective tenants related to the landlord. The analysis of variance[1] shows method of rent determination to be a stronger influence than farm size on farm rent. This result of the analysis might be expected in the light of the superiority of influence exercised by method of rent determination over farming type. Interaction between farm size and method of rent determination is more significant than the interaction between farming type and method of rent determination, indicating, as observed above, that among farm size-groups the general findings of Table 20 are more faithfully followed.

Frequency of rent determination procedures.

Procedures that have determined rent at the last rent change do not occur in equal numbers throughout the evidence. The occasions of each, shown as a percentage of the total number of occasions and in terms of acreage representation, are given in the Appendix[2]. Clearly from the chronology of procedures given earlier, negotiation with sitting tenants is the most frequent. It accounts for 73% of all rent determinations; a percentage which becomes 75.5% when expressed in terms of acreage represented. Consequently the nine other procedures share between them no more than one quarter of the total number of occasions and the occurrence of each of them must appear insignificant in comparison with the number of sitting tenant negotiations. This dwarfing should not be allowed to minimize the significance of their role in the post-war farm rent story.

A clearer conception of their significance is gained when neg-

---

[1] v. Appendix pp. 191, 192.
[2] cf. Table App. 7. Appendix p. 199.

DIAGRAM 9

RELATIONSHIP OF OPEN MARKET RENT TO RENTS DETERMINED
BY OTHER PROCEDURES WITHIN FARM SIZE-GROUPS.

1957

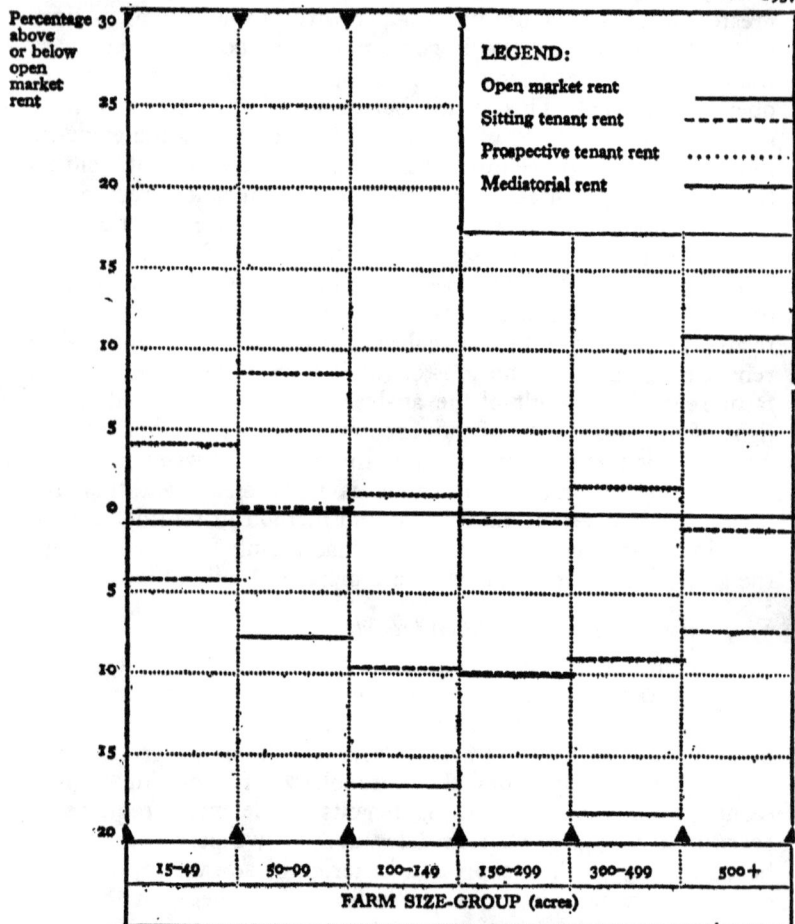

LEGEND:

Open market rent

Sitting tenant rent

Prospective tenant rent

Mediatorial rent

Percentage above or below open market rent

FARM SIZE-GROUP (acres)

15-49   50-99   100-149   150-299   300-499   500+

otiation with sitting tenants is excluded from the calculations and the occasions of each of the other nine procedures are expressed as a percentage of the reduced total. Table 25 gives the result. Nearly a quarter of the rent determination procedures are unknown and of this quarter the majority occurred in or before 1945[1]. On one out of every two of the known occasions the landlord negotiated with prospective tenants. The majority of these negotiations took place in open market conditions, as the successful tenant was not related either to the landlord or to his established tenants. Negotiations with a relative of the landlord were the least frequent of all and are of little significance. Letting by tender accounts for 8% of the total. And one in every ten is a mediatorial procedure; the chance of arbitration or independent valuation being two to one.

TABLE 25

FREQUENCY OF RENT DETERMINATION PROCEDURES,
EXCLUDING NEGOTIATION WITH SITTING TENANT.

1957

PROCEDURE	FREQUENCY OF OCCURENCE BY HOLDINGS			
	%	No.	%	No.
Prospective tenant: open tender	7.7	264	7.7	264
negotiation with— stranger;	30.9	1,066		
relative of tenant;	21.5	743	54.8	1,893
relative of landlord	2.4	84		
Mediatorial: independent valuer;	3.5	121		
arbitrator	6.6	228	10.1	349
Other procedures	3.7	129	3.7	129
Procedure unknown	23.7	819	23.7	819
TOTALS:	100.0	3,454	100.0	3,454

The percentage of "other procedures" is but 4%. The majority of these were on county council estates where the Council declined to negotiate rent or tenancy terms with prospective candidates; when completing the questionnaire the county land agent, understandably, was reluctant to classify the procedure as negotiation. A similar attitude was adopted by the National Coal Board over a few of their lettings. On other holdings in this category rent changed *pro tanto* with change of acreage. Here and there holdings had been sold by owner-occupiers to purchasers who had granted a lease to the vendors and negotiations for rent in the course of these vendor and purchaser transactions are classified among "other procedures".

[1] cf. p. 109 ante.

If the number of holdings given in each procedural category of Table 22 are expressed as a percentage of the total number of holdings of each farming type the incidence of rent determination procedures among farming types can be demonstrated. Among the holdings contributing to the Table, 18.5% of the rent determination procedures were negotiation with prospective tenants, 3% mediatorial and 78.5% negotiation with sitting tenants. Compared with these general averages, the Grass types have the highest percentages of prospective tenant negotiations, the Intermediate types the highest percentages of mediatorial procedures and the Arable types the highest percentage of sitting tenant negotiations. Among the Grass types, the mixed livestock holdings have the highest percentage of prospective tenant negotiations and of the two modes of livestock farming, the upland mixed livestock farms have the highest percentage of all—24%. These percentages are highly significant. It is just these two farming types which reveal high mediatorial rents and low open market rents: the relatively greater number of prospective tenant negotiations points to a relatively strong supply of farms to let and a relatively weak market, a state of affairs well in accord with the evidence of low open market rents. Mediatorial procedures have the highest percentages on the general mixed farms and the corn, sheep and dairying holdings; the percentages are identical for each type of farming and stand at 4%. Alluvial arable and mixed farms of the Arable type boast the highest percentage of sitting tenant negotiations. This high percentage has a high reciprocal in a relatively low percentage of prospective tenant negotiations and points to a short supply of new tenancies, a state of affairs exactly contrary to the weak supply of mixed livestock holdings. Again the position of open market rent and mediatorial rent corresponds: open market rent soars above the mediatorial rent, thereby declaring a strong market and arbitration rent awards out of touch with it.

When figures for holdings arranged in farm size-groups and rent determination procedures given in Table 25 are treated in the same way, the highest percentages of prospective tenant negotiations occur among farms in the smallest size-groups, 15 to 99 acres, and in these size-groups are found the lowest percentages of sitting tenant negotiations. Indeed with one exception prospective tenant percentages move in regular inverse ratio to farm size, and sitting tenant percentages in direct ratio to farm size. The one exception is the incidence of procedures among the largest farms of all, 500 acres and over. The anomaly here is not serious and can undoubtedly be attributed to the influence of the high proportion of upland mixed livestock holdings in this size group. The highest incidence of mediatorial procedures occurs among farms from 150-299 acres; these are the holdings where recourse to arbitrators and independent valuers has been most frequent.

Rent increase and determination procedures.

It is not possible with the majority of the holdings of the survey to show what increase, if any, the rent last determined gained over the immediately preceding rent and by comparing the degrees of increase to discover how methods of rent determination affected the increases. But with holdings where the rent change occurred in the current year (1957) it is possible to compare the degrees of increase because the survey records the rent of the immediately preceding year (1956).

Rental increases consequent upon landlord's improvements and causes other than a general rent review are not comparable either with each other or with increases resulting from a rental review or change of tenancy. The very high percentage of general rental reviews within the mediatorial procedure classes shown in Table 27[1] clearly indicates that the vast majority of changes of rent from all other causes except change of tenancy enumerated in Table 26[2] will have been negotiated with sitting tenants. This means that the average rent increases negotiated with sitting tenants are not comparable with those awarded by arbitrators and independent valuers—the rent increases of the mediatorial class, or with open market increases and increases of other prospective tenant negotiations. On the other hand, the high percentage of general rent reviews among the mediatorially determined rents enables the increases awarded by arbitrators and valuers to be compared with those gained in open market and other prospective tenant negotiations.

Prospective tenant negotiations determined the rent of 338 holdings of the sample in 1957; of this number 129 were negotiated with prospective tenants related neither to established tenants of the landlord nor to the landlord himself and thus the rents determined by them satisfy the definition of open market rent framed earlier. Awards of arbitrators and independent valuers determined the rent of 95 of the holdings which changed rent in 1957.

Open market rent averaged £3.09 per acre (adjusted) and was 31% above mediatorial rent. Rent determined by open tender was

[1] v.p. 129 post.
[2] v.p. 126 post.

9% higher than open market rent. This particular difference between open market rent and mediatorial rent is greater than the corresponding difference among the averages of all years given in Table 20. The greater difference in 1957 bears out the earlier observation that the margin between open market rent and mediatorial rent is probably greater than the averages of Table 20 indicate because there were proportionately less mediatorial procedures in the earlier years than in the later years by which time market rents had enjoyed the cumulative advances of the earlier years; while prospective tenant negotiations were more numerous proportionately in the earlier years than in the later years.

The difference however is greater between the degrees of rental increase. Open market negotiations resulted on average in an increase of 64% over the rent of the previous year, but mediatorial procedures advanced the rent no further than 37%. Thus when entire rents are compared open market rent is 31% above mediatorial rent, but when actual rental increases are compared open market gains are 71% above the mediatorial achievements, although below the open tender advances. The contrast of the differences between the entire rents and the differences between the degrees of increase however is mainly a mathematical[1] function and is not indicative of differences in the original rents.

---

[1] If two rents are equal an advance of 60% in one and 30% in the other will result in ultimate indices of 160 and 130 respectively; the 60% increase is 100% higher than the 30% increase but the resulting 160 index is only 23% higher than the resulting 130 index.

CHAPTER NINE

CAUSES OF RENT CHANGE

Knowledge of the causes of rent change throws light upon the stability and mutability of rents. With this in view, the survey is concerned with causes *per se*. An attempt is now made to relate cause and rent level where possible. Time did not allow enquiry to range beyond the last rent change. The figures therefore are not comprehensive of all changes throughout the period covered by the survey. By noting the last rent change only, a record of rent changes is obtained which reflects the overall frequencies of change, because the most frequent cause of rent change overall has the greatest chance of being the most frequent among the causes of the last rent changes.

A predetermined schedule of possible causes of rent change was drawn up, a course which eased the work and made for uniformity of statement. Rents are likely to change, it was supposed, with a change of tenancy, as the outcome of a general rent review, as a consequence of landlord's improvements or the alteration of farm boundaries or the terms of tenancy—especially terms touching repair obligations. And change may be provoked by a combination of two or more of these causes. No provision was made for recording other causes of rent change, but a return of "not known" was provided for.

Frequency of causes of rent change.

Causes of rent change are compared for frequency of occurence in Table 26. General rent review occurs most frequently, accounting for 42% of all the causes. It is of even greater consequence than this percentage implies because 6% of the causes are a combination of general rent review and improvements made by the landlord. Improvements made by the landlord are in fact the next most frequent cause: as a single cause they account for 17% of the total. The additional 6% just noted gives them pride of place over change of tenancy, with a percentage of 18%. Apart from these three causes and combinations of them, the only other cause occurring with significant frequency is alteration of boundaries, accounting for 6% of all causes.

This general run of percentages does not hold year by year.

TABLE 26

FREQUENCY OF CAUSES OF LAST RENT CHANGE 1945-1957.

FREQUENCY OF CAUSES OF LAST RENT CHANGE BY HOLDINGS FOR EACH YEAR OF OCCURRENCE

CAUSE OF LAST RENT CHANGE	1945 and earlier	1946	1947	1948	1949	1950	1951	1952	1953	1954	1955	1956-1957	All years Holdings	All years Average rent per acre (adjusted)
	Holdings %	Holdings %	Holdings %	Holdings %	Holdings %	Holdings %	Holdings %	Holdings %	Holdings %	Holdings %	Holdings %	Holdings %	Holdings %	INDEX
0. Change of tenancy	28.3	37.9	43.6	22.2	16.4	21.8	18.6	18.6	14.5	13.6	19.6	13.1	17.6	100.0
1. General review	8.6	25.3	24.0	55.6	49.9	46.7	44.4	55.0	56.3	47.9	35.0	44.8	42.3	88.8
2. Improvements	2.2	15.8	6.8*	6.8	13.0	16.9	14.6	13.8	13.5	19.6	25.5	22.9	17.5	94.4
3. Boundary alteration	3.6	8.4*	14.3	5.6	9.5	5.2	4.9	3.9	4.5	6.6	7.5	7.7	6.3	88.8
4. Repair obligation, alteration	0.1*	—	—	—	—	—	0.2*	—	—	0.1*	—	0.1*	0.0*	82.3
5. Other change in tenancy agreement	0.5*	—	—	1.1*	0.3*	0.8*	0.5*	0.3*	0.4*	0.9	0.5*	1.0	0.7	87.5
6. Combination of 1 and 2	0.5*	1.0*	0.8*	5.1	2.6*	5.0	12.9	4.5	6.8	6.9	7.1	6.5	5.9	92.2
7. Combination of 0, 1 and 2	0.2*	1.0*	0.8*	—	2.3*	0.7*	1.4*	1.0*	1.0	1.0	1.4	1.0	1.0	105.6
8. Combination of 0, 1 and 4	—	—	—	—	—	—	—	—	0.1*	0.1*	—	0.1*	0.0*	109.5
9. Combination of 0, 1, 2 and 4	—	—	—	—	—	0.2*	—	—	0.1*	0.1*	0.2*	0.0*	0.1*	104.7
10. Other combinations	0.8	5.3*	3.7*	1.1*	1.1*	1.0*	1.6	2.3	2.3	2.4	2.4	2.6	2.2	103.0
11. Not known	55.2	5.3*	6.0*	2.5*	4.9	1.7*	0.9*	0.6*	0.5*	0.8	0.8	0.2*	6.4	72.4
All holdings: Number	1,294	95	133	356	347	463	630	937	1,364	1,502	1,750	3,790	12,661	
Rent per acre (adjusted) (£)	1.61	1.62	1.71	1.81	1.73	1.89	1.92	1.97	2.05	2.17	2.21	2.35	2.13	

Table 26 shows how the passing years since 1945 modify the pattern. The panorama of the years shows clearly the grip of the 1947 legislation upon tenure. During the year 1946-1947, four out of every ten causes of rent change were change of tenancy and one in every four a general review of rent. In 1948, the first year of the effectual working of the 1947 Agriculture Act, changes in tenancy were halved in number and general rent review doubled. Changes of tenancy show a slight decline in numbers from 1948 onwards. General rent reviews continue to account for about half of the causes and in the later years become more frequently a joint cause with landlord's improvements. Improvements as a single cause suffer a set back at the time of the 1947 legislation. Recovery from 1949 is steady and in the later years what had been lost by change of tenancy was gained by improvements. An interesting feature of these yearly percentages is the way alteration of boundaries doubles its normal percentage in 1947, the year immediately prior to the fixation of tenancy by the 1947 Agriculture Act.

Stability of rents.

Since the rent changes of Table 26 are those last occurring, it is possible by enumerating for each year the holdings on which a rent change is recorded to gain a notion of the stability of farm rents. From among the 12,661 holdings in the sample, 3,790 or 30% suffered rent change in 1956 or later, that is during the last two years of the period covered by the survey. Hence on 70% of the holdings rent has remained stable for two years. On the same principle, rent on 56% of the holdings has remained stable for three years; on 44% for four years; on 33% for five years; on 26% for six years; on 21% for seven years; on 17% for eight years; and so on until a core of 10% of the holdings is reached, on which rent has remained static for twelve years or more. According to these figures the chances of rent changing are even after a period of three to four years since the last rent change; in other words for that length of time the odds are against a change of rent and after then they switch in favour of it. Thus the figures indicate a tendency for rent to change with slightly less frequency than the triennial change imposed as a minimum by the provisions of the Agricultural Holdings Act, 1948 for general rent review arbitrations.

Causes and procedures.

Certain causes of rent change are in the nature of things associated with specific rent determination procedures. Cause and procedure associated in this way will tend to equalise the frequency of each and the occasions when a particular cause occurred will equal in number the occasions when an associated procedure was followed. When a tenancy changes, for example, the rent is more likely to be determined by negotiation with a prospective tenant than with a sitting tenant, although the latter is not unheard of: in 13% of the cases where the cause of rent change was change of tenancy the rent had been determined by negotiation with a sitting tenant in occupation under a previous tenancy. The close natural association between change of tenancy as a cause of rent change and negotiation with a prospective tenant as a procedure of rent determination is seen in the near parallel of the percentages of prospective tenant procedures in the chronology of Table 21 and the percentages of change of tenancy year by year in Table 26. There is no point in giving specific figures of numerical relationship between these naturally associated causes and procedures.

Arbitration and independent valuation, on the contrary, are procedures not in the nature of things associated with particular causes of rent change. Admittedly, settlement by mediatorial procedure is unlikely between prospective tenants and landlords, although the survey evidence is not entirely devoid of examples. General rent review, landlord's improvements, and alteration to boundaries and terms of tenancy are causes of rent change where the chances of rent determination being referred or not to arbitration or independent valuation are not biased either way by the cause of rent change.

What in fact happened is important for the findings of the survey. The evidence is arranged in Table 27. The occasions of each cause of rent change are given as a percentage of the total number of rents determined by a particular mediatorial procedure. Without exception the figures for each of the three mediatorial procedures show an overwhelming percentage of rent changes as caused by general rent review. If cases where a general rent review combined with another cause are added to the number of general rent reviews, the average percentage is 86%. From this high percentage figure it can be inferred that arbitrators and independent valuers are in the vast majority of cases employed to determine whole rent and not, as might be supposed, increments to rents consequent upon improvements, boundary adjustments or modifications of tenancy agreements.

Cause of rent change and level of rent.

Included in Table 26 is an index of the average rent per acre (adjusted) of holdings within each causal class[1]. The average rent of the holdings where the last rent change was caused by change of tenancy is taken as the base. The association of cause of rent change and rent determination procedure is reflected by this index. Rents consequent upon general rent review only are obviously

TABLE 27

FREQUENCY OF CAUSES OF LAST RENT CHANGE
BY HOLDINGS WITHIN MEDIATORIAL PROCEDURE CLASSES.

CAUSE OF LAST RENT CHANGE	MEDIATORIAL PROCEDURE CLASSES					
	Independent valuer		Agreed arbitrator		Minister-appointed arbitrator	
	Holdings		Holdings		Holdings	
	No.	%	No.	%	No.	%
0. Change of tenancy	6	5.0	3	2.3	—	—
1. General review	91	75.2	96	73.2	85	87.7
2. Improvements	6	5.0	8	6.1	2	2.1
3. Boundary alteration	3	2.5	2	1.5	—	—
4. Repair obligation alteration	—	—	—	—	1	1.0
5. Other change in tenancy agreement	1	.8	—	—	—	—
6. Combination of 1 and 2	11	9.1	14	10.7	7	7.2
7. Combination of 0, 1 and 2	1	.8	1	.8	1	1.0
8. Other combinations	2	1.6	6	4.6	1	1.0
9. Not known	—	—	1	.8	—	—
TOTALS:	121	100.0	131	100.0	97	100.0

negotiated with sitting tenants and on average are approximately 11% (index 88.8) below the average rent of holdings where the last rent change followed a change of tenancy. Change of tenancy as just intimated generally opens the way for negotiation with prospective tenants. The close association between these procedures and causes is reflected in the difference of 11% between the average rent following change in tenancy and the average rent after a general rent review, for, as has been seen[2], it is by an exactly equal percentage that the average prospective tenant rent is ahead of the average sitting tenant rent. Rents adjusted in response to alteration of boundaries and change in terms of tenancy agreement approximate, on the evidence of the index to Table 26, very closely to the average rent consequent upon general rent reviews, and thereby hint of a hidden element of general rent review wherever rents are

[1] The analysis of variance by a single one-way test shows that these figures for average rent per acre within causal classes are significant. The figures from the analysis of variance are as follows:
Degrees of Freedom {Between Classes. 11 / Within Classes. 12,644} Mean Squares {55.1 / 1.42}

[2] v.p. 105 ante.

I

adjusted primarily on account of alteration to the boundaries of a holding or to the terms of tenancy.

Alteration of rent caused by a landlord's improvements on a holding will in the nature of the case be a fractional increase and not a comprehensive one. The rent index of Table 26 is an index of whole rents, and on those holdings where improvements by the landlord were the cause of the last rent change, the average rent is appreciably higher than the average rent of holdings where a general rental review was the cause of the last change. One explanation of this can be that the holdings on which the landlords had made improvements are for some reason basically higher rented than the holdings which had had a general rental review. The higher rent of the improved holdings can be more reasonably explained, however, by postulating that the holdings had had a general rental review just before the landlord made the improvements which were the cause of the last rent change. This supposition is supported by the index of the average rent of those holdings where the cause of the last rent change was a combination of a general rental review and landlords' improvements. The combined causes lift the average rent of these holdings above the average rent of holdings where a general rental review is the sole cause of the last rent change. The additional rent may with reason be attributed to the landlords' improvements. The joint effort of the general rental reviews and landlords' improvements does not lift the average rent as high as the average rent of those holdings where the landlords' improvements only are the cause of the last rent change. The slightly lower rent of the holdings with the combined causes strongly suggests that the holdings where landlords' improvements were the sole cause of the last rent change have in fact had a recent general rental review.

The rent of the improved holdings is over and above the average rent of those holdings which had a general rental review only by about 5% and this percentage may be taken as indicative of the degree to which, on average, landlords' improvements have advanced rents. Further evidence corroborating the 5% improvements index in rent may be seen in the difference between the index figures for the average rent of the holdings where change of tenancy was the sole cause of the last rent change and the average rent of the holdings where change of tenancy was a cause combined with a general rental review and with landlords' improvements. There are not many holdings in this latter case, but such as occur have an index figure 5.6% higher than the index figure for the average rent of the holdings where change of tenancy was the sole cause of the last rent change. This 5.6% advantage can hardly be the consequence of change of tenancy having coincided with a general rental review; a general rental review of all farms on an estate is not likely to influence the letting price of one of the farms where the tenancy has terminated and rent negotiations are being conducted in the open market. It is more reasonable to suppose that the difference of 5.6% in rent is due to change of tenancy and landlords' improvements operating as combined causes of rent change and that the landlords' recent improvements were deliberately taken into account in the rental negotiations with the prospective tenants.

CHAPTER TEN

ESTATE CHARACTER: SIZE OF ESTATE

Meaning of "estate".

Attention in this and the following chapters is turned away from holdings and towards the estate, of which the holding is a part. An estate is a proprietorship superior to the holding, for the size, shape and land use of holdings and the terms of tenancy on which tenants occupy them are controlled by estate policy. An estate owner moreover sees farm rent from the opposite pole to the tenant's viewpoint. To the estate owner farm rent is revenue and not expenditure. Hence there is reason in the surmise that the rent of agricultural holdings is influenced by estate character. On this surmise the present survey has been directed to obtain evidence of the relationship between estate character and farm rent.

Study of the estate as an institution of economic significance is at present scanty. Precedents to guide the planning of the survey in this matter were sadly wanting. The only full-scale rent surveys that recognise the estate as an entity in itself are the surveys conducted in 1947-1952 by the Country Landowners' Association and the Ministry of Agriculture and Fisheries[1].

Unlike the agricultural holding which is the demised land of a particular tenancy, an estate can vary in size according to the stand point from which it is looked at. Estate size and shape are inter-dependent[2]. The land of one landowner may lie together neatly ringed in a compact block. Another's land may be scattered, like an archipelago, over far distances. Must it be said of the owner of the single block: he owns an estate? And of the owner of the scattered properties: he owns many estates? Or does the land of each proprietorship comprise an entire estate so that the physical difference between two estates is one of shape and not of size? To answer this question the survey has called in aid the abstract notion of management. One landowner, however widely dispersed his land may be, manages the lot as a single entity. Another regards his land as an empire of separate domains independently managed. Central control can mean no more than a tenuous oversight,

---

[1] v.p. 163 post.
[2] cf. D. R. Denman op. cit p. 22.

little concerned with local policy and management. Again it may be but the command of financial policy and accounting. On the contrary, scattered possessions may be the subject of constant and minute technical and financial control from a centre. Variations upon these three systems occur. The managerial criterion adopted by the survey sees a series of separate estates where local control is complete, or central control is no more than an attenuated oversight; and a single whole estate wherever central control is close, however scattered the parcels of land may be.

So intricate a definition of the estate is not an academical niggle. It has fundamental and practical importance for the survey. Whatever principle governs the identification of an estate, governs also, although indirectly, the selection of the sample of holdings[1]. And the classification of estates into size-groups is directly influenced by the definition of an estate. Managerial systems were investigated in order to identify estates only where the estate unit required was not obvious to the owner or agent.

Size and shape are not the only features of estate character. Tenure, finance policy, land use, ownership personality and other traits go to its making[2]. Any one of these could have provided a basis of reference for estate classification and the analysis of farm rents. As the estate aspect of the survey is only incidental to its main aims, the survey does not pursue a thoroughgoing enquiry into estate character and farm rents. What was asked for and received provides sufficient information about the estates for them to be classified by ownership personality and size.

Ownership personality is a term first used in the recent survey of agricultural estate finance[3]. A need was felt for a phrase which denotes the element in estate character that is contributed by the form of land proprietorship. An estate may be owned by a sole person, or by two or more persons associated together. This simple dichotomy is a primary classification of estate character. But the association of persons as estate owners takes different constitutional forms, a complication that makes finer classification possible and is the source of the felt need in systematic study for an appropriate phrase denoting that aspect of estate character which is dependent upon the form of proprietorship.

Lowest rents on largest estates.

The survey classifies estates into the following estate size-groups:

[1] As explained later, the selection of the sample had to observe a 10-holdings maximum per estate: cf. p. 188 post.
[2] cf. D. R. Denman, op. cit. pp. 19-32.
[3] cf. op. cit. p. 29.

0-999 acres; 1,000-1,999 acres; 2,000-3,999 acres; 4,000-5,999 acres; 6,000-9,999 acres; and 10,000 acres and over. Table 28 gives the average current rent per acre of the holdings in each estate size-group.

The average rents show a definite tendency for farm rents per acre to move in an opposite direction to estate size: the larger the estate the lower the rent. Where estate acreage is unadjusted for rough grazings this correlation is quite regular. Over estates running up to 999 acres the average rent is £2.14 per acre. On estates from 1,000-1,999 acres the rent is £2.10; on estates 2,000-3,999 acres it is £1.94; on estates 4,000-5,999 acres it is £1.93 and finally on the largest estates, those from 6,000-9,999 acres and 10,000 acres and above it is £1.71 and £1.28 per acre respectively. Similar clear correlation between estate size and farm rent has been demonstrated in the recent survey of the finances of agricultural estates previously mentioned[1]. Rough grazings, it might be supposed, are in large measure responsible for the drop in rent per acre in the largest estates. Certainly the percentage of land used for rough grazings in each estate size-group moves upwards as estate size rises—the group of smallest estates has only 6% and the estates 10,000 and above acres 35.2%. But when acreages are adjusted to allow for rough grazings the phenomenon of farm rents moving in indirect ratio to estate size remains.

Farming type distribution is not a cause. The constancy of the decline in rent per acre with increase in estate size even after making allowance for rough grazing acreage suggests that the distribution of farming types within estates is not the cause of the correlation. Nevertheless, a relatively high number of dairying holdings with their high rents might pertain to the smaller estates and a preponderance of upland mixed livestock holdings with their low rents to the larger estates. If this were so, it could be the explanation of the relationship of estate size and farm rent.

In Table 28 the holdings of the estate size-groups are arranged in farming type classes. The figures do not support the supposition just made. Estates in the size-group 1,000-1,999 acres have a lower acreage percentage of upland mixed livestock holdings than is found on the estates below 1,000 acres. Estates 2,000 and over acres show only very slight increase in the percentage of upland mixed livestock acreage as estate size increases; with the exception of the largest estates of all which have a fairly sharp increase. Acreage percentage of dairy holdings is almost equal in the three estate size-groups—0-999 acres; 1,000-1,999 acres; and 4,000-5,999

---

[1] cf. op. cit. p. 133.

acres; and again in the remaining estate size-groups—2,000-3,999 acres; 6,000-9,999 acres and 10,000 acres and over. These percentages refute the supposition that low rented farming types predominate on large estates and vice versa.

That farming type distribution could account for the correlation of estate size and farm rent is further repudiated by the levels of the average rents per acre of each farming type in the respective estate size-groups. Grass type average rents fall regularly as estate size increases, with the exception of the slight aberration of the average rent on estates in the size-group, 4,000-5,999 acres, where the average is slightly higher than the normal trend requires. The aberration only occurs while the acreages are unadjusted to allow for rough grazings. Adjustment of acreage brings down the average rent, but this rather undermines than supports the supposition that farming type distribution is a clue to the farm rent and estate size correlation. If the supposition were sound, the percentage of rough grazing acreage in this estate size-group should be greater than the corresponding acreage in the smaller estate size-group immediately preceding it: in fact the acreage in the former is substantially less and hence the average rent rises when adjustment is made to allow for rough grazings. More striking still, the rent per acre of the upland mixed livestock holdings itself drops regularly as estate size increases, except for holdings in the estates of the 4,000-5,999 acres size-group, where it is abnormally high. This abnormally high upland rent has a less depressing effect than is usual upon average rents, and is largely the cause of the slight aberration of the average Grass type rent in this estate size-group.

Furthermore, the rent per acre of the dairy holdings also falls with the increase in estate size, and with them the fall is regular. Even if the acreage percentage of dairy holdings had been higher on the smaller estates than on the larger estates, and the acreage percentage of upland mixed livestock holdings had moved in direct ratio with estate size, the supposition that farming type distribution is the cause of the correlation would not have been vindicated: the evidence of the correlation running through the rents of dairy holdings and upland mixed livestock holdings themselves would still require explanation. The analysis of variance[1] while establishing that both farming type and estate size are significant factors influencing rent per acre, shows farming type to be by far the stronger influence of the two, so strong indeed that by comparison estate size is an insignificant influence. On the other hand the analysis shows also a marked degree of interaction

[1] v. Appendix pp. 191-193.

TABLE 28
AVERAGE CURRENT RENT PER ACRE FOR EACH ESTATE SIZE-GROUP BY FARMING TYPE.

1957

FARMING TYPE	ESTATE SIZE acres					
	0–999	1000–1999	2000–3999	4000–5999	6000–9999	10,000+
	£	£	£	£	£	£
Rent per acre, unadjusted						
GRASS Mainly dairying	2.63	2.55	2.42	2.42	2.40	2.40
Dairy and mixed	2.10	2.09	2.08	1.90	1.82	1.97
Mixed livestock (upland)	.96	.94	.61	.88	.61	.35
Mixed livestock (lowland)	2.05	1.92	1.68	1.75	1.55	1.80
INTERMEDIATE Mixed with dairying	2.38	2.20	2.14	2.15	2.02	1.94
General mixed	1.94	2.07	1.91	1.99	1.63	1.68
Corn, sheep and dairying	1.62	1.90	1.92	1.79	1.73	1.78
ARABLE Heavy land	2.48	2.10	2.23	2.03	2.26	2.08
Light land	1.96	1.95	2.12	2.04	1.99	1.80
Alluvial and mixed	2.36	2.14	2.50	2.38	2.27	2.18
SPECIALISTS	3.21	2.89	2.74	3.72	2.68	.48
ALL TYPES	2.14	2.10	1.94	1.93	1.71	1.28
Rent per acre, adjusted						
	£	£	£	£	£	£
GRASS Mainly dairying	2.72	2.64	2.53	2.52	2.53	2.49
Dairy and mixed	2.21	2.21	2.16	2.00	2.00	2.16
Mixed livestock (upland)	1.46	1.53	1.28	1.45	1.37	.99
Mixed livestock (lowland)	2.14	2.05	1.81	1.82	1.78	1.98

INTERMEDIATE Mixed with dairying	2.43	2.25	2.19	2.20	2.09	2.00
General mixed	2.02	2.12	1.96	2.06	1.74	1.74
Corn, sheep and dairying	1.73	2.05	2.03	1.85	1.76	1.79
ARABLE Heavy land	2.50	2.13	2.24	2.05	2.31	2.11
Light land	1.98	2.00	2.14	2.06	2.01	1.83
Alluvial and mixed	2.40	2.19	2.54	2.39	2.29	2.24
SPECIALISTS	3.32	3.00	2.83	3.79	2.79	1.66
ALL TYPES	2.27	2.22	2.14	2.10	2.01	1.82

Percentage of total acreage

	%	%	%	%	%	%
GRASS Mainly dairying	18.0	17.7	10.5	15.2	8.4	7.5
Dairy and mixed	16.3	16.0	12.5	13.8	8.3	9.0
Mixed livestock (upland)	8.1	5.9	13.1	13.5	19.6	38.5
Mixed livestock (lowland)	6.5	4.7	4.9	4.7	5.7	3.7
INTERMEDIATE Mixed with dairying	10.8	13.1	12.3	13.9	13.0	9.1
General mixed	15.3	14.4	13.3	12.5	14.7	11.3
Corn, sheep and dairying	1.4	1.9	2.3	2.4	2.0	2.1
ARABLE Heavy land	8.5	7.5	9.1	6.4	9.7	2.3
Light land	8.9	11.9	14.4	14.4	12.5	8.2
Alluvial and mixed	5.1	5.9	6.4	2.3	3.5	4.7
SPECIALISTS	1.1	1.0	1.2	.9	2.6	3.6
ALL TYPES	100.0	100.0	100.0	100.0	100.0	100.0

between these two factors. This interaction suggests that among holdings of similar farming type estate size exerts an influence on rent, a suggestion further supported by the next paragraph.

Correlation strong in Grass types. While the figures of Table 28 show that the manner of farming type distribution is not an adequate explanation of the correlation of farm rent per acre and estate size, they hint also of farming type being in some way concerned with the phenomenon. The correlation does not run with equal regularity in all farming types. It is most regular among the Grass types and the mixed with dairying holdings of the Intermediate type. It is not entirely absent from the average rents of the other farming type classes, but in them it is far less obvious; especially among the Arable types and the heavy land arable holdings in particular. Grass farming types and mixed with dairying holdings of the Intermediate type are numerically dominant in all estate size-groups; in no estate size group is the percentage less than 58%. This predominance of farming types whose rents display the correlation of farm rent and estate size may in some measure account for the correlation itself in the average rents of the estate size-groups. If this were so, it would only be a mathematical explanation of the figures; it would not wholly solve the riddle and explain why the correlation is so marked among average rents of the numerically predominant holdings.

Farm size and estate rent per acre. Farm size distribution like farming type distribution appears to offer a possible explanation. Are not the lower rents of the larger estates the consequence of greater numbers of larger holdings on these estates? Analysis of estate acreage into farm size-groups as in Table 29 reveals a distinct tendency for the percentage of acreage of smaller holdings to diminish as estate size increases, and for the percentage of acreage in the largest farms of all (500 acres and over) to increase with estate size. But these tendencies are not the sole or even main cause of the estate size and farm rent relationship.

A glance at the average rents of the several farm size-groups within each estate size-group shows that the relationship of farm rent per acre and estate size is independent of the distribution of holdings in size-groups within estates, for the average rent of holdings in particular farm size-groups itself falls as estate size increases. Take, for example, holdings 500 acres and over: on estates less than 1,000 acres the average farm rent is £1.91 per acre (unadjusted); on estates 1,000-1,999 acres it drops to £1.66; on estates 2,000-3,999 acres it declines further to £1.33; on estates 4,000 to 5,999 it becomes £1.44; and in the two size-groups of the largest estates of all it falls to £1.04 and £.66 per acre respectively. The correlation follows through more or less faithfully all farm size-groups above the range 50-99 acres.

TABLE 29

AVERAGE CURRENT RENT PER ACRE FOR EACH
ESTATE SIZE-GROUP BY FARM SIZE.

1957

FARM SIZE-GROUP	ESTATE SIZE (acres)					
acres	0–999	1000–1999	2000–3999	4000–5999	6000–9999	10,000 and over
Rent per acre, unadjusted						
	£	£	£	£	£	£
15–49	2.51	2.66	2.57	2.81	2.80	2.57
50–99	2.30	2.32	2.24	2.29	2.30	2.11
100–149	2.16	2.27	2.15	2.00	1.95	1.87
150–299	2.09	2.13	2.11	1.95	1.88	1.77
300–499	2.00	1.91	1.81	1.85	1.78	1.45
500 and over	1.91	1.66	1.33	1.44	1.04	.66
All farm size-groups	2.14	2.10	1.94	1.93	1.71	1.28
Percentage of total acreages						
	%	%	%	%	%	%
15–49	7.7	4.3	3.7	5.2	4.8	4.0
50–99	16.3	11.2	9.0	10.1	11.3	7.5
100–149	16.8	14.9	13.0	13.1	10.1	7.8
150–299	35.9	38.9	34.7	32.4	24.1	20.9
300–499	16.4	18.1	21.1	23.8	20.8	14.0
500 and over	6.9	12.6	18.5	15.4	28.9	45.8
All farm size-groups	100.0	100.0	100.0	100.0	100.0	100.0

The analysis of variance[1] shows farm size to be a stronger influence on farm rent per acre than estate size. Farm size however unlike farming type does not suppress the influence of estate size into insignificance. The two factors show an interaction, significant but less so than between farming size and estate size, thereby supporting the observation just made, that in some farm size-groups, but not in all, the estate size and farming rent correlation holds good.

[1] v. Appendix pp. 192, 193.

Ownership personality and estate rent per acre. The inverse ratio
between rent per acre and estate size which is so clearly apparent
in the figures of this chapter is looked at again later on[1], when it
will be seen that ownership personality is an influential factor.

Estate size and rent movement.

Average rent per acre in 1945 of holdings grouped according
to the size of estate to which they belong moves, in general, like
current rent, in indirect ratio to estate size. Table 30 gives the
figures. The average rent of the estates in the 2,000–3,999 acres
group displays a slight aberration from the normal trend, as it is
a fraction lower than the average rent of the next largest estate
size-group, 4,000–5,999 acres. The aberration is in some measure
due to the relatively high rent of the 4,000–5,999 acre size-group,
which, in turn, is partly due to the relatively high percentage
of local authority estates in this size-group[2]. For 1956 and 1958 the
relationship of rent average and estate size does not depart from
the pattern of 1945. Correlation of rent per acre and estate size
is not therefore a peculiarity of current rent.

Although rent on the smallest estates (0–999 acres) is on average
the highest per acre, it has been the least vigorous over the years
1945–1958. Between 1945 and 1956 it increased 44.8%. By 1957
the increase has jumped to 53.7%; and for 1958 an increase of 59%
is forecast. At the other extreme are the estates of the 2,000–3,999
acres size-group; these estates increased their average rent 57.1%
from 1945 to 1956; 68.8% by 1957; and alterations are forecast for
1958 which will give an increase of 73.2%. Estates in the size-
group 1,000–1,999 acres appear to be affected by the sluggish
character of the rent of the smallest estates next in size below them.
Rent increases on the estates of the remaining size groups (4,000–
5,999 acres, 6,000–9,999 acres and 10,000 and over) run neck and
neck between 1945 and 1956 and are in the neighbourhood of 54%.
By 1957 the rent increase on the 6,000–9,999 acres estates has
slackened off; a lack of vigour which is carried forward to affect
the increase for 1958. Nonetheless, in all years, rent increase in this
size-group has been greater than the rent increase of the smaller
estates, up to 2,000 acres. While rent per acre is higher the smaller
the estate no similar correlation appears between rate of rent
increase and estate size. Middle-size estates, 2,000–3,999 acres, show
the greatest increase. The smallest increase is on the estates next
below them in size, running up to 2,000; and it is these least vigorous

---

[1] v.p. 152 post.
[2] cf. p. 155 post.

rents that are the highest per acre. The rapidly moving rent of the 2,000-3,999 acres estates is the very rent which shows a slight deviation from the otherwise regular inverse ratio between estate size and rent per acre; a deviation which suggests that despite its strides forward current rent on these estates is still low, relative to the rent of the other estate size-groups.

TABLE 30
AVERAGE RENT PER ACRE BY ESTATE SIZE 1945-1958.
(Sample 10,413 holdings: 1,616,270 acres).

ESTATE SIZE-GROUP	RENT PER ACRE £				INDEX 1945 = 100			TOTAL ACREAGE OF SAMPLE
acres	1945	1956	1957	1958	1956	1957	1958	%
0-999	1.34	1.94	2.06	2.13	145	154	159	15.8
1000-1999	1.28	1.95	2.07	2.14	152	162	167	21.0
2000-3999	1.12	1.76	1.89	1.94	157	169	173	25.4
4000-5999	1.15	1.77	1.93	1.98	154	168	172	13.1
6000-9999	1.02	1.58	1.67	1.74	155	164	171	10.7
10,000 and over	.79	1.22	1.32	1.36	154	167	172	14.0
All estate size-groups	1.13	1.74	1.86	1.92	154	165	170	100.0

CHAPTER ELEVEN

ESTATE CHARACTER: OWNERSHIP PERSONALITY

Forms of ownership personality.

The forms of ownership personality recognised in the survey are real persons, companies, trusts, local authorities, Government departments and charities.

These terms need elucidation. Real persons is a term used to distinguish persons in the popular sense and the fictitious personality which the law creates to fashion loose associations of people into a body corporate, endowed with all the attributes of a real person. A real person can never be confused with a charity, a company or a local or central Government authority. But between real persons and trustees confusion may arise. Two people, husband and wife for example, owning land together are in the eyes of the law joint tenants, holding the land in trust for themselves. Trusts of this kind are not expressly created; they arise by implication. Persons who are at law implied trustees are often unaware of their legal status; in their own mind and to the lay world at large they are, and act as, real persons. The present survey adopts the same attitude and regards the trustees of implied trusts as real persons and not as trustees vested with the title to the land on behalf of beneficiaries.

Estates classified as trust estates are those which are expressly owned by trustees, who as trustees and owners have contributed information to the survey. A body of trustees who would be accepted as holding an estate on trust might also satisfy the definition of a charity, as used for the present survey. In that event the estate would be counted among the charity estates. Similarly, where an estate company or other type of company acts as a trustee, the estate would be pigeon-holed for survey purposes with the estates owned by companies. Sometimes a company fulfills the requirements of a charity and then its charity role determines the character of the estate it owns.

Charity estates are usually owned by a body corporate, which may or may not be a body of trustees or a company. The essential distinction is the exemption from income tax these estates enjoy and their immunity to surtax and estate duty. They are immune from estate duty because the charitable bodies who own them are immortal and hence not subject to inheritance taxation. Immunity from surtax is enjoyed because this tax is personal and inapplicable to bodies corporate. Exemption from income tax is statutory and specifically bestowed. Charities are exempt from income tax on rents from land let by them, but only in so far as the income from the rents is applied to charitable purposes. Whether the body, or institution, is a charity or not is a question of law. The Inland Revenue use well-established general working rules by which charities are distinguished from tax-paying bodies. The present survey follows the Inland Revenue in this and accepts as charity estates those whose owners are exempt from income tax.

Local authorities and Government departments are designations easily understood. They do not call for further comment, except to say that the estates owned by the boards of nationalised industries, of which the National Coal Board is an example, and estates belonging to similar quasi-Government bodies, are classified with estates of Government departments; as also are the estates of the Crown Commissioners and those of the Duchies of Cornwall and Lancaster.

Charity estate rent the highest.

Ownership personality on the evidence of the analysis of variance[1] is, like estate size, a significant influence affecting the level of farm rent per acre. When average current rents per acre on estates differing in ownership personality are compared, the rent of charity estates is the highest. Table 31 gives the figures. Current rent per acre over the acreage of charity estates, unadjusted for rough grazings, is £2.33, or £2 6s. 7d. Rent of local authority estates holds second place with an average of £2.12, or £2 2s. 5d. per acre. Company estates are next in order with an average rent of £2.01, or £2 0s. 2d. per acre. Below them come trustee estates with an average rent of £1.94, or £1 18s. 9d.; the estates of real persons with an average rent of £1.86, or £1 19s. 7d. per acre; and lowest of all Government department estates with an average rent of £1.64, or £1 12s. 9d. per acre.

Significance of farming type distribution. As will be seen in a moment, the supremacy of charity estate rents and the rents of local authority estates is partly a consequence of farming type distribution. But there is another cause of the supremacy because when arranged according to the ownership personality of estates to which they belong the average rents of all Grass type holdings follow the same order of precedence as the average rents of owner-

[1] Single one-way classification, Appendix p. 191.

TABLE 31   AVERAGE CURRENT RENT PER ACRE FOR EACH OWNERSHIP PERSONALITY CLASS BY FARMING TYPE.

1957

FARMING TYPE	OWNERSHIP PERSONALITY					
	Charity	Real persons	Company	Trust	Local Authority	Government department
	£	£	£	£	£	£
Rent per acre, unadjusted.						
GRASS	2.31	1.68	1.92	1.85	2.16	1.12
Mainly dairying	2.65	2.47	2.31	2.47	2.72	2.74
Dairy and mixed	2.16	2.03	1.93	2.12	2.06	1.92
Mixed livestock (upland)	1.13	.63	.86	.97	.56	.36
Mixed livestock (lowland)	2.22	1.86	1.67	1.70	2.42	1.40
INTERMEDIATE	2.23	1.96	2.02	1.92	2.59	2.04
Mixed with dairying	2.38	2.10	2.19	1.97	2.86	2.28
General mixed	2.14	1.87	1.88	1.88	2.16	1.88
Corn, sheep and dairying	2.03	1.79	1.92	1.72	—	1.39
ARABLE	2.48	2.08	2.12	2.06	2.89	2.17
Heavy land	2.42	2.19	2.14	2.11	2.81	2.32
Light land	2.16	1.99	2.06	1.97	2.80	1.88
Alluvial and mixed	3.04	2.11	2.47	2.14	3.16	2.52
SPECIALISTS	2.32	3.12	2.47	2.69	.48	3.09
ALL TYPES	2.33	1.86	2.01	1.94	2.12	1.64
Rent per acre, adjusted.						
	£	£	£	£	£	£
GRASS Mainly dairying	2.70	2.58	2.40	2.52	2.87	2.91
Dairy and mixed	2.29	1.14	2.08	2.23	2.23	2.06
Mixed livestock (upland)	1.74	1.33	1.38	1.55	1.03	0.96
Mixed livestock (lowland)	2.23	1.98	1.86	1.80	2.45	1.68

INTERMEDIATE Mixed with dairying	2.36	2.89	2.02	2.29	2.15	2.39
General mixed	2.04	2.21	1.91	1.99	1.93	2.16
Corn, sheep and dairying	1.51	—	1.73	2.09	1.84	2.18
ARABLE Heavy land	2.35	2.82	2.12	2.17	2.22	2.45
Light land	1.90	2.81	2.01	2.11	2.02	2.18
Alluvial and mixed	2.56	3.17	2.18	2.58	2.14	3.07
SPECIALISTS	3.31	1.87	2.84	2.49	3.26	2.33
ALL TYPES	2.08	2.58	2.07	2.15	2.09	2.38

Percentage total acreage.

	%	%	%	%	%	%
GRASS Mainly dairying	9.0	24.2	14.5	16.9	12.9	12.7
Dairy and mixed	7.9	12.4	9.9	10.4	15.7	10.8
Mixed livestock (upland)	28.6	8.1	12.1	5.1	15.7	1.8
Mixed livestock (lowland)	3.8	1.7	6.4	5.8	4.9	6.6
INTERMEDIATE Mixed with dairying	9.7	12.0	14.2	16.8	11.0	15.8
General mixed	10.4	7.4	13.4	18.8	13.4	18.2
Corn, sheep and dairying	.9	—	.8	3.6	2.0	4.3
ARABLE Heavy land	8.8	7.4	8.3	6.4	7.5	5.4
Light land	12.8	6.5	12.0	12.7	11.6	13.8
Alluvial and mixed	6.6	4.8	7.6	1.5	4.4	8.6
SPECIALISTS	1.5	15.5	1.0	2.0	0.9	2.0
ALL TYPES	100.0	100.0	100.0	100.0	100.0	100.0

K

ship personality groups throughout the entire sample. Table 31 illustrates this. Charity estates lead with an average rent of £2.31 per acre; then local authorities, companies, trusts, real persons and Government departments. As with the overall- figures, charities and local authorities tend to draw together into a distinctive sector of the rent range; real persons, trusts and companies into another; and Government departments make a third. Among the Intermediate and Arable farming types, the same affinities are seen. With the Intermediate types, local authorities and charities have the highest rents; the only difference from the general pattern is the supremacy of local authority rent over charity rent. Rents of companies, real persons and trusts cling close together, but are the lowest rented of the series, and Government departments jump three steps to come next after charities. Rents of the Arable farming types follow exactly the order of the rents of the Intermediate types. Rents in the Specialist classes are anomalous; the anomalies would be significant if the number of Specialist holdings were greater. As it is, the evidence turns the normal order of precedence on its head and rents of charities and local authorities occupy the lowest position, while at the top are the rents of real persons, followed by those of Government departments, trusts and companies.

That farming type is part cause of the rent level relationship is indicated when average rents are adjusted for rough grazings acreages. Charities then lose place to local authorities, as charity estates have the least percentage of rough grazings in their acreage (2.31%) and local authority estates the second highest percentage (20.98%).

What the adjustment of acreage indicates becomes more patent when the acreages of specific farming types within ownership personality classes are compared. Table 31 does this. Local authority estates have the highest percentage of mainly dairying farms, with their relatively high rents, and in an opposite direction they have the second lowest percentage of Intermediate type holdings. Charity estates have the lowest percentage of upland mixed livestock acreage with their relatively low rents. Estates of real persons and trusts, on the other hand, carry the second and third highest percentages of upland livestock acreage while Government department estates have the highest percentage of all. It is significant that among Intermediate and Arable types, the rent of Government department estates outdistances the rent of real persons, trusts and companies, for these farming types have no high percentage of upland mixed livestock acreage to keep the rent figure depressed.

Too much regard however must not be paid to the distribution of farming type as a cause of rent level relationships. Ownership personality itself has a definite influence upon rent, as the above comparisons of the average rent of the principal farming types show. Admittedly and understandably, the acreage of upland mixed livestock holdings exercises a significant influence upon average rent, but the order of precedence of the overall rents is clearly followed also by the rents within this farming type class. Charity estates within the class come first with an average rent of £1.13 per acre; then trusts with a rent of £0.97 per acre, followed by companies at £0.86 per acre; real persons at £0.63 per acre; local authorities at £0.56; and Government departments at £0.36 per acre. There are only two shifts from the overall order of precedence —trusts change place with companies, an interchange of no consequence, and local authorities fall to second lowest. The evidence so far shows that ownership personality affects the level of rent both by the attitude of the owner to rent itself and to the type of farm owned. The high rents of charity lands, for example, are the consequence of deliberate ownership policies, the selection of land and holdings of specific farming types.

Significance of farm size. When holdings within ownership personality groups are separated into farm size-groups and average rents compared, local authority rents take the lead in the two smallest size-groups 15-49 acres and 50-99 acres (as shown in Table 32). In the next size-group, 100-149 acres, local authority rent is mid-way; and in the size-groups of the larger holdings it is the lowest of all.

Only among the small holdings, 15-99 acres, does local authority rent surpass all others. Of the total acreage of the local authority estates a high percentage is in county council smallholdings estates, and in consequence 92% of the total acreage is occupied by holdings between 15 and 99 acres[1]. On these smallholdings estates only does local authority rent excel. Rent on the remainder of the local authority acreage makes a poor showing; 50% of its total area is in holdings of over 500 acres with an average rent of 6s. 6d. per acre. The overwhelming proportion of the acreage of local authority estates in county council smallholdings and the relatively high rents of these smallholdings are together responsible for lifting the

---

[1] County Councils, under the Agriculture Act, 1947, and the Agricultural (Miscellaneous Provisions) Act, 1954, as smallholding authorities, are required to provide smallholdings; before 1954 to a maximum of 75 acres per holding and after 1954 to a maximum of 50 acres per holding.

overall average rent of local authority estates into a leading position with the overall rent of charity estates.

TABLE 32
AVERAGE CURRENT RENT PER ACRE FOR EACH
OWNERSHIP PERSONALITY CLASS BY FARM SIZE.

1957

FARM SIZE-GROUP	OWNERSHIP PERSONALITY CLASS					
acres	Charity	Real persons	Company	Trust	Local Authority	Government department
	Rent per acre, unadjusted					
	£	£	£	£	£	£
15–49	2.72	2.62	2.63	2.53	3.12	2.16
50–99	2.48	2.25	2.33	2.15	2.57	2.11
100–149	2.51	2.10	2.25	2.15	2.15	1.90
150–299	2.41	2.02	2.08	2.06	1.33	1.97
300–499	2.17	1.80	1.80	1.78	1.07	1.76
500 and over	2.20	1.07	1.58	1.44	.32	.87
All size-groups	2.32	1.86	2.01	1.94	2.12	1.64
	Percentage of total acreage					
	%	%	%	%	%	%
15–49	2.8	4.0	3.8	4.1	27.0	6.3
50–99	6.6	10.5	10.4	9.8	35.7	10.2
100–149	10.6	13.8	15.0	13.0	7.8	11.1
150–299	33.8	34.9	32.9	34.6	5.9	25.9
300–499	25.6	18.2	21.0	22.0	5.0*	18.2
500 and over	20.6	18.6	16.9	16.5	18.6*	28.3
All size-groups	100.0	100.0	100.0	100.0	100.0	100.0

Local authority rent enjoys supremacy of place only in the specific case of holdings less than 100 acres. If these are set aside the rent of charity estates is left unquestionable master of the field in all size-groups. Rent of company estates takes second place. Companies' rent however is much closer to the rents of trusts, real persons and Government departments, than it is to charity rent. Indeed, in the size-group 300–499 acres, rents of companies, trusts and real persons and are almost identical at about £1 16s. per acre, while the charity rent is £2 3s. 6d. per acre. Government department rent in this size-group is no exception to the general rule, which places it below the rents of companies, trusts and real persons. In the larger size-group it vies with local authority rent for the unenviable bottom place. In fine, with the exception of local authority estates, the evidence of the farm size-groups reveals faithfully the ownership personality order of precedence of the overall average rents.

Significance of fixed equipment. At first glance the figures give the impression that the provision of fixed equipment and electricity supplies might account in some way for the difference in average rent within ownership personality classes. Charity estates have the highest percentage of holdings (65.3%) where farmhouse and buildings are provided and both are connected to electricity supplies. On further scrutiny the impression fades. First because on charity estates the rent per acre of holdings with homesteads and electricity supplies is no higher than the rent of holdings not so equipped. The high percentage of holdings with homesteads connected to electricity supplies does not therefore account for the relatively higher average rent per acre of the charity estates. Secondly the order of precedence of the overall average rents of the ownership personality classes is closely, but not at all points, followed by the average rents of holdings equipped with homesteads and electricity supplies. In the lead are local authority estates with an average rent of £2.66 per acre; then charity estates at £2.35 per acre; Government department estates at £2.19 per acre; company estates and trust estates at £2.11 per acre; and the estates of real persons at £2.04 per acre. Charity and local authority rents are well in the lead and those of companies, trusts and real persons hang close together in an inferior position. Government department rent jumps to third place. In this only is there a difference from the order of precedence of the overall averages. Further evidence pointing in the same direction is the relatively low percentage of holdings (42.3%) on the local authority estates with homesteads connected to electricity supplies. Against this must be set the equally low percentage (46.8%) on estates of Government departments of holdings similarly equipped. But for the low percentage of fully equipped holdings on the local authority estates, with their high average rent, it would be reasonable to see in the low percentage on Government department estates a possible explanation of the low position of Government department rent in the order of precedence of the overall averages.

When holdings with main water supplies are isolated from the others, and the average rent of ownership personality classes compared, the order of precedence observed in the overall averages emerges substantially. Charity and local authority rents take the lead; local authority rent averages £2.82 per acre and charity rent £2.43 per acre. Government department rent does not occupy the lowest position, as in the general order, but has third place with an average of £2.26 per acre. On the estates of real persons, companies and trusts rents are lowest, with averages in the order of £2.15 per acre. Rents of holdings supplied with water through an estate system follow faithfully the order of the overall figures; local authority and charity rents lead and those of Government departments rank lowest. On holdings with other forms of water supply—from farm sources and other unpiped supplies—the normal order of precedence is lost, except for the leading position of charity estates. However water is supplied rent on the charity estates never falls below second place. The most significant divergence from the normal is the low position of local authority rent among holdings without a proper water supply or with a water supply from a source on the farm or from some other unpiped source.

Supremacy of charity rent among the overall average rents is not due, therefore, to a relatively high percentage of holdings with main water supply; indeed, charity estates have 58.8% of their holdings so equipped and fall short of the achievements of both local authority estates with 64.2% and company estates with 60.7%. This relatively high percentage of holdings with main water supply on the estates of local authorities probably accounts in part for the lead so often taken by the rents of these estates. Estates of Government departments have the lowest percentage of holdings with main water supply, 49%, and this may be partly responsible for their low position in the order of precedence of the overall average rents and the average rents of the Grass farming types. The low percentage of holdings supplied with main water on these estates is probably a consequence of terrain and location, for a high percentage of their acreage is rough grazing land. Indifferent water supply and poor quality, inaccessible farm land interact and keep farm rents low.

Ownership personality and rent movements 1945-1958.

Evidence from the holdings in the sample whose rent changes from 1945-1957 and proposed changes by 1958 are known, has been arranged in ownership personality classes. The results are given in Table 33. These show how the average rent of each class stands in relation to the average rent of other classes for the years 1945, 1956, 1957 and 1958 and the degrees of rent movement over the years.

In 1945 rents of local authority estates and charity estates were in the lead—local authority rent somewhat in advance of charity rent. Rents on the estates of trusts, companies and real persons were close to each other and formed a sector decidedly below the level of charity and local authority rents. At rock bottom stood the rent of Government department estates. By 1956 charities just manage to take the lead from local authorities, but both rents are well in advance of the rent of other ownership personality classes. Rents on the estates of trusts and companies go ahead and leave the rents on the estates of real persons behind. Government department estates still show the most depressed rents, but there is little difference between the level of their rent and the level of rent on estates of real persons. In 1957 the same order of precedence is followed although the rent of charity estates is more securely in the lead. Proposals for 1958 do not forecast a change in the relative positions.

The consistently low rent of the Government department estates nonetheless displays the greatest vigour in its rate of increase from 1945-1956. Over these eleven years the increase is 67%. Other personality classes cannot approach this achievement and at best can show the 59% increase gained by rents of company estates. Increase in the rent of the charity estates comes third, followed by the increase in the rents of estates of trusts and real persons. Local authority rent which in magnitude competes so closely with charity rent for the leading position is the most sluggish and rises only 44% over the eleven years.

Over the twelve years 1945-1957 rent movement in all ownership personality classes was greater than in the eleven years period. The most impressive movement is the advance in the rent of Government department estates by 81% of their 1945 level. Movement in the rent of company estates, the next most vigorous class, is 70%. Movement in local authority rents is again smallest, a meagre 50%—barely over half the achievement of Government department rent. Forecasts for 1958 follow suit: the greatest advance, to 85%, is in Government department rent, and the least in local authority rent.

Rates of movement between 1956 and 1957 are of course reflected in the percentages just cited. They are, however, more clearly seen when 1957 rent stands on a 1956 base. Government department rent has the highest percentage increase of 8.7%, followed by charity rent with an increase of 7.4%, and company rent with 7.1%. Advances in the rents of real persons and trusts are almost equal, 6.5% and 6.7% respectively. Sluggish local authority rent increases only 4%. Figures forecast for 1958 indicate an abrupt slowing down in the advance of Government department rent, and a quickening of local authority rent. Government department rent is forecast to advance 2.3%, and local authority rent 5.3%. The latter figure is the highest forecast; charity and company rents promise a 4% increase and rents on estates of real persons and trusts 3%.

TABLE 33

AVERAGE RENT PER ACRE BY OWNERSHIP PERSONALITY
CLASS 1945–1958.

(Sample 10,413 holdings: 1,616,270 acres).

OWNERSHIP PERSONALITY CLASS	RENT PER ACRE £				INDEX 1945 = 100			TOTAL ACREAGE OF SAMPLE
	1945	1956	1957	1958	1956	1957	1958	%
Charity	1.30	2.03	2.18	2.27	156	168	175	7.0
Real persons	1.12	1.69	1.80	1.86	151	161	166	58.2
Company	1.16	1.84	1.97	2.05	159	170	177	9.0
Trust	1.16	1.77	1.89	1.95	153	163	168	11.9
Local Authority	1.39	2.00	2.08	2.19	144	150	157	3.1
Government department	.96	1.60	1.74	1.78	167	181	185	10.8
All ownership personality classes	1.13	1.74	1.86	1.92	154	165	170	100.0

Ownership personality and estate size.

The correlation of rent per acre and estate size may be affected by ownership personality; and the relationship of ownership personality and rent per acre may be influenced by estate size. Figures showing something of the interaction of estate size, ownership personality and rent per acre are given in Table 34.

Estates are arranged in size-groups and ownership personality classes. On the estates of real persons only do average rents consistently display the indirect ratio between estate size and rent per acre: from an average rent of £2.10 per acre on the smallest estates (0-999 acres) the averages fall regularly to £1.14 per acre on estates 10,000 acres and over. On charity estates the indirect ratio is apparent over the estate-size range 1,000 acres-5,999 acres. Rent per acre on the estates of larger acreage, 6,000 acres and over, tends to rise with acreage. The indirect ratio is conspicuous but not regular among the rents of companies, trusts and Government departments. Local authority rents are outstandingly erratic: far from the rents on estates 4,000 acres-9,999 acres being proportionally lower than the rent on estates below 1,000 acres, they average nearly 31% above it. From these figures the correlation between rent per acre and estate size, so clearly patent in the overall average rents of estate size-groups, appears to be a peculiar preserve of the estates of real persons. Although not altogether alien to estates of other ownership personality, it is but indifferently associated with them. Of the 2,440 estates in the sample 58.7% are estates of real persons. This percentage of total estates is matched fairly closely by the percentage of estates of real persons in all estate size-groups. Estates of real persons obviously dominate and bias the results of the survey. It is their influence that is responsible for the correlation of estate size and rent per acre in the overall averages of the estate-size groups.

Ownership personality rents set out in estate size-groups display certain relationships which correspond to what is observed in the overall averages of the ownership personality classes. A faithful reproduction is wanting. Charity rent is highest in all but two size-groups; in one of these exceptions, charity rent has second place and in the other third place. Government department rents are consistently in the lowest place, except in the same two size-groups. The size-groups responsible for these exceptions are the 4,000-5,999 acres group and the 6,000-9,999 acres group. In other respects also the rents of these groups are exceptional. Local authority rent in both is in advance of all other rents; this is not surprising. What is remarkable is the level of the local authority rent: in one size-group it is 46% above group average and in the other 63% above group average. This outstanding performance occurs in these two estate size-groups only; local authority rent in one only of the other estate size-groups is as high as second place. It is the abnormally high rents of these two size-groups that weaken the correlation between estate size and rent per acre on local authority estates. The county council smallholdings estates tend to fall within the size range of these two estate size-groups and are the cause of the aberrant averages. Apart from the particular unchallengeable position of local authority rent in the two estate size-groups, company rent is in general the most favoured after charity rent. In three of the estate size-groups it holds second place, and in two, third place. On estates of real persons and trusts the rents are low in all estate size-groups and hence follow more closely the order of precedence of the overall averages of the ownership personality classes.

The number of estates in each estate size-group and ownership personality class is also shown in Table 34. In all ownership personality classes, but that of local authorities, the weight of numbers is in the lowest estate size-groups (0-999 acres to 2,000-3,999). Local authorities unlike other ownership personality classes show a relatively high percentage of their estates in the estate size-range 4,000 acres and over. The exceptionally high rents

TABLE 34
AVERAGE CURRENT RENT PER ACRE FOR EACH ESTATE SIZE-GROUP AND OWNERSHIP PERSONALITY CLASS.

1957

OWNERSHIP PERSONALITY CLASS	RENT PER ACRE AND PERCENTAGE DISTRIBUTION OF ESTATES BY OWNERSHIP PERSONALITY — ESTATE SIZE GROUP (acres)												PERCENTAGE DISTRIBUTION OF ESTATES BY ESTATE SIZE-GROUPS — ESTATE SIZE-GROUP (acres)							TOTAL ESTATES	
	0–999		1000–1999		2000–3999		4000–5999		6000–9999		10,000 and over		0–999	1000–1999	2000–3999	4000–5999	6000–9999	10,000 & over	All sizes		
	£	%	£	%	£	%	£	%	£	%	£	%	%	%	%	%	%	%	%	No.	%
Charity	2.50	11.2	2.32	8.9	2.3	4.5	1.96	3.0	2.07	5.8	2.29	5.0	63.0	19.7	8.6	2.4	3.4	2.9	100	208	8.5
Real persons	2.10	64.3	2.07	56.3	1.90	59.3	1.88	54.5	1.44	43.0	1.14	31.7	52.8	18.1	16.5	6.4	3.6	2.6	100	1,431	58.7
Trust	2.01	8.2	2.09	13.7	2.07	11.0	1.77	10.2	2.01	8.3	1.33	9.2	39.8	26.1	18.3	7.1	4.1	4.6	100	241	9.9
Local Authority	2.14	4.4	2.29	0.9	1.66	2.8	2.83	8.4	2.79	12.4	1.58	12.5	46.9	3.6	9.9	12.6	13.5	13.5	100	111	4.5
Government department	2.03	7.2	1.96	12.6	1.85	16.6	1.96	15.0	2.0	18.2	0.56	26.6	29.8	20.1	22.9	8.7	7.6	11.1	100	288	11.8
Company	2.34	4.7	2.19	7.6	1.97	5.8	2.09	9.0	1.74	12.4	1.88	15.0	34.2	21.7	14.3	9.3	9.3	11.2	100	161	6.6
All classes		100.0		100.0		100.0		100.0		100.0		100.0	48.1	18.9	16.3	6.8	5.0	1.9	100	2,440	100.0

of local authority estates in the estate size range 4,000-9,999 acres and the abnormally high percentage of their number in that estate size range, due to the concentration of county council smallholdings estates, override the contributions of local authority estates in other estate size-groups and enable the overall average rent of this ownership personality class to attain precedence over the overall average rents of all other types of estate, except the charity estates. Charity estates themselves are somewhat oddly distributed among the estate size-groups. An exceptionally high percentage of their number (63%) is in the smallest size-group. As a general rule rent per acre is higher on these smallest estates than on the larger estates. The high percentage of charity estates in the smallest size-group would be, therefore, an explanation of the supremacy of charity rent among the overall averages of the personality classes, had not charity rent displayed a tendency to rise with estate size on estates above 6,000 acres and also been the highest in all estate size-groups, except the two where local authority rent steals the limelight.

CHAPTER TWELVE

EARLIER SURVEYS AND OTHER COMPARISONS

Comparison of the results of the present survey with those of other surveys, if perfectly made, would show how rents have moved since the time of the earlier surveys, how far the figures of the present survey differ from or agree with those of other contemporary surveys, and reveal whether or not certain trends (e.g. the correlation of farm rent and farm size) are peculiar to the present survey. Unfortunately perfect comparisons are not possible because in aim, scope and sample the present survey differs from the others. Imperfect comparisons can be made, nonetheless, after proper adjustments. And where for want of necessary figures the evidence cannot be adjusted, it may yet be possible by imperfect comparisons to detect parallel trends. It is intended now to make broad comparisons of the results of the present survey, the evidence of the three extensive earlier surveys, previously mentioned[1], and certain figures of farm rents in Scotland obtained from Government surveys of selected farms.

The earlier surveys.

The three earlier surveys are the survey of agricultural rents carried out by the Ministry of Agriculture and Fisheries in 1938[2]; the portion of the National Farm Survey 1941-43 that deals with the rent of holdings; and the series of enquiries into agricultural rents and the expenses of landowners carried out by the Country Landowners' Association and the Ministry of Agriculture and Fisheries at intervals from 1947-1952[3].

Agricultural rents 1936/37. Early in 1938 the Ministry of Agriculture and Fisheries asked some 500 landowners to submit particulars of the rent rolls of their estates for the years 1936 and 1937. The enquiry was based upon the estate and not upon the holding, but no definition of an estate is given in the report that

---

[1] v.p. 25 ante.

[2] *Statistical Study of Agricultural Rents: Statement of Results.* Ministry of Agriculture and Fisheries, 1939.

[3] *An Enquiry into Agricultural Rents and the Expenses of Landowners in England and Wales, 1946 and 1947: 1949 and 1950, etc.* Country Landowners' Association.

presents the results. An area of 1.6m. acres was covered by the enquiry; an acreage representing approximately 8% of the total acreage of let land under crops, grass and rough grazings at that time. Representation of total let acreage differed from county to county within a range of 28% for Durham and less than 1% for Caernarvon, Glamorgan, Anglesey and Carmarthen. No figures are given of the distribution of the holdings in the sample in size-groups or farming types, hence it is impossible to say how representative the sample is of the holdings pattern or farming type pattern of the national universe; or to compare the structure of the sample with the structure of the sample of the present survey. The figure of the present survey which answers nearest to the 8% representation of the enquiry of 1938 is the 11.5% of the total acreage under crops, grass and rough grazings in holdings of 15 acres and over, wholly or partly let; the two percentages are not strictly comparable as the acreage represented by the percentage of the earlier survey is probably, but not certainly, representative of holdings smaller than 15 acres.

The results of the two surveys are comparable in so far as the 1938 enquiry gives figures for what it calls contract rent—similar in all respects to the contractual rent of the present survey; and the acreages used in the calculations are inclusive of crops, grass and rough grazings unadjusted for rough grazings. Rents per acre, therefore, are comparable, other things being equal, with the rent per acre figures of the "unadjusted" acreages of the present survey. Although the constitution of the sample is not known, it is freely admitted that a high proportion of the total acreage was drawn from large estates and 37.8% of the total was in the ownership of public and semi-public bodies (e.g. the Ecclesiastical Commissioners, Commissioners of Crown Lands). This percentage is high compared with the corresponding percentage of 14.3% of the present survey[1].

For both years 1936 and 1937 the enquiry gives the average contract rent as £1.05 per acre. Commenting on this figure and comparing it with a figure of £1.25 per acre, estimated by Crop Reporters in 1931 as the national average rent per acre for that year, the report of the 1938 enquiry considers the drop in its own figure to £1.05 per acre to be a consequence of the size of the holdings and estates in the sample and not indicative of a fall in

---

[1] The percentages do not represent the same thing in each survey. The earlier survey did not include estates owned by Government Departments and county councils and includes among its public and semi-public bodies owners like the Ecclesiastical Commissioners whose estates in the present survey are counted as "charity estates".

average rent. The average size of holding used for the Crop Reporters' estimate was 73 acres, and the average size holding in the 1938 enquiry was 155 acres.

As a national average figure for farm rent per acre, the £1.05 is more acceptable than a figure that might be obtained by attempting to adjust the proportionate representation of holdings in the 1938 sample, to the proportionate representation of the holdings covered by the Crop Reporters' figures. Raising the number of small holdings represented in the 1938 sample to bring it closer to the proportion of small holdings in the 1931 sample is unlikely to influence the national average rent per acre very much. The sample used for the present survey illustrates this. The average size of the holdings of the present sample is 155 acres (a figure exactly equal to the average size of the holdings in the 1938 survey); and if the present sample is raised to correspond to the proportionate national distribution of holdings in the size-groups, the proportions of the numbers in the smaller size-groups increase and the average size of holding drops to 125 acres. But the change in average rent per acre is only £0.04. The average rent per acre of £1.05 in 1936/37 would not alter much by merely increasing the number of small holdings in the sample. To alter it so that it approaches the £1.25 per acre of the 1931 figures would require adding to the sample smallholdings of considerably higher rent per acre than those of the small holdings already in the sample; and this would mean bringing into the sample high-rented holdings whose size is often too tiny to allow them to be counted among the farms of the country[1].

National Farm Survey 1941/43. This survey was nation-wide and records information about every holding of 5 acres and upwards in England and Wales. From this complete record of the "universe" of holdings, a random sample was selected for detailed analysis and presentation of results. The sample was approximately 14% of the total number of holdings of 5 acres and over in England and Wales. Small holdings are more numerous than large holdings and consequently an arbitrary scale of proportions was used which raised the proportion of holdings selected progressively with the size of holding. The sampling procedure of the present survey has achieved a result similar in principle, but not in magnitude. Table 35 compares the percentage representation in size-groups of the two samples.

[1] The Crop Reporters' figures show an average rent of £3.05 per acre for 1931 for holdings from 1-5 acres. cf. *Agricultural Out-put of England and Wales,* 1930-31. p. 51.

TABLE 35

REPRESENTATION OF POPULATION OF HOLDINGS IN
NATIONAL FARM SURVEY AND PRESENT SURVEY.

NATIONAL FARM SURVEY		PRESENT SURVEY	
Size-group	Sample as percentage of population	Size-group	Sample as percentage of population of wholly rented holdings
acres	%	acres	%
5–24	5	15–49	7.8
25–99	10	50–99	9.2
100–299	25	100–149	11.4
300–699	50	150–299	14.0
700 and over	100	300 and over	16.2

While the percentage of holdings selected in the present sample
rises in direct ratio with the magnitude of the size-group, the rate
of rise is very much slower than in the sample of the 1941/43
survey. The earlier survey includes the very small holdings between
5 and 14.9 acres and consequently there is no comparison between
the two samples at this point. Percentages in the size-groups 100-
299 acres are nearly equal. But as would be expected from the
difference in the rates of rise, the percentages in the higher size-
groups are very much lower in the present sample than in the
earlier sample. Moreover, the percentages of the earlier sample
related to the universe of rented and owner-occupied holdings
together. These differences in sample must be borne in mind when
comparing the respective results.

The National Farm Survey gives figures for what it calls "actual
rents paid". No reference is made to abatements and arrears of
rent and it is reasonable to suppose that this expression is synony-
mous with the term "contractual rent" as used in the present
survey. On this supposition, the figures of the 1941/43 survey and
the present survey are comparable. Since the figures of the earlier
survey include the rents of holdings from 5-14.9 acres and the
estimated rents of owner-occupied holdings, it is necessary to adjust
them before comparison is made. Comparison of absolute figures
is significant wherever it is possible to subtract from the 1941/43
evidence the figures relating to owner-occupied holdings, and
holdings from 5-14.9 acres. Subtraction is possible only as regards
the sample as a whole and not for separated portions of it such as the
farming type classes, farm size-groups and other categories. Hence
comparison of the absolute average rents of these categories is
not significant. A similar limitation however does not prevent the
comparison of relative rent levels in each category.

Although subtraction of the incommensurable figures is possible, the process is not straightforward. It is approached by a devious route winding among the many published Tables of the 1941/43 survey and calls in aid the Agricultural Statistics 1939/44 and the unpublished census of holdings and acreages prepared in 1950 by the Ministry of Agriculture and Fisheries for F.A.O.[1]

The official statistics for 1944 give the acreage of holdings from 5-14.75 acres; the National Farm Survey 1941/43 gives the average rent per acre of holdings from 5-25 acres[2]. Multiplying the former figure by the latter gives an approximate estimate of the total rent of all holdings from 5-14.75 acres. This figure when subtracted from the total rent in 1942[3], calculated by multiplying the acreage under crops and grass (excluding rough grazings) by the average rent, gives a figure for total rent of all holdings of 15 acres and over in 1942; and the acreage of holdings 5-14.75 acres subtracted from the total acreage under crops and grass, gives a total acreage for all holdings of 15 acres and over. The percentage of this total acreage in owner-occupation in 1942 and the acreage of rough grazings in owner-occupation is also given in the National Farm Survey 1941/43[4]. So it is possible to calculate the acreage in owner-occupation for both types of land use and to combine the answers to give an "adjusted" total acreage of all holdings of 15 acres and over in owner-occupation. The total estimated rental value of owner-occupied land in 1942 can be calculated by multiplying the "adjusted" acreage so calculated by the average estimated rent per acre[5]. This figure subtracted from the figure for total rent of all holdings of 15 acres and over, gives the total rent of all let land in similar sized holdings. The total acreage of this let land, calculated by subtracting the acreage of owner-occupied holdings from the total acreage of holdings 15 acres and over (including rough grazings), divided into the total rent of the let land gives the average rent per acre for all land under crops, grass and rough grazings in holdings of 15 acres and over; a rental figure commensurable with the average rent per acre of the unadjusted acreages of the present survey.

Figures from the 1941/43 survey adjusted in this way give a national average rent of £1.06 per acre of crops, grass and rough grazings. This compares with the national average current rent

---

[1] cf. n.3 p. 38 ante.
[2] v. Table A.5. *National Farm Survey 1941-43.*
[3] This year is used as it was the only full calendar year of the period of the survey and was central to the period.
[4] v. Table A.3. op. cit.
[5] v. Table A.8. op. cit.

(1957) of £1.9 given by the unraised sample of the present survey and the £1.94 per acre given by the raised sample. Between 1942 and 1957 the national average rent increased 79% on the verdict of the unraised sample, and 83% on the verdict of the raised sample. If the figures of the 10,413 sample of the present survey used for measuring rent movements from 1945 to 1957 are adjusted by raising the sample and the results compared with the 1942 national average rent, the increase in rent since 1942 is shown to be 81%. The percentage increases shown by making these three comparisons are not exactly the same, but the differences are very slight and the concensus of the results points to an increase in rent in the neighbourhood of 80% between 1942 and 1957. Comparison of the 1945 national average rent as calculated from the raised smaller sample of the present survey and the 1942 figures shows an increase in the national average rent of 10% between the years 1942 and 1945.

Calculation of county average rents from the 1941/43 evidence adjusted for comparison in the manner just described has also been made. The results are given in Table App. 6[1] and compared with the current county average rents of the unraised and raised samples of the present survey. Table App. 6 sets the county average rents in order of magnitude for both 1942 and 1957. On both occasions Cheshire tops the list and Merioneth takes the lowest place. Of the leading counties in 1942, six remain with the first ten in 1957, namely Cheshire, Somerset, Shropshire, Staffordshire, Flint and Cambridgeshire. Two counties, Middlesex and Lancashire, fall far from the level of the upper ten. Leicestershire and Worcestershire, counties among the leading ten in 1942, are within the first fifteen counties in 1957. The severe displacement of Middlesex and Lancashire has its counterpart in the greatly improved fortunes of Kent and Essex, counties which move up from seventeenth and fifteenth on the list in 1942 to fifth and sixth in 1957. Two other counties that improved their position and move into the leading ten are Lincolnshire and Herefordshire; but these shifts are not so impressive as the ascents of Kent and Essex, for Herefordshire occupied eleventh place in 1942 and Lincolnshire twelfth place.

In the lowest places on the lists there is little change. Nine of the counties among the lowest ten in 1957 were in the same humble position in 1942, namely Cumberland, Northumberland, Glamorgan, Montgomery, Caernarvon, Radnor, Cardigan, Brecon and Merioneth. The only movement in and out of the lowest ten places is the exchange between Carmarthen and Westmorland;

[1] v. Appendix p. 198 post.

L

Carmarthen was fortieth on the list in 1942 and falls to forty-fourth in 1957; and Westmorland elevates itself from forty-eighth to forty-second place. Although the counties occupying the lowest ten places have barely changed as a group between 1942 and 1957, there have been changes in the order of sequence among themselves. The most outstanding is the elevation of Breconshire from being second from the bottom in 1942 to forty-fifth in 1957. Cumberland's decline is also worth special mention: from forty-third in 1942 the county falls to forty-eighth in 1957.

Rent movement in some counties has been far greater than the national average of 79%. Somewhat surprisingly the percentage increase of Breconshire is remarkable, being as much as 222%; even so the average rent of the county in 1957 does not lift it out of the ranks of the lowest ten counties. Suffolk's percentage increase by 135% is the second highest and is doubtless largely responsible for the improved position of the county—from being thirty-seventh on the list in 1942 it jumps to twentieth in 1957. Hampshire's change of fortune is very similar, an increase of 134% helps to lift the county from forty-second place to thirtieth. Other counties where the percentage increase of average county rent is above 100% are Kent, Devon, Rutland, Hertford, Norfolk, Surrey, Denbigh and Westmorland. Even so Kent only among these counties of exceptionally improved fortunes moves into the leading ten counties. Middlesex shows the smallest movement in county average rent, a mere 10% increase; this is almost certainly a major contributary cause in its fall from second place in 1942 to eighteenth place in 1957. Two other counties, Radnorshire and Cardiganshire, show but small increases in county average rent. Both were so low on the list in 1942 that fortune's ill favour cannot depress them much further and together with Merioneth they occupy the lowest positions in 1957.

Similar comparisons of other features of the two surveys cannot be made because it is impossible to subtract from the 1941/43 figures the information relating to 5-14.9 acre holdings or to adjust acreages to make them comparable. Although item for item comparisons cannot be made, it is possible to make a fairly satisfactory comparison of two sets of related figures: the relationship of the average rents per acre of farming type classes to the national average rent per acre; and the similar relationship of farm size-group average rents.

These relationships in both surveys are compared in Table 36. The Table shows for each survey how the average rents of farming type classes and farm size-groups stand above or below the national average. Deviation one way or the other is expressed as a percentage of the national average.

While both sets of figures show the rents of mainly dairying holdings and those of alluvial arable and mixed farms to be the highest, displaying the greatest positive deviation, the figures of the present survey demonstrate a considerable improvement in the relative position of rents of Arable farms. Indeed, the heavy arable land farms wrest the honour of third place from the mixed with dairying farms. Rent of the dairying and mixed farms of the Grass group which in 1942 was far superior to that of light arable land was in 1957 almost on a level with it. Another noticeable contrast is displayed by the rent of mixed upland livestock holdings: in 1942, as would be expected, its deviation was the greatest negative deviation of all, 46%; but by 1957 this furthest negative deviation has become 68%.

Comparison of the relative levels of farm size average rents is not so satisfactory, as the farm size strata differ in each survey and it has not been possible to adjust acreages for rough grazings. The positive deviation of the rent of the smallest size-group is much less in 1957 than in 1942, probably because in the earlier survey the average size of holding in this group was smaller than the average size in the corresponding group of the present survey. The most noteworthy feature of this comparison is the improvement in the rent of farms in the 100-299 acres size-group. Each survey uses this size-range in its classification and hence comparison is more worthwhile. In 1942 the average rent of the 100-299 acres size-group shows a 6% negative deviation, and in 1957 there is a 10% positive deviation.

Country Landowners' Association surveys. In 1947 the Country Landowners' Association[1] in conjunction with the Ministry of Agriculture and Fisheries commenced a series of extensive enquiries into agricultural rents and the expenses of landowners. The first survey of the series covered the years 1938 and 1946; after that the periods covered were 1946/47; 1949/50 and 1950/51. The series was an attempt to pick up the thread of the enquiry into agricultural rents conducted by the Ministry of Agriculture and Fisheries with the assistance of the C.L.A. in 1938 and already referred to. These four post-war enquires are modelled on the earlier work and stand therefore upon an estates basis and not a holdings basis. Each follows the pattern of the one immediately preceding it, with here and there a refinement or elaboration.

---

[1] At that time known as the Central Landowners' Association.

For the purposes of comparison the entire series may be taken as one enquiry.

TABLE 36

DEVIATION FROM NATIONAL AVERAGE RENT PER ACRE OF THE AVERAGE RENT PER ACRE OF FARMING TYPES AND FARM SIZE-GROUPS IN 1942 AND 1957.

FARMING TYPE	PERCENTAGE DEVIATION FROM NATIONAL MEAN OF AVERAGE RENT PER ACRE			
	National Farm Survey		Present Survey	
	+	−	+	−
GRASS Mainly dairying	42		32	
Dairy and mixed	12		7	
Mixed livestock (upland)		46		68
Mixed livestock (lowland)		17		4
INTERMEDIATE				
Mixed with dairying	13		14	
General mixed		6		
Corn, sheep and dairying		28		4
ARABLE Heavy land arable		6	17	
Light land arable		16	6	
Alluvial and mixed	71		23	
FARM SIZE-GROUP				
acres				
5–24	93			
15–49			38	
25–99	19			
50–99			19	
100–299		6	10	
300 and over		24		21

At certain points, like the enquiry of 1938, the series lends itself to comparison with the present survey. It gives figures for contractual rent over acreages of crops, grass, rough grazings and woodlands. The contractual rent therefore is comparable with the present survey in terms of the land use to which the let land is put. Each enquiry relates to a pair of years; the intention being to show how rent and expenditure change between the two years. The number of estates and acreage in the sample used for each enquiry of the series were not constant[1]. On two occasions, 1946 and 1950, the periods overlap and two surveys exist for each year, the area and number of estates in each survey varying somewhat. The enquiry with the greatest number of estates is that for 1946/47 and the enquiry with the least number of estates that for 1950/51; the area of let agricultural land, rough grazings and woodland covered in 1946/47 is 1.8m. acres, and in 1950/51 is 1.3m. acres.

Every one of these enquiries was extensive in area. For the 1938/46 survey, the area of crops, grass and rough grazings (including woodland) in the 1946 sample amounted to 10.8% of the total land under crops, grass and rough grazings, let in holdings of 5 acres and over in 1950. The corresponding percentages of the other enquiries are: 1947 11.8%; 1949 9.4%; 1950 9.4%; and 1951 8.6%.

In size of sample, therefore, every one of these enquiries is not dissimilar to the present survey. There is, however, in the C.L.A. surveys no attempt to select a sample at random as representative of the national distribution of let holdings or estates. It is difficult to compare the holdings structure of the 1938/46 sample with that of the present survey as no information is given, not even the indirect evidence provided by the distribution of holdings in rent per acre groups. Reports of the later enquiries, for 1946/47 to 1950/51, give the distribution of holdings in size-groups. This makes comparison possible. For all the enquiries, the size and number of estates are given and in this respect comparison is possible.

Of the total number of holdings of the 1946/47 enquiry 64% are between 5 and 49.9 acres and the corresponding percentages of the enquiries of 1949/50 and 1950/51 are but slightly less than this. Compared with the sample of the present survey, these samples have a very high percentage of tiny holdings. The present survey does not cover holdings of less than 15 acres, and the number of holdings from 15-49 acres in the 12,661 holdings of the sample is only 24.3% of the total number. This marked difference is borne out in the average size of holding: this varies from 92 acres in 1946/

[1] Acreages of agricultural land and rough grazings and the number of estates in each enquiry are as follows:—

    1938: 1,576,144 acres (309).
    1946: 1,642,898 „ (309).
    1946: 1,818,831 „ 2nd Survey—(253).
    1947: 1,808,268 „ (353).
    1949: 1,432,469 „ (276).
    1950: 1,436,112 „ (276).
    1950: 1,324,066 „ 2nd Survey—(253).
    1951: 1,314,237 „ (253).

47 to 113 acres in 1950/51; in none of the C.L.A. enquiries does the average size of holding approach the 155 acres of the average size of holding in the present survey.

Despite this wide divergence of conformation between the samples, a not altogether invalid comparison can be made by introducing the evidence of the Ministry of Agriculture's survey of 1938 and the results of the first post-war C.L.A. survey covering the years 1938 and 1946. The report of the later survey laments the difficulty of reconciling the figure for average rent per acre in 1937, as given by the earlier survey, with the average rent per acre for 1938 produced by the later survey: the earlier survey gives an average rent per acre of £1.05 in 1937[1], and the later survey an average rent per acre of £1.21 in 1938. Between these two figures is a margin of 15%; too great to be the consequence of a change in average rent between the years 1937 and 1938. On the other hand, a figure for average rent in 1946 of £1.3 per acre given by the 1938/46 survey is identical with the average rent per acre for 1946 as given by the 1946/47 survey. It is reasonable to suppose, therefore, that the sample of estates and holdings was approximately similar on both occasions. The distribution of holdings in the 1946/47 sample is known, and indeed gives the 64% of small holdings quoted above and the average size of holding as 92 acres. Hence it can be supposed that the sample for 1938 in the 1938/46 survey had a similar high percentage of very small holdings and an average size of holding in the region of 90-100 acres. Now the average size of holding of the 1938 enquiry is given as 155 acres. Clearly the sample on that occasion, as the report admits, did not have a high proportion of tiny holdings. The absence of high numbers of very small holdings in the 1938 sample and their inclusion in the 1938/46 enquiry undoubtedly accounts for the margin of 15% between the average rent of each enquiry.

This proposition is corroborated and light thrown upon the relationship between the results of the present survey and those of the C.L.A. series by calculating the margin between the figure given by the present survey for the average rent per acre in 1945 and the corresponding figure in 1946 given by the C.L.A.'s 1938/46 and 1946/47 enquiries. The average size of holding of the present survey for the year 1945 is 155 acres, exactly similar to that of the 1938 enquiry with its £1.05 per acre average rent. Average rent in 1945 as given by the present survey is £1.13 per acre, and that for 1946 given by the two C.L.A. surveys is £1.3. The margin between the two is exactly 15%.

[1] v. p. 157 ante.

These equal margins of 15% are hardly fortuitous. They point, it is suggested, to a similarity in the distribution of holdings in the samples used for the 1938 enquiry and the present enquiry, and to a corresponding difference in the distribution of holdings in these samples and those of the C.L.A. series. They also show the 1938 survey and the present one running together, parallel with the C.L.A. series. Each corroborates and supports the other. And the £1.05 average rent for 1937 can with fair confidence be compared with the average rents for the years referred to in the present survey.

The average size of estate in the C.L.A. series varies very slightly from survey to survey, and in general is round about 6,000 acres. Compared with the average size of estate of the present survey amounting to 2,550 acres, an average size of 6,000 acres is high. The difference in average size is no doubt partly the consequence of a difference in the definitions of "estate" as used for the present survey and for the C.L.A. series. In respect of Crown Lands only do the C.L.A. surveys adopt a managerial criterion and follow to some extent the principle of the present survey. Otherwise the word "estate" is used of "the whole of the agricultural property in the ownership of a person, family, body or institution"[1].

Two important trends in the relationship of farm rents and estate size demonstrated by the results of the present survey are also traceable through the evidence of the C.L.A. series.

One of these trends is the correlation of farm rent per acre and estate size. Dr. Dawe commenting on the evidence of the first of the "paired years" surveys, 1946/47, writes "in general as the size of the estate increases the rent per acre decreases". Comparison of average rent per acre by estates arranged in estate size-groups is made for 1946, 1947, 1950 and 1951 in Table 37 from the results of the C.L.A. surveys. The published information has been recast for the purpose and presented in estate size-groups corresponding to the classification used in the present survey. The correlation between estate size and farm rent per acre is conspicuous in the figures for each year, but is not so clearly demonstrated as in Table 28 of the present survey.

The other trend is rent movement related to estate size. Percentage increases gained by the rents of one year, the year of advance, over the rents of an earlier year, the base year, are given in Table 37 for the four pairs of years of the C.L.A. series, with 1946, 1947, 1950 and 1951 as years of advance. The information

---

[1] cf. *The Rent of Agricultural Land in England and Wales* 1870-1946. Central Landowners' Association, 1950. p. 9.

TABLE 37

AVERAGE RENT PER ACRE BY ESTATE SIZE FROM COUNTRY LANDOWNERS' ASSOCIATION SURVEYS 1946-1951.

ESTATE SIZE	1946		1947		1950		1951	
	Rent per acre	Increase over 1938	Rent per acre	Increase over 1946	Rent per acre	Increase over 1949	Rent per acre	Increase over 1950
acres	£	%	£	%	£	%	£	%
0-999	1.55	26.0	1.56	0.6	1.69	4.3	1.71	2.4
1000-1999	1.44	7.5	1.52	2.0	1.79	5.3	1.77	4.7
2000-3999	1.43	6.7	1.53	3.4	1.61	3.2	1.75	4.8
4000-5999	1.39	8.6	1.48	2.8	1.63	3.8	1.82	7.7
6000-9999	1.42	8.4	1.41	3.7	1.54	2.7	1.50	2.7
10,000 and over	1.21	8.0	1.20	2.6	1.46	8.1	1.51	9.4

is arranged in estate size-groups after the present classification scheme. Between 1938 and 1946, the smaller estates (0-999 acres) advanced their rents far more successfully than the larger estates, especially those of the mid-range, 1,000-3,999 acres; achievement of the largest estates takes second place. After 1946 the rate of rent increase on the smaller estates slackens abruptly. By 1951 the smallest estates have the poorest showing and greatest advances are with the rents of the middle sized estates. This change in direction is paralleled by the course of rent movements since 1945 recorded by the present survey[1], and supports its evidence.

Farm Rents in Scotland, 1951/56.

For a period running back from 1951 into the war years official information on farm rents in Scotland was obtained from yearly returns of cropping and other items rendered by the tenant farmers. Although these official statistics are the best available for the earlier years they cannot be read as reliable guides to the national levels of farm rent without making allowances for gaps and inconsistencies by searching analysis and systematic collation of the evidence. This has not yet been done and, on the advice of the Department of Agriculture for Scotland, the figures are not used for comparison here with those of the present survey of English farm rents.

Since 1951 statistics of the total rent of whole-time farms in Scotland have been gathered by the Department of Agriculture

[1] cf. Table 30, p. 141 ante.

through a different procedure. Each year a random sample of farms is selected representative of the distribution of farming types throughout Scotland. From these farms information on production, farm expenditure and rent is obtained by officials of the Department who visit each selected holding. The sample each year has been approximately 7% of the national total of wholly and partly tenanted farms, capable of providing full-time occupation for the tenant farmer. The samples are exclusive of very small holdings and information on these is separately returned. The term rent in this instance is used inclusively of rent actually payable—a near approximation to the contractual rent of the present survey—and the rental value of owner-occupied land.

Figures from these yearly enquiries have been prepared by the Department of Agriculture for comparison with those in the present survey. Only very limited comparison is possible. Actual rent payable by tenants can be extracted from the aggregate of actual rents and rental values of owner-occupied holdings. But when this is done the result is the total rent figure for Scotland's whole-time farms. The information does not give the rent per acre figure. Year by year, comparison therefore, shows the yearly change in the sum of the rent bill, but only crudely the change in the unit value of rent, as the total rent figures are not adjusted for shrinkage or expansion of rented acreage. On the evidence of these gross figures Scotland's farm rent advanced 12.6% between 1951 and 1956, whereas farm rent in England and Wales, on the evidence of the present survey increased 24.5% in the corresponding period. The ratio of owner-occupied holdings to tenant holdings has increased lately[1] and it is reasonable to suppose that the total rent bill in Scotland, year by year, would have been higher but for the slowly diminishing total acreage of let land. Even so, the figures as they stand are substantial evidence of the comparative sluggishness of the movement of farm rent in Scotland since 1951.

An additional cause of the comparatively slow increase in total rent is the relatively low percentage of specific rent changes in Scotland. Farms in Scotland on average have experienced a rent change once every 12 years since 1951, compared with the three to four years change in England[2]. The amount by which rents have specifically increased in Scotland, however, is not behind the English achievement. Between 1951 and 1956 the average specific rent increase in Scotland has been 31.8%, and the corresponding increase of rent in England and Wales, estimated from the evidence of the present survey, has been 20.8%.

[1] v. *Agricultural Statistics*, Department of Agriculture for Scotland.
[2] v.p. 127 ante.

CHAPTER THIRTEEN

FARM RENT AND AGRICULTURAL INCOME

Movements in farm rent since the late 1930's shown by the evidence of these and earlier surveys, reflect changes in the landowner's revenue from his land. Landowners can be said to share the total income of agriculture with the farmers who occupy and operate the farms and with the agricultural workers who comprise the labour force. Although the purpose of this report is strictly objective and the text is confined to factual evidence, the comparisons it makes would be incomplete if its figures of rent movement were not compared with the movement in incomes of farmers and agricultural workers. Farm rent, moreover, is gross revenue to a landowner and not income. Out of this revenue he has to pay, among other things, for the repair and renewal of buildings and other items of fixed equipment. The balance is his income and is dependent upon the cost of building works. This chapter therefore compares in a simple straightforward manner the movement of rent and the movements of farming income, of the earnings of agricultural workers and of building costs and shows how the shares in the total agricultural income enjoyed by the landowner, the farmer and the agricultural worker have changed proportionately.

Changes in rent, farm income, earnings and costs are measured from either a 1937/38 or a 1939 base. In these immediately prewar years the shares of the landowner, the farmer and the agricultural worker in the total agricultural income stood in a certain relationship to each other; likewise farm rent and building costs. The corresponding relationships in later years and at the present time depend upon the degrees of change in each item and upon the relationship in the basic year or years. These relationships may be judged as unjust or unacceptable. It is not the purpose of this report to make judgements of that kind. Assumptions of the merit or unworthiness of the relationships shown by the figures are not made, neither are they implied. Moreover, no attempt is made to discuss the economic implications of the relationships indicated by the figures. The figures in the Tables and in the comments that accompany them are simply factual presentations.

Rent movement and building costs.

The preceding comparisons of theresults of the present survey

and information from earlier surveys make it possible to compile
an index of rent movements from the late 1930's to 1957. Rental
revenue of the agricultural industry should be sufficient to provide
for the maintenance, replacement and improvement of agricultural
fixed equipment. If it in fact did so, and there were a state of
equilibrium in which costs of maintenance, replacement and capital
improvements were stationary, rents could remain unchanged
without detriment to the interests of landowner or tenant. The
agricultural economy is far from being stationary either in costs or
capital needs, and if equilibrium is yet to be obtained change in the
demands upon rental revenue should be answered by counter-
balancing change in rental revenuee itself. No attempt is made
here to measure changes in rental revenue against changing
demand for capital improvements, but simply to show how far
rental revenue has been able to keep up with the inflation of
maintenance and replacement costs.

A comparison of this kind would have been greatly facilitated
by evidence of movements in estate maintenance and replacement
costs. For reasons previously given[1] the present survey could not
include such evidence. The best therefore than can be done is to
compare the index of rental movements compiled from this and
earlier surveys with an index of building costs[2]. Table 38 gives an
index of building costs movements since the late 1930's and
compares it with the index of movements in farm rent.

TABLE 38

MOVEMENT OF FARM RENT AND BUILDING COSTS 1939–1957.

YEAR	INDICES OF CHANGE			
	1939 = 100		1945 = 100	
	Farm(i) rent	Building costs	Farm(i) rent	Building costs
1945	111	190	100	100
1957	183	365	164	192

(i) Calculation from smaller sample, raised.

Farm rent increased only 11% between 1939 and 1945, while
building costs in the same period spiralled to 90% above their
earlier level. The average yearly rate of increase in building costs
was 12% compared with a yearly farm rent increase of 1%. War-

[1] v.p. 31 ante.
[2] The building cost index is an estimate based on total costs, including materials,
wages and overheads, of new building work.

172 FARM RENTS

time rent almost stagnated, while building costs galloped ahead.
Between 1945 and 1957, farm rents increased 64% and building
costs 92%. The average yearly rate of increase in building costs
slowed down in this period to 8%, and the yearly rate of increase
in farm rents accelerated to 5%. Over the entire period 1939-1957,
farm rents lag far behind building costs; for a £1 rise in farm
rent, building costs increase nearly £3. In the latter years, farm
rents began to improve upon their earlier performance and in the
last year of all, 1956-57, they increased 7% against an increase in
building costs of no more than 3%, less than half what farm rent
achieved. Seen at large, the twenty years' picture shows farm rents
moving forward at a much slower pace than the more than three-
fold advance of building costs.

Farm rent movement and farming net income.

The failure of farm rent to march with building costs is by no
means the consequence of laggardly farming incomes. On the
contrary, farming incomes continually increase both during and
after the 1939-45 war years, as shown by the percentage changes in
incomes[1] in Table 39. Included also in this Table is an index of
changes in rent and interest. The latter index combines interest
on short term loans and farm rent calculated from the official
estimates of farm rent of holdings of all types previously mentioned[2]. Both indices are global for the United Kingdom and
therefore strictly comparable. The present survey provides evidence
from a wider sample than the official estimates of rent movements,

TABLE 39

FARMING NET INCOME, AGGREGATE RENT AND INTEREST
PAYMENTS AND FARM RENTS.

YEAR	PERCENTAGE CHANGE 1937–38 base		
	Farming net income %	Rent and interest %	Farm rents (surveys) %
1937–38 to 1945–46	267	12	11
1945–46 to 1956–57	194	80	72
1937–38 to 1956–57	461	92	83

[1] The indices of farming net income and rent and interest in this Table are based
on the items in the estimates of aggregate agricultural income and expenditure for the United Kingdom, made by the Agricultural Departments
for the *Annual Review and Determination of Guarantees.*

[2] v.p. 26 ante.

but only for England and Wales, and for holdings of 15 acres and over. The index of rent used in Table 38 is therefore not strictly comparable with the indices of farming incomes and rent and interest used in Table 39, but it has been included in Table 39 as substantial evidence of a slightly different order, against which movements in farming income can be compared with movements in farm rent.

Farming net income is a measure of the total profit accruing to the farmer after deduction of all costs of production, including depreciation of certain capital assets, and in this sense, represents the farmer's reward for his own and his wife's manual and managerial skills and the use of his "occupier's investment". Farming net income rose between 1937/38 and 1945/46 nearly 300%. Farm rent and interest, on the evidence of the "rent and interest" index, rose 12% only; and on the evidence of the present survey, rent rose 11% only. It must be remembered however that these rent figures do not represent net income to the landowner, in the same way as the farming income figure represents net income to the farmer. No maintenance costs or allowances for depreciation of fixed equipment have been set against rent; maintenance and replacement costs have to be met before the landowner's net income can be known. On the other hand interest on his occupier's investment has to be met by the farmer from farming net income, and it should be noted that over the period 1948/1957 a gross national expenditure of £236m.[1] on buildings and similar works was matched, from 1947/48-1956/57, by a net increment in occupier's capital of £665m.[2] These figures do not distinguish between landlord's and owner-occupier's expenditure on buildings and similar works, but they are a sufficient indication that investment by tenants in occupier's capital was probably nearly three times as great as the investment by landlords in new buildings and improvements.

From 1945/46 to 1956/57, although the movement in farming net income did not match the tremendous leap of the immediately previous period, the farmer's income rose a further 194% above its 1937/38 level. Rent and interest at the same time rose a further 80% over 1937/38, and rent on the evidence of the survey rose by a corresponding 72%. Nevertheless it is important to observe that the rate of increase in rent and interest during this period is faster than the rate of increase in farming net incomes, when 1945/46 instead of 1937/38 is taken as the base year. A major reason for this is the low level from which the rent, and the rent and interest

[1] National Income and Expenditure, 1958, H.M.S.O.
[2] Hansard H. of C., Vol. 584, 21st March, 1958.

figures start to increase in 1945, after remaining almost static during the war years, and the high level in 1945/46 of farming net income. Despite their relatively favourable rate of increase over the 1945/46 level, farm rents throughout the entire twenty years' period only manage to increase about 83%, on the showing of the surveys, and 92% according to the rent and interest index. Both of these percentages are relatively slight compared with the nearly five-fold growth of farming net incomes.

Clearly the slow movement in farm rents cannot be laid to the account of low profitability. It is a matter of shares in what may be called the social contribution. This phrase has been coined to express the surplus earned by agriculture over and above certain of its costs of production and available to recompense the landowner, the farmer and the agricultural worker for their efforts and capital investment. Rent is the contribution to the landowner before deduction of repairs and management expenditure and depreciation; and is not strictly comparable with the other two shares in the social contribution. The true share of the landowner is therefore overstated in Table 40. Were figures available of the percentages of rent expended on repairs and management and making good depreciation, the landowners' share of the social contribution would be seen to be much lower. The social contribution rose progressively over the war years and after, but its distribution between rent and interest, wages and farming net income changed. The share of the social contribution in agriculture which was rent and interest fell, and made way for an equivalent improvement in those shares which were farming net income and wages.

Table 40 gives some indication of how the shares have altered by comparing the proportions of the social contribution of agriculture which were rent and interest, wages, and farming net income in 1937/38 and 1956/57[1].

In 1937/38, 26% of the social contribution went to rent and interest; 34% to farming net income; and 40% to wages. Over the next twenty years, the social contribution increased 320%; £165 millions available for distribution in 1937/38 approximates to £700 millions in 1956/57. Had the rent and interest share remained unchanged, the item "rent and interest" in 1956/57 would have amounted to £180 millions, which is 26% of the total £700 millions;

---

[1] This table is based on the Departmental estimates of aggregate farming net income and expenditure used in Table 39 (see note 1 p. 172). Farming gross profits are obtained by subtracting from total farm revenue costs of feeding stuffs, fertilizers, seeds, fuel oil, other machinery costs, imported livestock and "other expenses" and depreciation of vehicles and machinery.

TABLE 40
DIVISION OF SOCIAL CONTRIBUTION BETWEEN RENT
AND INTEREST, LABOUR COSTS AND FARMING NET INCOME
FOR 1937–38 AND 1956–57.

FACTOR INCOME	PERCENTAGE OF SOCIAL CONTRIBUTION	
	1937–38	1956–57
	%	%
Rent and interest	26.1	11.9
Labour costs	40.0	42.8
Farming net income	33.9	45.3
Social contribution	100.0	100.0

and rent and interest would have increased 318.6% between 1937 and 1957. Even such an increase as this would have been below the increase in building costs. In fact, the share of rent and interest in the social contribution fell to 12%, and consequently the increase in rent and interest has been only 92% between 1937/38 and 1956/57. The share of the farming net income in contrast rose from 34% to 45%. Wages over the same period improved their share only slightly, rising from 40% to 43% of the total, making an increase of 349% in labour costs between 1939 and 1957.

Rent movement and workers' earnings.

The comparisons so far made do not show movements in the earnings of the agricultural worker himself. Comparisons of current and 1937/38 agricultural wage rates are difficult to make as there is a lack of comprehensive statistics for the years before 1947. Some notion of what has happened to the earnings of the individual agricultural worker can be obtained by looking at the average minimum wage rates of 1937 and the statutory minimum wage rate of 1957. The average in 1937 was 33/7½d. per week. By 1957 it had risen to 150/- per week, an increase of 346%. Labour has been scarce in many parts during and after the war years and workers have usually earned more than the minimum wage, and incentive money and overtime pay have added to their earnings. A calculation of agricultural earnings for the year ending September 1937[1] puts total average weekly earnings, including the payments for piecework, overtime, bonuses and so on, at nearly 37/- in 1937, or 10% above the average minimum wage. In 1957, official statistics

[1] cf. *Ministry of Labour Gazette.* The figures for 1937 should not be taken as completely authentic. The sample on which they are based mainly consisted of farmers suspected of paying less than minimum wages, and the average earnings figure provided is therefore probably on the low side.

show the average weekly earnings of all agricultural workers to be 174/8d., an increase of about 372% upon the 1937 earnings and 16% above the minimum wage. This percentage increase over 1937 is higher than the minimum wage rates suggest; but whichever is taken, the figures point to an impressive rise in the earnings of the individual worker. Admittedly these gains are behind the 461% rise in farming net incomes, but they are far above the 83% increase in farm rent.

CHAPTER FOURTEEN

GENERAL OBSERVATIONS

Certain general observations need to be made in conclusion. Further comment is necessary on the possibility of bias in the figures of the foregoing Tables and text and on the extent to which adjustments might be made to allow for it. Something should be said also about the probable outcome of the Agriculture Act, 1958 on the future of farm rents, and on the possibility of continuing the collection of information on farm rents.

Bias and adjustment of the figures given.

The presence of bias in the figures of the tables and text of the foregoing chapters has been exposed wherever possible by comparing the pattern of average rents of all holdings arranged in a selected manner—e.g. by farming types—with the pattern of average rents of holdings with a particular selected feature—e.g. farm size—arranged in a similar manner. For example, the pattern of the average rents of the farming types provide a standard against which are compared the patterns of the average rents of holdings of uniform size or standard of equipment, farming type by farming type. In general it has not been possible to make adjustments for abnormalities disclosed by such analysis, as it is not possible to determine the degree of bias. Where, for example, the average rent of dairy farms without a mains water supply is abnormally low it is not possible to say whether the average rent of all dairy farms in the sample is unduly depressed because of an abnormally high percentage of dairy farms without a mains water supply. A normal or national percentage of dairy farms without a mains water supply would have to be known before the degree of bias could be determined. For similar reasons, the average rent of holdings in rent determination classes and other categories cannot be adjusted to allow for what might be abnormal representation of holdings of a particular farming type or size or other character form.

It is possible, however, to make certain adjustments to the rent figures to allow for:

(*a*) a difference between the representation of estate size in the

M

sample and the representation of estate size in the holdings of the
preliminary survey; and

(b) a possible difference between the distribution of holdings
by farming type in the sample and the corresponding distribution
in the national picture.

These adjustments are explained and attempted in the next
three sections of this chapter.

Size of estates and national average rent. The present survey adds
a third and perhaps the most substantial contribution to the stock
of evidence demonstrating the inverse ratio between rent per acre
and estate size. Neither the present findings nor the earlier evidence
disclose the causes behind this fact. That the phenomenon is of
crucial importance to estate finance and of no little consequence to
the national farm budget, can hardly be denied. It demands close
analytical study to comprehend it. But whatever explanation
lies behind it, the very fact of its existence shows how closely tied
are the two separate worlds of agriculture and landownership.
And what is more, it adds to the mounting evidence of the need for
statistical information about the distribution of estates in this
country.

If such statistical information had been available when the present
survey was planned, the survey would almost certainly have been
mounted on an estates basis and not upon a holdings basis and
would have embraced estate expenditure as well as estate rental
revenue. And there would have been no cause to impose a ten-
holdings maximum when selecting the sample. This as explained
later[1] was the principle devised to limit the burden the return of
questionnaires would impose on estates of many holdings. A survey
on an estates basis would have sought particulars of total rent rolls
and expenditure bills, and the burden of providing the information
would have been, for a well managed large estate, no heavier than
for a small estate.

The ten-holdings per estate maximum undoubtedly spared
owners of large estates a great deal of work and probably has to its
credit the participation in the survey of a number of landowners
who would otherwise have been unable to co-operate. Certainly
without it the representation of estates would have been narrower:
prescribing a quota of holdings for one estate limited the contribution demanded from that estate and in the selection process
turned attention upon other estates instead of proceeding to fill
up the sample with holdings from the one estate.

The maximum principle, however, has resulted in the under-

[1] v.p. 188 post.

representation of small holdings[1]. Somewhat paradoxically it has
also meant the over-representation of small estates and the under-
representation of large estates. How serious this may be is illustrated
by Table 41 which shows for each estate size-group the total
overall and total rented acreage of the estates from which holdings
have been selected and compares these acreages with the total
acreage of the selected holdings themselves. The large estates
provide the highest percentages of the total estate acreages, but
almost the reverse obtains with the total acreage of the holdings
in the sample.

On this evidence the larger estates are inadequately represented
in the calculation of the national average rent per acre. Adjustment
can be made by weighting the evidence of the sample by the proportions of the total rented estate acreage in each estate size-group.
When this is done the current national average rent per acre falls
from £1.9 to £1.78. This difference illustrates how estate representation can be a material factor influencing farm rent averages.
It is not proposed to substitute the figure of £1.78 per acre for
the previously calculated current national average, as there is no
means of telling how representative of the pattern of estates
throughout the country are the estates of the present sample.
Admittedly the sum of the rented acreages of these estates covers
27.7% of the total area of rented holdings, but the pattern of estates
comprising the reciprocal 72.3% may be far different from the
pattern of estates of the selected sample. A high percentage of
the land might be held in small estates. If this were so, the sample,

TABLE 41
PERCENTAGE DISTRIBUTION IN ESTATE SIZE-GROUPS OF
OVERALL ESTATE ACREAGE, RENTED ESTATE ACREAGE AND
ESTATE ACREAGE USED IN SAMPLE.

1957

ESTATE SIZE	PERCENTAGE OF TOTAL		
	overall estate acreage	rented estate acreage	estate acreage used in sample
acres	%	%	%
0–999	6.9	10.1	16.8
1000–1999	10.4	14.0	21.6
2000–3999	18.0	21.4	26.3
4000–5999	12.9	14.6	12.1
6000–9999	14.7	14.6	10.0
10,000 and over	37.1	25.3	13.2
Total acreages	6,229,092	4,766,039	1,973,934

[1] v.p. 188 post.

as it is at present, would more perfectly represent the estates
universe than it appears to do.

Perhaps it is pertinent to suggest, as the sample appears to overweight the smaller estates and hence to throw up too high a current
national average rent, that the national average of £1.90 calculated
from the sample, unraised for farm size representation, should
be the accepted figure rather than the slightly higher £1.94 per
acre of the raised sample.

Farming type and national average rent per acre. No national
statistics have been compiled of the acreage or number of rented
holdings in the farming type classes used in this and the National
Farm Survey 1941/43; the latter gives farming type acreages
inclusive of let and owner-occupied holdings. It is not possible
to tell, therefore, how far the representation, by acreage and
holdings, of farming types in the sample of the present survey
corresponds to the pattern of acreage and holdings in farming
types throughout the country. There would be no cause to mention
this had not the findings of the present survey, like those of the
National Farm Survey 1941/43, demonstrated a close association
between certain farming types and rent per acre.

Fortunately, both the present survey and the National Farm
Survey 1941/43 show also a fairly constant association of farming
type and farm size: mainly dairying farms, for example, are on
average smaller holdings than most others; and corn, sheep and
dairying farms tend to be large. If throughout the country
mainly dairying farms out-number other farming types among all
smaller holdings, they probably occur in the same proportion among
the rented smaller holdings of the country and among the holdings
in the smaller farm size-groups of the sample of the present survey.
To the extent that this is true they will make their peculiar contribution of high rent per acre to the sum of the total rent of the
holdings of the smaller farm size-groups in proportion to their
numbers. Hence, when the sample is raised to conform with the
national distribution pattern of rented holdings by farm size, the
process will at the same time raise the rent contribution from
mainly dairying holdings in proportion as they occur in the size-
groups of the sample and in conformity with what can reasonably
be supposed to be the proportionate contribution of mainly dairying
farm rents to the total national rent. To the degree to which farming
type is associated with farm size, the same consequences will follow
for other farming types when the sample is raised to conform
to the distribution of rented holdings by farm size.

Modification of farming type average rent. By virtue of the relationship between farming type and farm size it is possible to adjust the figures for the average rent per acre of farming types in accordance with tolerable estimates of the total acreage of let holdings in the country in each farming type. The estimates take from the evidence of the sample the percentage of the acreage in each farm size-group that is under a specific farming type (e.g. 29.8% of the acreage of all holdings 15-49 acres is mainly dairying farms) and multiply this percentage by the acreage of let land in this size-group, as given by the Ministry of Agriculture's 1950 census for the country at large. The product gives an estimate of the acreage of let land under the farming type and in holdings 15-49 acres. A figure of total rent for this acreage is then computed by multiplying the acreage by the average rent per acre of holdings of that size and farming type. This process is repeated for each farm size-group and the result summed to give the total acreage of let land in the country under each farming type and the corresponding total rent. From these two figures there is calculated for each farming type the rent per acre figure, which is a modification of the average rents for farming types given in Table App. 1[1].

Average rents per acre modified in this way do not differ much from the average farming type rents of Table App. 1. The differences are set out in Table 42 which compares the modified and the original rents.

Significance for farm rents of the Agriculture Act, 1958.

Premium element in open tender rents. For the purpose of classifying rent determination procedures "open market" rents were distinguished from "open tender" rents. The former are rents negotiated between a landlord who has vacant possession of a holding to offer and prospective tenants who are strangers alike to the landlord and his established tenants. The latter are rents determined by soliciting tenders from prospective tenants. The distinction was drawn, and "open market" defined in the manner described and adopted as a standard against which to measure rents determined by other procedures, because it was hoped in this way to avoid the criticism of some who perceive what they call a "premium payment" in freely negotiated, relatively high farm rents, especially if these rents are the outcome of open tendering.

The distinction made must not be taken as evidence of acquiescence of the premium theory. On the contrary, the theory does not commend itself to the logic of simple economic factors. The word

[1] v. Appendix p. 194 post.

TABLE 42
MODIFICATION OF AVERAGE CURRENT RENT PER ACRE FOR EACH FARMING TYPE BY RAISING SAMPLE TO NATIONAL AVERAGE OF FARM SIZE-GROUPS.

FARMING TYPE	ORIGINAL RENT PER ACRE	MODIFIED RENT PER ACRE	PERCENTAGE MODIFICATION
	£	£	%
GRASS			
Mainly dairying	2.50	2.57	+2.8
Dairy and mixed	2.03	2.08	+2.5
Mixed livestock (upland)	.61	.67	+9.8
Mixed livestock (lowland)	1.82	1.87	+2.7
INTERMEDIATE			
Mixed with dairying	2.16	2.21	+2.3
General mixed	1.90	1.93	+1.6
Corn, sheep and dairying	1.82	1.85	+1.6
ARABLE			
Heavy land	2.23	2.22	—0.4
Light land	2.01	2.03	+1.0
Alluvial and mixed	2.33	2.36	+1.3
SPECIALISTS			
Market gardens	3.46	3.59	+3.7
Mainly poultry	2.15	3.49	+62.3
Mainly pigs	2.61	2.71	+3.8
Other types	1.73	1.90	+9.8

"premium" is frequently used in the technical parlance of the surveying profession. Usually in landlord and tenant negotiations it denotes a capital payment made by a tenant to a landlord in consideration of the landlord's reducing the rent of the demised premises, and is calculated with reference to the amount of the reduction as the yearly equivalent of the capital payment. But for the premium the rent would be much higher. It is difficult to see how far farm rent, however high it may be, can be in part a premium in this sense, as it is a periodic revenue payment to the landlord and not a capital payment.

The premium payment case is usually supported by the argument that the tenant bids beyond what he knows to be the true market rent of the farm in order to secure possession of it. He bids high relying all the while on his right to compel the landlord to refer the question of rent to arbitration within three years of the beginning of the tenancy, which he hopes to enter upon, and confident of the ability of the arbitrator to spot the excess in the rent and to reduce it accordingly. On this hypothesis, the arbitrator should reduce the rent to the true open market rent and rid it of the noxious premium. But on the showing of the present survey, arbitrators, in the majority of cases, would be inclined to reduce the rent well below the open market value. On average, open market rent is 14% below open tender rent and mediatorial rent 24% below open tender rent. An open tender rent for three years reduced to a mediatorial rent thereafter for the next four years, would almost be equivalent to an open market rent for seven years. It could be maintained, therefore, that a tenant who offers a high open tender rent with his eye on the possibility of an early arbitration revision is doing no more than offering an open market rent for seven years—a normal basic period for a lease of an agricultural holding.

Apparently very little evidence exists to support the presumptions of the premium payment theory. The theory confuses two markets, an imaginary one and a real one: an imaginary free market for let farms and the market as it actually exists, with the supply of let farms shortened as a consequence of tenurial restriction. Both markets would give a market rent, but the market rent of the latter with its shortened supply would be higher than the market rent of the former. The latter, nonetheless, is a true market rent and the tenant who offers it should not be accused of offering a premium to gain possession. A landlord who offers a holding to let by tender is surely not seeking premium payments, but inviting the unhampered demand forces, competing in a restricted market, to express their price option.

There is more weight in the view which sees open tender quotations as expressions of true market worth, than there is in the premium theory. And it would not be unreasonable to combine the figures of "open market" rent and "open tender" rent given by the present survey into a single "market rent". If this were done the overall average of the survey would, on average, put "market rent" at 17% above mediatorial rent; and this margin would vary between 33.3% for general mixed arable farms, and figures which put mediatorial rent 67.7% above "market rent" for upland mixed livestock holdings.

Consequences of "market rent" enactment.

Parliament has recently modified the enactment requiring arbitrators to "determine what rent should be properly payable"[1] by providing that this phrase shall mean "the rent at which the holding might reasonably be expected to be let in the open market by a willing landlord to a willing tenant"[2]. The re-phrasing clarifies the intentions of Parliament, removes all ambiguity and states unequivocally that arbitrators must allow the dictates of the market and not some theoretical notion of a rent properly payable

[1] v. *Agricultural Holdings Act, 1948.* Section 8.
[2] *Agriculture Act, 1958.* Section 2.

to influence their minds when awarding farm rents.

What this can mean for the future movement of farm rents is implicit in the findings of the present survey. The evidence of Tables 22 and 24 and the accompanying Diagrams points to mediatorial rents being awarded in solemn disregard of market opinion. Where the market is weak, as with upland mixed livestock holdings, the rents awarded are far above the market level; where the market is strong, as with general mixed arable holdings and others, the awarded rent is well below the open market level.

Evidence of rent movement since 1956 shows a jump of 6.9% in the national average by 1957, and a further jump of 3.2% by 1958. More than one cause is responsible for these movements. The high percentage of general rent reviews among the causes of rent change suggests that the main cause is a belated stirring among farm rents to move them in the direction of most other costs and prices of the post-war inflationary period. Rent movement consequent upon the recent enactment of the "open market" provision for farm rent arbitrations will start at another spring. There will probably be response to upward moving prices and costs by the revision of total farm rents in the next few years, but surely an additional and dominant feature will be the raising of sitting tenant rents to their open market equivalent. Some notion of what this rise might be can be gained from the margin between sitting tenant rents of all kinds (including mediatorial rents) and the "market rent" when this is conceived as the average of the open market rent as used in this survey and the open tender rent.

Market rent thus conceived is 14.6% in advance of the average for all sitting tenant rents. This may be taken as roughly indicative of the measure of increment in average farm rent which the new enactment will stimulate. But it must be remembered that not all holdings are at present occupied by tenants paying a sitting tenant rent. If the proportions of these other holdings in the sample are taken account of and due weight given to the acreage throughout the country in farm size-groups among which margins between "market rent" and sitting tenant rent differ, the estimated advance in the national average rent consequent upon the new enactment hardly alters, being slightly higher at 15%.

Rent revisions of a general kind following an arbitrator's award can only take place triennially. Not all landlords will have to wait three years from the passing of the Agriculture Act, 1958, before they can proceed to revise rents in accordance with its provisions. Others will not take advantage of the occasions provided for them. On the evidence of the frequency of change given in Table 26 it is reasonable to speculate that the increase of 15% just mentioned will take four years to reach its full stature.

Future surveys.

Although in size of sample the present survey matches the National Farm Survey 1941/43, it cannot claim to be so perfectly representative of the holdings of the country at large. The sample used in 1941/43 was selected from returns over the entire field of rented holdings. Some will say this was achieved because enquiry was made of the tenants and occupiers of the holdings and on this argument they advocate a yearly return of farm rent along with the statistical data given yearly as statutory returns from the farms of this country. In fact it was not the occupiers of the holdings who returned rental information in 1941/43; each occupier was visited by an officer of a war-time War Agricultural Executive Committee who completed a comprehensive questionnaire on the spot.

In theory the notion of occupiers and tenants making return of rental information is sound, but in practice it would be risky and the results uncertain. Rent can mean so many different things: the rent reserved by written tenancy agreement, the actual rent payable, with or without modification of the rent terms of the agreement; rent due plus arrears of rent; rent and interest on improvements; rent inclusive or exclusive of usual outgoings; and combinations of these conceptions. A return left to the mercy of a tenant or occupier of the farm would need to carry a ponderous and complicated definition of rent and introduce different abstract ideas such as the tenancy year.

Since farm rents so long ice-bound have begun to thaw and move upwards and so many millions of private and public money are being poured into farm improvements, the question of rent is and will continue to be one of paramount significance in any view of the agricultural economy of the nation. Information about farm rents should not be left to the hazards of *ad hoc* haphazard surveys varying in scope, style and selection as in the past. There should be a regular, periodic (not necessarily yearly) and systematically planned gathering of facts and figures.

Undoubtedly, short of visiting each holding, as was done in 1941/43, the estate in receipt of the rent is a more reliable source of rent information. Not only is the estate a reliable source where the surveys depend upon postal returns, but it is possible on an estate basis to deal with a far greater area of land more quickly than is possible on a holding basis. Surveys of estate rentals, moreover, can with ease be extended to surveys of estate expenditures,

But the estate approach can never commend itself until statistics have provided knowledge of the distribution of estates throughout the country, thus making possible the selection of a representative sample for survey.

This then is the first step in the development of future systematic surveys. A census of land ownership would itself require regular periodic revision. What followed as a rent survey would depend upon whether at each census of land ownership, samples were chosen afresh for the study of rents, or whether a more or less permanent selection of estates, periodically checked for its adequacy of representation were used as a permanent source of information. There is much to commend the latter alternative.

Until some knowledge of the pattern of estates in this country is obtained, schemes of this kind are mere pipe-dreams. If a periodic census, or survey, of estates is itself beyond the realms of possibility, rental surveys will have to continue on a holdings basis. The present survey has laid the foundation and it should be possible to erect an edifice of systematic surveys upon it that would be far less costly than the haphazard attempts of the past.

APPENDIX A

SAMPLE AND VARIANCE

The preliminary return.

The number of owners of agricultural land in England and Wales is unknown. Nevertheless, an attempt was made to approach every one of them at the outset of the survey. Owners of the larger estates are usually represented by land agents or surveyors and the preliminary questionnaires[1] were sent to their professional representatives. A considerable number of owners received their questionnaires directly through the offices of the Country Landowners' Association. Others were approached in person. Many land agents are retained by more than one landowner and it was not possible to tell how many landowners were indirectly sent preliminary questionnaires via their agents. Consequently the measure of response as a percentage of the number of landowners who received questionnaires is not known.

What is known is the acreage and number of let holdings in England and Wales for the year 1950[2] and against this "universe" of holdings the extent of the response to the preliminary questionnaires can be measured, both as a percentage of total acreage and as a percentage of the total number of holdings.

The acreage of land under crops, grass and rough grazings in England and Wales in wholly let holdings of 15 acres and over in 1950 was 15m. acres. When to this figure is added the acreage of land under similar use in partly let holdings of 15 acres and over, a grand total of 17m. acres is obtained. Preliminary questionnaires were returned from 2,900 estates covering over 6½m. acres. A portion of this estate acreage is "in hand" to the estate owners, a further portion is woodland and some is in holdings of less than 15 acres. When allowance is made for these portions and holdings, a net acreage of 4,766,039 acres is obtained. This net acreage is 31.8% of the 15m. acres of wholly let holdings just mentioned, and 27.7% of the 17m. acres inclusive of the partly let holdings.

Response to the preliminary questionnaires was not uniform throughout the country. Some counties responded more generously than others. Table App. 8[3] shows the response from each county as

---

[1] v. p. 206 post for a facsimile of the form used.
[2] v.n. p. 3 p. ante.
[3] Appendix p. 200 post.

a percentage of the total area of crops, grass and rough grazings in the county in wholly let holdings of 15 acres and over. From the English counties, taken together, the response is 28.2% and from the Welsh counties together 24.7%. At one extreme the response from the counties is as high as 49.7%, as with Radnorshire at the other it is no more than 8.5% as with Cardigan.

The number of holdings 15 acres and over wholly let in England and Wales in 1950 was approximately 120,800. Preliminary questionnaires were received for 34,872 holdings, a return which is 27.9% of this total number of wholly let holdings. Table App. 8 shows the corresponding response by counties. In the lead are Middlesex with 52.5% and Huntingdonshire with 49.2% respectively; and at the rear Cardiganshire with 6.2%.

The sample.

It was hoped from the preliminary returns to select for the survey proper a 20% sample of the national total of let holdings. Although the return of 29% was large enough for this purpose, the hope was not realised. As a principle of procedure, the number of holdings selected from each estate was limited to a maximum of ten. This device was employed to keep within reasonable bounds the work which would otherwise have fallen upon landowners of large estates. Unfortunately the holdings of the preliminary return were distributed among estates, counties and size-groups in a way which made the imposition of the 10-holdings maximum exceedingly wasteful and greatly reduced the sample of holdings ultimately selected. On estates where holdings were small the number of holdings discarded for every one selected was greatest, consequently the 15-99 acre size-groups suffered the highest percentage of rejection.

Each holding mentioned on a preliminary questionnaire was classified by county and acreage. The sample was selected at random from the holdings so classified. In some counties the total number of larger holdings selected reached 20% of the number in the whole county in a particular farm size-group and at that point no further selection was made. Stopping at the 20% level in this way tended to curtail the number of holdings in the sample, and together with the 10-holdings per estate maximum narrowed the sample to 14,225 holdings or 11.8% of the national total of wholly let holdings.

A main questionnaire was sent to the owner (or his agent) of each holding selected. Completed questionnaires suitable for inclusion in the survey numbered 12,661, an 89% response. The sample comprises these holdings. The response is considered satisfactory. Failure to achieve a better response was due to a variety of causes. The most frequent was change in tenure of the holding subsequent to the return of the preliminary questionnaire; e.g. a tenancy had terminated and the holding had been taken "in hand". Sometimes an acreage had been incorrectly returned on the preliminary questionnaire showing what was in fact a holding less than 15 acres as larger and eligible for inclusion in the survey. Here and there holdings for which a preliminary return had been made had later been amalgamated with other holdings. Change of owner through death, or sale of the estate, and change of agent were sometimes responsible. A few owners did not have the information required and could not complete the main questionnaires. A number of owners refused point blank to go further than the preliminary return. Now and again an owner or agent would complete main questionnaires for one estate only and not for others in his ownership or stewardship.

The sample finally selected of 12,661 holdings is 10.5% of the total number of wholly let holdings of 15 acres and over in England and Wales. In acreage the sample covers 1,973,934 acres and represents 13.1% of the total acreage under crops, grass and rough grazings in wholly let holdings of 15 acres and over, and 11.5% of the total acreage when partly let holdings are included.

The factors that prevented the sample reaching the 20% ideal did not operate with equal effect county by county. Percentage representation both of the number and acreage of holdings in each county vary widely. Table App. 8 shows the county percentages of holdings and acreage. Counties with the highest acreage representation are Berkshire and Northumberland both with 18.4% and Radnorshire with 17.8%; counties with the lowest representation are Pembrokeshire with 4.2% and Breconshire with 4.8%. Counties best represented by percentage of holdings are Sussex with 16.9% and Hertfordshire with 16.8%; and the worst represented in this way are Pembrokeshire with 3.5% and Cardiganshire with 3.3%.

Percentage representation varies also with the size-group. As a rule, the larger the holdings the greater the percentage representation. For the country at large, the sample carries 13.6% of the total acreage of holdings 500 acres and over; and for other size-groups the corresponding percentages are—holdings of 300-499 acres 14.1%; holdings of 150-299 acres 12.6%; 100-149 acres 10.3%; 50-99 acres 8.1%; and 15-49 acres 6.7%. When the sample is raised to compute the national average current rent per acre[1] the average rent per acre of each size-group is multiplied by the acreage of that size-group in the country; the products are added together to give an aggregate national rent and this is divided by the total acreage of the holdings to arrive at a national average rent. Similar principles under-lie the calculations of the county average rents of the raised sample.

Answers were received to all questions asked for each holding in the sample of 12,661 holdings, with the exception of the question on rent in 1945. Information on this point was received from 10,413 holdings of the sample. This reduced number was used when calculating the national average rent per acre in 1945 and wherever rent figures for 1945 were compared with those of later years. The smaller sample represents 8.6% of the total number of wholly let holdings of 15 acres and over in England and Wales; and in acreage represents 10.7% of the total acreage under crops, grass and rough grazings in wholly let holdings of 15 acres and over, and 9.4% of the total acreage when partly let holdings are included. In structure the reduced sample does not differ materially from the larger sample. The average size of holding (155 acres) is the same in each, and, as Table 1 indicates, when each sample is raised to calculate the national average rent per acre for 1957 there is a difference of £0.02 only between the results.

Analysis of Variance.

An analysis of variance of the results of the survey was carried out to test:

1. whether there is significant correlation between rent per acre and the following single factors:
> county;
> ownership personality;
> estate size;
> farm size;
> farming type;
> water supply;
> method of rent determination;
> repair liabilities;
> fixed equipment.

2. the relative significance of the influence on rent per acre of each factor in the following pairs of factors:
> number of cottages and size of farm;
> estate size and farming type;

[1] v.p.   ante.

estate size and farm size;
rent determination and farming type;
rent determination and farm size;
farming type and farm size.

3. the significance of the interaction between each factor in the pairs of factors of (2) above, assuming that each factor separately has a significant influence on rent per acre.

The first test was made by a single one-way classification and the results are as follows:

SINGLE ONE-WAY CLASSIFICATION

| TABLE NO. | DEGREES OF FREEDOM* | | MEAN SQUARES |
	BETWEEN CLASSES p - 1	WITHIN CLASSES N - p	
2	13	12,642	221 1.24
7	5	12,650	236 1.38
11-12	9	12,646	92 1.40
15	4	12,651	329 1.37
18	3	12,652	11 1.47
20	11	12,644	123 1.36
29	5	12,650	42 1.45
32	6	12,649	67 1.44
17	51	12,604	52 1.23

It is clear from these results that variation between classes is greater than within classes.

* Some of the figures given here do not correspond with the number of categories set out in the Tables because the degrees of freedom above are calculated according to the total number of categories used in the survey and these have been reduced in one or two Tables for clarity of presentation.

The second test was made by a double one-way classification and the results are as follows:

DOUBLE ONE-WAY CLASSIFICATION

| TABLE NO. | DEGREES OF FREEDOM* | | | MEAN SQUARES |
	BETWEEN HORIZONTAL CATEGORIES p - 1	BETWEEN CATEGORIES q - 1	RESIDUAL N - pq	
8	5	13	12,556	178 583 1.3
16	11	5	12,584	7,199 1,067 1.28
22	13	11	12,457	31 89 1.2
24	5	11	12,584	11 275 1.3
28	5	13	12,556	.82 21,482 1.24
29	5	5	12,620	11 233 1.37

The second column shows the number of degrees of freedom between those categories of each Table which are arranged in a horizontal direction and the third column, the degrees of freedom between those categories of each Table which are arranged in a vertical direction.

* v.n.p. 191.

The third test to show the interaction between the two factors of each pair of factors produced the following results:

INTERACTION OF TWO FACTORS

TABLE NO.	FITTING Constants p+q—2	INTER-ACTION (p-1) (q-1)	TOTAL pq-1	WITHIN GROUPS N-pq	MEAN SQUARES
8	18	65	83	12,556	91.7 15.2 33.4 1.3
16	16	55	71	12,584	233 41.7 40.7 1.28
22	24	143	167	12,457	142.0 2.2 22.3 1.2
24	16	55	71	12,584	117.5 4.5 30.0 1.3
28	18	65	83	12,556	77.7 24.4 36.0 1.24
29	10	25	35	12,620	120.5 5.8 31.8 1.4

* v.n.p. 191.

APPENDIX B

ADDITIONAL TABLES

TABLE APP. 1

AVERAGE CURRENT RENT PER ACRE FOR EACH FARMING TYPE.
1957

FARMING TYPE	RENT PER ACRE		HOLDINGS	
	adjusted	unadjusted	No.	Acreage
	£	£		
GRASS				
Mainly dairying	2.60	2.50	2,668	262,251
Dairy and mixed	2.15	2.03	1,924	259,972
Mixed livestock (upland)	1.29	0.61	1,198	291,380
Mixed livestock (lowland)	1.95	1.82	859	99,281
Total Grass	2.12	1.69	6,649	912,884
INTERMEDIATE				
Mixed with dairying	2.21	2.16	1,373	237,929
General mixed	1.97	1.90	1,601	269,626
Corn, sheep and dairying	1.90	1.82	143	39,242
Total Intermediate	2.07	2.01	3,117	546,797
ARABLE				
Heavy land	2.25	2.23	882	147,923
Light land	2.04	2.01	1,238	235,080
Alluvial and mixed	2.36	2.33	507	100,182
Total Arable	2.17	2.14	2,627	483,185
SPECIALIST				
Market garden	3.50	3.46	116	7,098
Mainly poultry	2.33	2.15	24	1,262
Mainly pigs	2.66	2.61	15	1,560
Other types	2.63	1.73	113	21,148
Total Specialist	2.88	2.19	268	31,068
ALL FARMING TYPES	2.13	1.90	12,661	1,973,934
ALL TYPES—RAISED SAMPLE	—	1.94	163,500	17,188,517

TABLE APP. 2
DISTRIBUTION OF HOLDINGS OF EACH FARMING TYPE IN RENT PER ACRE GROUPS.

1957

FARMING TYPE	HOLDINGS IN EACH RENT PER ACRE GROUP									
	Under £1		£1–£2		£2–£3		£3–£4		£4 and over	
	No.	Acres	No.	Acres	No.	Acres	No.	Acres	No.	Acres
GRASS										
Mainly dairying	80	10,838	650	75,232	945	101,683	622	52,707	371	21,791
Dairy and mixed	167	24,578	731	111,656	674	90,527	252	26,367	99	6,786
Mixed livestock (upland)	645	231,098	409	49,933	113	8,991	21	1,077	10	291,380
Mixed livestock (lowland)	86	13,484	353	47,686	307	32,115	75	4,189	38	1,807
INTERMEDIATE										
Mixed with dairying	44	10,528	451	95,775	555	93,202	239	30,742	84	7,682
General mixed	121	25,160	732	134,446	551	89,809	148	16,538	48	3,599
Corn, sheep and dairying	7	2,496	68	20,403	56	14,804	8	1,285	4	254
ARABLE										
Heavy land	35	3,353	335	59,427	356	61,625	114	17,852	41	147,881
Light land	72	11,921	528	118,809	447	80,783	126	16,200	64	7,028
Alluvial and mixed	14	2,996	148	36,707	208	39,595	76	13,230	60	7,496
SPECIALIST										
Market garden	1	28	5	145	31	2,736	33	2,592	46	7,098
Mainly poultry	3	332	3	246	12	522	4	128	2	34
Mainly pigs	—	—	3	224	7	1,032	1	19	4	285
ALL TYPES	1,275	336,812	4,262	750,689	1,719	617,424	871	182,935	12,543	1,951,773

TABLE APP. 3   AVERAGE RENT PER ACRE FOR EACH FARMING TYPE 1945–1958.

FARMING TYPE	AVERAGE RENT PER ACRE £				INDEX 1945=100			HOLDINGS	
	1945	1956	1957	1958	1956	1957	1958	No.	Acreage
GRASS									
Mainly dairying	1.57	2.37	2.50	2.55	141.0	159.2	162.4	2,202	213,008
Dairy and mixed	1.28	1.90	2.01	2.07	148.4	157.0	161.7	1,638	217,357
Mixed livestock (upland)	0.41	0.60	0.63	0.64	146.3	153.6	156.1	1,007	246,005
Mixed livestock (lowland)	1.21	1.69	1.80	1.85	139.7	148.8	152.9	692	83,056
Total Grass	1.06	1.58	1.68	1.72	149.1	158.5	162.3	5,539	759,426
INTERMEDIATE									
Mixed with dairying	1.23	1.97	2.12	2.20	160.2	172.4	178.9	1,208	208,044
General mixed	1.14	1.73	1.86	1.90	151.8	163.2	166.7	1,338	229,407
Corn, sheep and dairying	0.97	1.67	1.80	1.86	172.2	185.6	191.8	121	33,659
Total Intermediate	1.17	1.84	1.97	2.03	157.3	168.4	173.5	2,667	471,110
ARABLE									
Heavy land	1.23	1.95	2.14	2.25	158.5	174.0	182.9	611	96,507
Light land	1.14	1.80	1.98	2.06	157.9	173.7	180.7	981	184,820
Alluvial and mixed	1.40	2.07	2.20	2.32	147.9	157.1	165.7	397	78,157
Total Arable	1.22	1.90	2.07	2.17	155.7	169.7	177.9	1,989	359,484
SPECIALIST									
Market garden	2.34	3.30	3.40	3.52	141.0	145.3	150.4	100	6,072
Mainly poultry	1.37	1.89	1.98	2.00	140.0	144.5	146.0	18	1,001
Mainly pigs	1.60	2.64	2.62	2.64	165.0	163.7	165.0	13	1,481
Other types	1.10	1.59	1.65	1.66	144.5	150.0	150.9	87	17,696
Total Specialist	1.42	2.05	2.12	2.16	144.4	149.3	152.1	218	26,250
ALL FARMING TYPES	1.13	1.74	1.86	1.92	154.0	164.6	169.9	10,413	1,616,270
ALL TYPES—RAISED SAMPLE	1.17	1.80	1.92	—	153.8	164.1	—	163,500	17,188,517

TABLE APP. 4
AVERAGE CURRENT RENT PER ACRE FOR EACH
FARM SIZE-GROUP.

1957

| FARM SIZE-GROUP | RENT PER ACRE | | HOLDINGS | |
| | adjusted | unadjusted | | |
acres	£	£	no.	acreage
15–49	2.79	2.62	3,080	95,156
50–99	2.41	2.27	2,958	214,518
100–149	2.23	2.13	2,097	258,631
150–299	2.16	2.05	3,074	644,533
300–499	1.98	1.82	1,013	375,618
500 and over	1.70	1.17	439	385,478
All size-groups	2.13	1.90	12,661	1,973,934
All size-groups—Raised sample	—	1.94	163,500	17,188,517

TABLE APP. 5
AVERAGE RENT PER ACRE FOR EACH FARM SIZE-GROUP
1945–1958.

| FARM SIZE-GROUP | RENT PER ACRE £ | | | | INDEX 1945 = 100 | | | HOLDINGS | |
acres	1945	1956	1957	1958	1956	1957	1958	no.	acreage
15–49	1.72	2.52	2.65	2.72	146.5	154.1	158.1	2,484	77,322
50–99	1.41	2.18	2.26	2.34	154.6	160.3	166.0	2,423	175,369
100–149	1.30	1.97	2.09	2.16	151.5	160.7	166.2	1,753	216,435
150–299	1.19	1.85	1.99	2.06	155.5	167.2	173.1	2,580	540,518
300–499	1.03	1.63	1.75	1.82	158.3	169.9	176.7	828	306,685
500 and over	.62	1.00	1.09	1.13	161.3	175.8	182.3	345	299,914
All size-groups	1.13	1.74	1.86	1.92	154.0	164.6	169.9	10,413	1,616,270
All size-groups Raised sample	1.17	1.80	1.92	—	153.8	164.1	—	163,500	17,188,517

TABLE APP. 6

AVERAGE RENT PER ACRE FOR EACH COUNTY 1942-1957.

		PRESENT SURVEY: 1957				NATIONAL SURVEY: 1942	Increase on 1942 rent
Order	COUNTY	RENT PER ACRE		Order	COUNTY	RENT PER ACRE	
		Sample	Raised sample				
		£	£			£	%
1	Cheshire	3.26	3.19	1	Cheshire	1.937	68.4
2	Somerset	2.57	2.68	2	Middlesex	1.930	9.8
3	Shropshire	2.51	2.64	3	Shropshire	1.734	44.7
4	Stafford	2.50	2.55	4	Somerset	1.729	48.6
5	Kent	2.49	2.52	5	Cambridge	1.528	55.8
6	Essex	2.45	2.43	6	Stafford	1.500	66.6
7	Flint	2.40	2.53	7	Leicester	1.486	46.0
8	Cambridge	2.38	2.43	8	Lancashire	1.432	40.3
9	Lincoln	2.28	2.33	9	Worcester	1.417	53.1
10	Hereford	2.28	2.29	10	Flint	1.404	70.9
11	Warwick	2.23	2.26	11	Hereford	1.342	69.8
12	Huntingdon	2.21	2.40	12	Lincoln	1.341	70.0
13	Wiltshire	2.20	2.24	13	Warwick	1.328	68.6
14	Leicester	2.17	2.17	14	Derby	1.288	66.9
15	Worcester	2.17	2.19	15	Essex	1.245	96.7
16	Rutland	2.17	2.23	16	Bedford	1.219	59.9
17	Derby	2.15	2.12	17	Kent	1.196	108.1
18	Middlesex	2.12	1.97	18	Cornwall	1.183	42.8
19	Devon	2.10	2.25	19	Buckingham	1.175	63.4
20	Suffolk	2.10	2.08	20	Huntingdon	1.171	88.7
21	Oxford	2.07	1.97	21	Northampton	1.171	65.6
22	Sussex	2.04	2.05	22	Wiltshire	1.157	90.1
23	Nottingham	2.02	2.05	23	Dorset	1.151	64.2
24	Lancashire	2.01	2.62	24	Oxford	1.123	84.3
25	Gloucester	1.99	2.00	25	Anglesey	1.077	37.4
26	Surrey	1.99	2.00	26	Gloucester	1.074	85.2
27	Hertford	1.97	1.95	27	Devon	1.043	101.3
28	Bedford	1.95	2.03	28	Nottingham	1.038	94.6
29	Northampton	1.94	1.94	29	Sussex	1.023	99.4
30	Hampshire	1.92	1.94	30	Monmouth	1.021	50.8
31	Norfolk	1.92	1.93	31	Rutland	1.012	114.4
32	Buckingham	1.92	1.94	32	Hertford	0.957	105.8
33	Dorset	1.89	1.93	33	Berkshire	0.957	92.2
34	Denbigh	1.89	1.81	34	Pembroke	0.943	42.0
35	Berkshire	1.84	1.94	35	Norfolk	0.937	104.9
36	Yorkshire	1.70	1.71	36	Yorkshire	0.912	86.4
37	Cornwall	1.69	1.87	37	Suffolk	0.891	135.6
38	Monmouth	1.54	1.54	38	Surrey	0.891	123.3
39	Anglesey	1.48	1.49	39	Durham	0.886	54.6
40	Durham	1.37	1.48	40	Carmarthen	0.857	35.3
41	Pembroke	1.34	1.42	41	Denbigh	0.833	126.8
42	Westmorland	1.28	1.35	42	Hampshire	0.819	134.4
43	Glamorgan	1.28	1.17	43	Cumberland	0.734	37.6
44	Carmarthen	1.16	1.06	44	Northumberland	0.699	60.2
45	Breconshire	1.14	1.11	45	Glamorgan	0.686	86.5
46	Northumberland	1.12	1.17	46	Montgomery	0.673	58.9
47	Montgomery	1.07	1.09	47	Caernarvon	0.550	47.2
48	Cumberland	1.01	1.30	48	Westmorland	0.544	135.2
49	Caernarvon	0.81	0.75	49	Radnor	0.484	23.9
50	Radnor	0.60	0.80	50	Cardigan	0.437	16.7
51	Cardigan	0.51	0.73	51	Brecon	0.354	222.0
52	Merioneth	0.51	0.48	52	Merioneth	0.303	68.4
	England and Wales	1.90	1.94		England and Wales	1.061	78.7

TABLE APP. 7

DISTRIBUTION OF RENT DETERMINATION PROCEDURES BY ACREAGE AND HOLDINGS.

PROCEDURE	TOTAL YEARLY RENT £	ACREAGE						HOLDINGS	
		Total		Rough		Wood			
		Acres	%	Acres	%	Acres	%	No.	%
A. *Prospective tenant procedures:*									
i) open tender	92,942	47,121	2.39	15,385	32.65	149	0.32	264	2.08
ii) negotiation with—									
a) stranger;	267,323	132,982	6.74	21,806	16.40	947	0.71	1,066	8.42
b) relative of tenant;	208,754	105,863	5.36	17,571	16.60	625	0.59	743	5.87
c) relative of landlord	26,031	22,704	1.15	11,116	48.96	32	0.14	84	0.66
B. *Sitting tenant procedures:*									
i) negotiation	2,892,425	1,495,266	75.75	147,915	9.89	6,454	0.43	9,207	72.72
ii) mediatorial									
a) by agreed arbitrator;	49,360	25,704	1.30	1,405	5.47	142	0.55	131	1.03
b) by Minister-appointed arbitrator;	31,882	18,324	0.93	4,150	22.65	55	0.30	97	0.77
c) independent valuer	45,081	23,298	1.18	1,277	5.48	117	0.50	121	0.96
C. *Other procedures*	33,978	21,994	1.11	7,005	31.85	275	1.25	129	1.02
D. *Procedures unknown*	96,117	80,678	4.09	20,659	25.61	1,109	1.37	819	6.47
TOTALS:	3,743,893	1,973,934	100.00	248,289	12.58	9,905	0.50	12,661	100.00

TABLE APP. 8

PERCENTAGE REPRESENTATION OF NATIONAL AND COUNTY ACREAGES(i) AND NUMBERS OF HOLDINGS(ii) IN PRELIMINARY RETURNS AND IN SAMPLE (12,661 Holdings).

COUNTY	PERCENTAGE OF COUNTY TOTAL			
	Acreage		Holdings	
	Prelim'ary returns	Sample	Prelim'ary returns	Sample
	%	%	%	%
Bedfordshire	24.5	11.6	39.6	12.8
Berkshire	45.8	18.4	35.3	14.7
Buckinghamshire	25.0	13.0	42.5	15.8
Cambridgeshire	31.2	13.1	44.1	12.0
Cheshire	37.4	12.6	34.9	12.2
Cornwall	23.2	7.8	22.4	6.1
Cumberland	29.9	16.0	21.6	10.5
Derbyshire	24.8	10.9	22.6	9.9
Devonshire	24.1	7.7	22.8	6.9
Dorset	36.5	16.5	41.0	14.8
Durham	42.6	7.8	44.3	7.2
Essex	25.6	15.0	30.9	16.2
Gloucestershire	28.2	12.8	38.4	13.4
Hampshire	26.1	15.1	27.8	15.3
Hereford	27.8	13.3	25.8	11.8
Hertfordshire	27.0	11.4	42.6	16.8
Huntingdonshire	28.1	11.5	49.2	9.0
Kent	24.5	12.2	25.2	12.8
Lancashire	19.8	10.1	17.7	7.9
Leicestershire	19.8	10.5	28.2	12.7
Lincolnshire	35.0	13.0	34.6	12.3
Middlesex	32.2	5.5	52.5	6.3
Norfolk	37.8	13.7	44.1	12.4
Northamptonshire	25.9	8.2	33.9	10.4
Northumberland	36.4	18.4	38.9	16.6
Nottingham	28.6	13.0	30.2	13.5
Oxford	36.1	14.7	41.2	15.9
Rutland	11.1	9.6	14.0	11.9
Shropshire	24.5	12.8	27.4	9.9
Somerset	26.8	9.4	34.1	10.3

COUNTY	PERCENTAGE OF COUNTY TOTAL			
	Acreage		Holdings	
	Prelim'ary returns	Sample	Prelim'ary returns	Sample
	%	%	%	%
Staffordshire	26.2	10.9	21.7	8.4
Suffolk	29.9	14.8	35.0	16.3
Surrey	25.5	12.4	26.9	12.8
Sussex	29.3	17.3	28.9	16.9
Warwickshire	24.9	9.4	27.9	10.3
Westmorland	25.8	7.5	17.5	6.3
Wiltshire	27.3	13.2	35.5	12.4
Worcester	28.7	11.5	26.9	9.9
Yorkshire	22.3	8.8	21.5	8.1
Anglesey	32.2	10.7	29.8	9.1
Breconshire	12.7	4.8	15.4	6.7
Caernarvon	29.9	6.7	29.7	8.2
Cardigan	8.5	5.3	6.2	3.3
Carmarthen	18.2	5.9	15.4	5.0
Denbigh	29.0	11.1	31.3	12.4
Flint	36.8	12.2	38.2	10.7
Glamorgan	24.8	6.9	26.8	7.1
Merioneth	28.4	8.3	31.3	9.1
Monmouth	27.9	6.5	30.2	8.4
Montgomery	27.6	9.4	29.3	7.9
Pembroke	9.8	4.2	10.9	3.5
Radnor	49.7	17.8	26.6	13.7
ALL COUNTIES	27.7	11.5	27.9	10.5

(i) Crops, grass and rough grazings in holdings 15 acres and over wholly and partly let.

(ii) Wholly let, 15 acres and over.

TABLE APP. 9

DISTRIBUTION OF HOLDINGS OF EACH FARMING TYPE IN FARM SIZE-GROUPS.

1957

FARMING TYPE	15–49		50–99		100–149		150–299		300–499		500 and over	
	No.	Acreage	No.	Acreage	No.	Acreage	No.	Acreage	No.	Acreage	No.	Acreage
GRASS												
Mainly dairying	906	28,376	772	55,646	467	57,071	457	92,750	59	21,453	7	6,955
Dairy and mixed	399	12,671	457	33,303	306	48,750	540	110,199	108	38,909	24	16,140
Mixed livestock (upland)	285	8,592	263	19,132	180	22,015	247	51,976	104	39,347	119	150,318
Mixed livestock (lowland)	355	10,196	171	14,232	109	13,218	154	32,466	54	20,207	16	10,962
INTERMEDIATE												
Mixed with dairying	137	4,785	337	24,681	283	34,748	416	87,219	155	56,470	45	30,026
General mixed	286	9,145	357	26,169	238	29,633	499	105,924	174	64,450	47	34,395
Corn, sheep and dairying	6	187	21	1,732	19	2,448	55	11,797	23	8,606	19	14,472
ARABLE												
Heavy land	201	6,295	183	13,193	125	15,584	235	51,026	105	39,249	33	22,576
Light land	279	8,365	258	18,527	161	20,428	298	64,001	151	56,236	91	67,523
Alluvial and mixed	88	2,832	92	6,490	88	11,025	140	30,554	67	25,643	32	23,638
ALL SPECIALISTS	138	3,712	47	3,413	31	3,711	33	6,621	13	5,048	6	8,563

FARM SIZE-GROUPS
Acres

SAMPLES OF FORMS USED

i. MAIN QUESTIONNAIRE

UNIVERSITY OF CAMBRIDGE
FARM RENTAL SURVEY

NAME OF FARM	PARISH ....
NAME OF ESTATE	

County (See Code)	1 2 [ ]	Estate No.	3 4 5 [ ]	Approx. Acreage of the whole Estate	6 7 8 9 10 [ ] Ten 'ooo 'oo Tens Units thous

Number of Agricultural Holdings Comprised in the Whole Estate	11 12 13 [ ] 'oo Tens Units	Farm No.	14 15 [ ]	Total Acreage of Holding in Farm Tenancy (Nearest acre if possible) e.g. a farm of 1321 acres will be entered.................. If 321 acres	16 17 18 19 [ ] 'ooo 'oo Tens Units 1 3 2 1 0 3 2 1

Acreage of Rough Grazing included in Boxes 16 to 19	20 21 22 23 [ ] 'ooo 'oo Tens Units	Acreage of Woodland included in Boxes 16 to 19	24 25 26 [ ] 'oo Tens Units

CHARACTER OF THE HOLDING

If 'Grass' or 'Intermediate' type insert the No. applicable in box 27 and 'o'
in box 28. If 'Arable' or 'Specialist' type insert the No. applicable in box 28
and 'o' in box 27. ('o' must appear in box 27 or 28.)

GRASS TYPES (Two-thirds or more of farm cultivatable land under grass) **27** [ ]

1. MAINLY DAIRYING
2. DAIRY AND MIXED
3. MIXED LIVESTOCK (UPLAND) including Hill Farms and Livestock Rearing Farms
4. MIXED LIVESTOCK (LOWLAND)

INTERMEDIATE TYPES (Between one-third and two-thirds of cultivatable land under grass)

5. MIXED FARMING WITH SUBSTANTIAL DAIRYING
6. GENERAL MIXED FARMING
7. CORN, SHEEP AND DAIRYING

ARABLE TYPES (Less than one-third of cultivatable land under grass) **28** [ ]

1. HEAVY LAND ARABLE
2. LIGHT LAND ARABLE
3. ARABLE AND MIXED FARMING WITH ALLUVIAL ARABLE

SPECIALIST TYPES

4. MARKET GARDEN
5. MAINLY POULTRY
6. MAINLY PIGS
7. OTHER TYPES OF FARMING NOT SPECIFIED ABOVE

NOTE: If the tenancy agreement specifies a particular type of farming, this should govern the answer, whether or not the tenant is honouring the agreement.

MAIN QUESTIONNAIRE—*continued.*

	29	30	31	32
Current Gross Rent to Nearest £ (including interest on landowner's improvements)				
	'ooo	'oo	Tens	Units

e.g. a gross rent of £1234. 9s. will be shown as	1	2	3	4
a gross rent of £1234. 10s. will be shown as	1	2	3	5
a gross rent of £234 will be shown as..	o	2	3	4

	33 34 35 36		37		38 39 40
Gross Rent for Tenancy Year Preceding Current year (including interest on landowner's improvements)	'ooo 'oo Tens Units	**Was the Acreage then compared with Acreage now:** 0. THE SAME 1. MORE 2. LESS		**If the Acreage was different, State the Difference** (*If same, enter 'o' in the boxes*)	'oo Tens Units

	41 42 43 44		45		46 47 48
Gross rent for Tenancy Year ending in 1945 (including interest on landowner's improvements). (*If rent unknown enter 'o' in each box*)	'ooo 'oo Tens Units	**Was the Acreage then compared with Acreage now:** 0. THE SAME 1. MORE 2. LESS		**If the Acreage was different, State the Difference** (*If same, enter 'o' in the boxes*)	'oo Tens Units

	49 50 51 52
If the farm rent is to change in the next Tenancy year, the farm acreage remaining unchanged, state the new Gross Rent agreed (including interest on landowner's improvements). (*If there is no change of rent, or if the new rent is not yet known, or if there is to be a change in acreage, enter 'o' in the boxes*)	'ooo 'oo Tens Units

If the gross rent for the current year is inclusive of the following occupier's charges, state the sum in each case (to the nearest £) met by the landowner. (*Write 'o' in the boxes if there are no charges*)

	53 54 55		56 57 58
Occupier's Water Charges (Public)	'oo Tens Units	**Rates—Occupier's House**	'oo Tens Units

	59 60 61		62 63 64
Rates—Occupier's Cottages	'oo Tens Units	**Occupier's Drainage Rates**	'oo Tens Units

	65 66 67		68 69 70
Other Charges to Occupier	'oo Tens Units	(*Not to be filled in*) **Total sum of previous five Items** (Boxes 53-67)	'oo Tens Units

	71
If there is an owner's drainage rate, does the tenant pay it? 1. Yes. 2. No. (*Insert the No. which applies.*) *If there is no drainage rate, write 'o' in the box.*	

MAIN QUESTIONNAIRE—*continued.*

State the type of water supply provided under the tenancy (*Insert the No. which applies*)   72

o. Piped mains water supply
1. Piped water supply from private estate water system
2. Piped water supply from a source on the farm
3. Water supply on the farm but no piped supply
4. No water supply

What was the cause of the last change in rent? (*Insert the No. which applies*)   73

o. A change of tenancy
1. A general review of the rental value
2. Improvement carried out by the landowner
3. Alteration in the boundaries of the holding
4. An alteration of the repair obligations in the lease agreement
5. Some other change in the terms of the tenancy agreement
6. A combination of serials 1 and 2
7. A combination of serials o, 1 and 2
8. A combination of serials o, 1 and 4
9. A combination of serials o, 1, 2 and 4
10. Some other combination of serials
11. Not known

When was the last change in rent? (*Insert the No. which applies*)   74

o. 1945 or earlier   4. 1949   8. 1953
1. 1946   5. 1950   9. 1954
2. 1947   6. 1951   10. 1955
3. 1948   7. 1952   11. 1956

How was the last change in rent determined? (*Insert the No. which applies*)   75

o. BY NEGOTIATION with sitting tenant direct (or with his valuer)
1. BY NEGOTIATION with a prospective tenant who is a near relative of a tenant or a former tenant on the same Estate (or with his valuer)
2. BY NEGOTIATION with a prospective tenant who is a relative of the landowner (or with his valuer)
3. BY NEGOTIATION with a prospective tenant who is not a near relative of a tenant, or of a former tenant on the same Estate or of the landowner (or with his valuer)
4. BY ARBITRATOR appointed by agreement between the parties
5. BY INDEPENDENT VALUER appointed by agreement between the parties
6. BY AN ARBITRATOR appointed by the Minister of Agriculture
7. AS A RESULT OF A LETTING BY TENDER
8. BY OTHER MEANS
9. NOT KNOWN

MAIN QUESTIONNAIRE—*continued.*

The tenancy agreement: (*Insert the No. which applies*)

0. IS IN WRITING   1. IS NOT IN WRITING

76

What are the tenant's <u>LEGAL</u> liabilities for repairs and maintenance?
(*Insert the No. which applies*)

0. The tenant's liabilities are broadly similar to those set out in the Agriculture (Maintenance, Repair and Insurance of Fixed Equipment) Regulations, 1948. (Statutory Instrument 1948, No. 184.)

1. The tenant's liabilities are substantially **greater** than those set out in the Regulations mentioned in 0 above

2. The tenant's liabilities are substantially **less** than those set out in the Regulations mentioned in 0 above

3. The tenant's liabilities are uncertain.

77

Does the <u>TENANCY</u> provide, in addition to the land: (*Insert the No. which applies*)

0. Farmhouse with electricity and farm buildings with electricity

1. Farmhouse without electricity and farm buildings without electricity

2. Farmhouse with electricity and farm buildings without electricity

3. Farmhouse without electricity and farm buildings with electricity

4. Farmhouse with electricity but NO farm buildings

5. Farmhouse without electricity but NO farm buildings

6. Farm buildings with electricity but NO farmhouse

7. Farm buildings without electricity but NO farmhouse

8. Is the tenancy in land only, i.e. without farmhouse or farm buildings?

78

Does the <u>TENANCY</u> provide, in addition to the buildings in box 78: (*Insert the No. which applies*)

0. NO cottages

1. ONE cottage

2. TWO cottages

3. THREE cottages

4. FOUR cottages

5. FIVE cottages

6. SIX cottages

7. SEVEN cottages

8. EIGHT cottages

9. NINE cottages

10. TEN cottages

11. ELEVEN cottages or more

NOTE: A foreman's house or a flat for this purpose is a cottage

79

What was the month of completion of this form? (*Insert the No. which applies*)

0. November 1956	4. March 1957	8. July 1957
1. December 1956	5. April 1957	9 August 1957
2. January 1957	6. May 1957	10. September 1957
3. February 1957	7. June 1957	11. October 1957 or later

80

Status of the person completing this form: (*Tick the No. which applies*)

1. The landowner   3. The landowner's secretary, or member of office staff

2. The landowner's agent   4. The agent's secretary, or member of office staff

---

NOTE: If comments on doubtful answers are thought necessary, please send them on a separate sheet with the return

FARM RENTS

UNIVERSITY OF CAMBRIDGE
FARM RENTAL SURYEY

ii.

PRELIMINARY QUESTIONNAIRE

To be completed and returned to

DEPARTMENT OF ESTATE MANAGEMENT, 74 TRUMPINGTON STREET, CAMBRIDGE

Name and address of Estate:

Name and address of:

Owner	Agent
Tel. No.	Tel. No.

Total acreage of Estate:

Please provide the following information for each tenanted agricultural holding of **15 acres or more** on the estate.

Serial No.	Name of Holding	Parish	Acreage of holding (to the nearest acre if possible)	Code No. (Not to be filled in)
1				
2				
3				
4				
5				
6				
7				
8				
9				
10				
11				
12				